Study Guide

Criminal Law

TENTH EDITION

Joel Samaha
University of Minnesota

Prepared by

Lore Rutz-Burri
Southern Oregon University

Australia • Brazil • Japan • Korea • Mexico • Singapore • Spain • United Kingdom • United States

© 2011 Wadsworth, Cengage Learning

ALL RIGHTS RESERVED. No part of this work covered by the copyright herein may be reproduced, transmitted, stored, or used in any form or by any means graphic, electronic, or mechanical, including but not limited to photocopying, recording, scanning, digitizing, taping, Web distribution, information networks, or information storage and retrieval systems, except as permitted under Section 107 or 108 of the 1976 United States Copyright Act, without the prior written permission of the publisher.

For product information and technology assistance, contact us at
**Cengage Learning Customer & Sales Support,
1-800-354-9706**

For permission to use material from this text or product, submit all requests online at **www.cengage.com/permissions**
Further permissions questions can be emailed to
permissionrequest@cengage.com

ISBN-13: 978-0-495-81230-2
ISBN-10: 0-495-81230-7

Wadsworth
20 Davis Drive
Belmont, CA 94002-3098
USA

Cengage Learning is a leading provider of customized learning solutions with office locations around the globe, including Singapore, the United Kingdom, Australia, Mexico, Brazil, and Japan. Locate your local office at: **www.cengage.com/global**

Cengage Learning products are represented in Canada by Nelson Education, Ltd.

To learn more about Wadsworth, visit
www.cengage.com/wadsworth

Purchase any of our products at your local college store or at our preferred online store
www.CengageBrain.com

Printed in the United States of America
2 3 4 5 6 7 14 13 12 11

TABLE OF CONTENTS

1. Criminal Law and Criminal Punishment: An Overview — 1

2. Constitutional Limits on Criminal Law — 25

3. The General Principles of Criminal Liability: *Actus Reus* — 48

4. The General Principles of Criminal Liability: *Mens Rea,* Concurrence, Causation, and Ignorance and Mistake — 68

5. Defenses to Criminal Liability: Justifications — 88

6. Defenses to Criminal Liability: Excuse — 109

7. Parties to Crime and Vicarious Liability — 131

8. Inchoate Crimes: Attempt, Conspiracy, and Solicitation — 151

9. Crimes Against Persons I: Murder and Manslaughter — 175

10. Crimes Against Persons II: Criminal Sexual Conduct, Bodily Injury, and Personal Restraint — 200

11. Crimes Against Property — 225

12. Crimes Against Public Order and Morals — 247

13. Crimes Against the State — 268

Chapter 1
Criminal Law and Criminal Punishment: An Overview

LEARNING OBJECTIVES

1. To define and understand what behavior deserves criminal punishment.

2. To understand and appreciate the relationship between the general and special parts of criminal law.

3. To identify, describe, and understand the main sources of criminal law.

4. To define criminal punishment, to know the difference between criminal and non-criminal sanctions, and to understand the purposes of each.

5. To define and appreciate the significance of the presumption of innocence and burden of proof as they relate to criminal liability.

6. To understand the role of informal discretion and appreciate its relationship to formal criminal law.

7. To understand the text-case method and how to apply it to the study of criminal law.

KEY TERMS AND CONCEPTS

- **criminal liability**—response to behavior that deserves punishment; p. 6

- **torts**—private wrongs for which you can sue the party who wronged you and recover money; p. 8

- **crimes of moral turpitude**—criminal behavior that is inherently wrong or evil; p. 11

- **felonies**—serious crimes that are generally punishable by one year or more in prison; p. 11

- **misdemeanors**—minor crimes for which the penalty is usually less than one year in jail or a fine; p. 11

- **general part of criminal law**—principles that apply to all crimes; p. 12

- **special part of criminal law**—defines the elements of specific crimes; p. 12

- **common-law crimes**—crimes originating in the English common law; p. 13

- **codified**—putting laws (legal codes) into writing; p. 15

- **Model Penal Code**—the code developed by the American Law Institute to guide reform in criminal law; p. 16

- **analysis of criminal liability**—the act of analyzing statutes and cases to answer the question of whether a behavior deserves criminal punishment; p. 17

- **administrative crimes**—violations of federal and state agency rules; p. 19

- **federal system**—the organization of our government, its courts and criminal codes, into 50 autonomous states, one federal government, and the District of Columbia; p. 19

- **rates of imprisonment**—a number representing the number of prisoners per 100,000 people in the general population; p. 20

- **punishment**—intentionally inflicting pain or other unpleasant consequence on another person; p. 21

- **criminal punishment**—punishments prescribed by legislatures and imposed by the government (state or federal government); p. 22

- **retribution**—punishment based on just deserts; p. 22

- **prevention**—punishing offenders to prevent crimes in the future; p. 22

- **general deterrence (also called general prevention)**—aims, by threat of punishment, to deter criminal behavior in the general population; p. 24

- **special deterrence**—the threat of punishment aimed at individual offenders in the hope of deterring future criminal conduct; p. 24

- **incapacitation**—punishment by imprisonment, mutilation, and even death; p. 24

- **rehabilitation**—prevention of crime by treatment; p. 24

- **hedonism**—the belief that human beings seek pleasure and avoid pain; p. 25

- **rationalism**—the belief that individuals can, and ordinarily do, act to maximize pleasure and minimize pain; p. 25

- **deterrence theory**—the theory of punishment which suggests that rational people will not commit crimes if they know that the pain of punishment outweighs the benefits of committing the crime; p. 25

- **principle of utility**—permitting only the minimum amount of pain necessary to prevent the crime as punishment; p. 25

- **medical model of criminal law**—the view that crime is a disease and criminals are sick and that the appropriate response to criminal behavior is to cure the criminal; p. 27

- **incapacitation**—punishment by imprisonment, mutilation, or even death; p. 26

- **determinism**—the assumption that forces beyond offenders' control cause them to commit crimes; p. 27

- **indeterminate sentencing laws**—laws which make the actual sentence the offender receives dependent on how long it takes to rehabilitate the offender; p. 28

- **determinate sentences**—fixed sentences in which the actual sentence depends on the period of time specified by law, not by the rehabilitation of the offender; p. 29

- **presumption of innocence**—the premise that until the state proves defendants guilty of a crime, they are presumed not to have committed the crime; p. 29

- **burden of proof**—the requirement that the state must prove that the defendant has committed the crime without justification or excuse before he can be held criminally liable for the crime; p. 29

- **proof beyond a reasonable doubt**—the highest standard of proof, and the standard of certainty by which the jury must be convinced of the defendant's guilt before it can impose criminal liability; p. 29

- **reasonable doubt**—proof that prevents one from being convinced of the defendant's guilt or the belief; p. 29

- **bench trials**—trials in which the judge rather than a jury decides whether the defendant is guilty of the crime; p. 30

- *corpus delecti*—Latin for "body of the crime", it means the elements of the crime that the state must prove in order to prove criminal liability; p. 30

- **affirmative defenses**—defenses which require the defendant to present some evidence; p. 30

- **burden of production**—the requirement that the state or defendant put on (produce) some evidence. Generally the state has the burden of production, but sometimes, like with affirmative defenses, it makes sense to require the defendant produce evidence; p. 30

- **burden of persuasion**—the requirement that the state or defendant (whoever has the burden of production) produce enough evidence to convince (or persuade) the jury to a certain degree (generally, preponderance of the evidence); p. 30

- **preponderance of the evidence**—a standard of proof meaning more likely than not (or more than 50% certain); p. 30

- **discretionary decision making**—judicial criminal lawmaking power that leaves judges lots of leeway for making decisions based on their professional training and experience; p. 31

- **not guilty verdict**—a verdict that the trier of fact (the jury or the judge in a bench trial) will return if the state did not prove its case beyond a reasonable doubt; p. 32

- **guilty verdict**—the verdict that the trier of fact will return if it finds the state did prove its case beyond a reasonable doubt; p. 32

- **judgment**—the court's decision in a given case. At the trial level, the judgment will either be guilty or not guilty. On appeal, the judgment will either be: affirmed, reversed, or reversed and remanded; p. 34

- **opinion**—the courts written decision given its reasons for deciding the case as it did; p. 34

- **concurring opinion**—a written opinion by judges who agree with the judgment of the majority or the dissent, but they have a different reason for reaching their decision; p. 34

- **plurality opinion**—an opinion that represents the reasoning of the greatest number (but less than a majority) of justices; p. 34

- **case citation**—source reference to a case or other legal authority; p. 35

CHAPTER OUTLINE

I. What Behavior Deserves Criminal Punishment
   A. Not all wrongs are crimes.
   B. Behavior that deserves punishment warrants criminal liability.
   C. Criminal liability is reserved for conduct that unjustifiably and inexcusably inflicts or threatens harm.

II. Crimes and Noncriminal Wrongs
   A. Criminal law is one form of social control, but there are others. Criminal liability is the most extreme response to wrongdoing.
   B. Torts are similar to crimes in that they are a set of rules which apply to everyone in the community, and the power of the law backs them up.
   C. Torts are dissimilar to crimes in that they are brought by nongovernmental parties called plaintiffs who can only get money damages.
   D. Unlike crimes, there is no conviction or public condemnation if the party is found responsible for the wrongdoing.
   E. Conviction is the expression of the community's hatred or contempt for the convict. Criminal punishment expresses societal censure of the offender.

III. Classifying Crimes
   A. A response to an urge to make sense of criminal law.
   B. There are many ways to classify crimes.
   C. Crimes of Moral Turpitude and Crimes without Moral Turpitude
      1. Crimes of moral turpitude involve behavior that is inherently wrong or evil.
      2. Crimes without moral turpitude involve behavior that is only criminal because there is a law prohibiting it.
      3. Examples of Crimes of Moral Turpitude—murder and rape
      4. Examples of Crimes without Moral Turpitude—parking violations
   D. **Felony and Misdemeanor**—Classifications based on punishment
      1. Felonies—defined
      2. Misdemeanors—defined
      3. Distinction matters.
         a. Procedures for felonies are different.
         b. Prior felony convictions may enhance sentence.
         c. Legal consequences of felonies (for example, voting rights) that aren't there for misdemeanors

IV. The General and Special Parts of Criminal Law
   A. **The General Part**
      1. Broad propositions that apply to more than one crime
      2. Crimes of general applicability, such as attempt, conspiracy, solicitation
      3. Principles of complicity
      4. Principles of justifications and excuses

B. **The Special Part**
   1. Defines specific crimes; spells out the elements of the crime
      a. Crimes against persons
      b. Crimes against property
      c. Crimes against public order and morals
      d. Crimes against the state

V. **The Sources of Criminal Law**
   A. In addition to legislative and judicial lawmaking, there are several sources of criminal law. Most current criminal law is created by state legislatures or local governing bodies. Federal Congress and administrative agencies are also responsible for much of the current criminal law.
   B. **Common-Law Crimes**—Law that emerged over a long period of time and was based on customs and traditions passed down
      1. **State common-law crimes**: Many states have common law in their history, but most have now abolished it to some extent.
      2. **Federal common-law crimes**: There are no official federal common-law crimes; however, as judges interpret congressional acts and engage in judicial lawmaking, they are creating federal common law.
   C. **State Criminal Codes**—Periodically, states have been urged to abolish common-law crimes and establish a criminal law based solely upon criminal codes (called the codification movement).
   D. **The Model Penal Code (MPC)**—After several decades, the American Law Institute created a draft code in 1962 that abolished common-law crimes. Even states that have not strictly abolished their codes have been influenced by the MPC.
      1. MPC not adopted in total by any state, but followed by most of the states
      2. Structure of the MPC has "general part" and "special part"
      3. MPC defines criminal liability and answers which behavior deserves criminal punishment
   E. **Municipal Ordinances**—Municipalities have broad but not unlimited power to create local crime laws and determine the punishment for those crimes. Some of the limitations on this power includes constitutional limitations, the state's having a conflicting law, and the inability to create felonies or crimes for which the punishment is more than one year of jail time.
   F. **Administrative Agency Crimes**—State and federal agencies also make administrative rules that have criminal penalties. Administrative agencies base their authority to make administrative crime on rule-making authority that is delegated to them by Congress or state legislatures.

VI. **Criminal Law in a Federal System**
   A. There are fifty-two criminal codes in America—one for each state, the District of Columbia, and the U.S. Criminal Code for the federal government.
   B. These codes resemble one another but they differ significantly in both the definitions of crimes and the severity of punishment.

V. What is the Appropriate Punishment for Criminal Behavior?
A. The United States uses incarceration extensively as a punishment for criminal behavior. In addition, millions of Americans are on probation, parole, and other forms of community corrections.
B. Punishment takes many forms, but each must meet the four criteria (inflict pain, be prescribed by the law that defines the crime, be intentionally administered, and be administered by the state).
C. Distinguish between punishment and treatment—not always clear
D. There are two schools of thought concerning the purpose of punishment: retribution and treatment.
    1. **Retribution**—punishing individuals for their past crimes
        a. Retributionists assume that offenders choose behavior that makes their choice blameworthy, and they assume offenders have free will.
        b. Underpinnings of retribution: culpability and justice
        c. Problems with restitution: abstract notions of justice, how much is just desert; urge to retaliate isn't part of civilized society; free will debate; crimes without culpability requirement (for example, statutory rape)
    2. **Prevention**
        a. Types of prevention
            i. General deterrence—arguments in support and against
            ii. Special deterrence—arguments in support and against
            iii. Principle of utility, defined
            iv. Criticisms of deterrence theory in general
            iii. Incapacitation—arguments in support and against
            iv. Rehabilitation—arguments in support and against
E. **Trends in Punishment**
    1. Societies have justified punishment on grounds of the four types of prevention, but they have emphasized one over the others during different times and eras.
    2. Sentencing law changes to reflect the prevalent punishment philosophy of the time.
        a. indeterminate sentencing laws
        b. determinate sentencing laws-fixed sentences

VI. Presumption of Innocence and Proving Criminal Liability
A. **Presumption of Innocence and the prosecutions burden of proof**
B. **Burden of Proof of Criminal Conduct:** Prosecution has burden of proof to prove case beyond a reasonable doubt
C. **Proving the Defenses of Justification and Excuse:** Sometimes the burden of proof (meaning the burden of production-presenting evidence to the trier of fact and the burden of persuasion—convincing the trier of fact) switches to the defendant—for example in the case of affirmative defenses.

VII. Discretionary Decision Making
A. Although much of criminal law is based on formal laws and rules, invisible and informal discretionary decision making has a tremendous impact on what happens in the criminal justice process.
B. At each step in the criminal justice process, criminal justice practitioners exercise discretion that affects the outcome of the case.

VIII. The Text-Case Method
A. Two parts of the book
   1. The Text defines and explains concepts and principles.
   2. The Case Excerpts test your understanding (and get you to think critically by applying definitions, concepts, and principles to real cases).
B. **The Parts of the Case Excerpts**
   1. Each case has a title, a citation, a procedural history, the name of the judge who wrote the opinion, a section discussing the facts of the case, the court's decision or judgment, and the court's opinion. The court's (majority) opinion is made up of the court's holding and the court's reasoning—or why the court decided as it did.
      a. Majority opinions
      b. Concurring opinions
      c. Dissenting opinions
C. **Briefing the Case Excerpts**—In briefing a case, the important things that you should note are the important facts of the case, the legal issue that the court had to address, how the court decided the issues and why (the reasoning—the justifications the court gave for deciding how it did).
D. Summary of briefing cases—Not every case will have every part, so briefing cases gets easier with practice. Generally, briefs will always have a facts (what happened) section.

XI. Finding Cases
A. The ability to locate a case depends on understanding the components of the case citation. A case citation includes the volume of the reporter, the page number upon which the case starts, and the year of the decision.

CHAPTER SUMMARY

Not all wrongs are crimes, and using the criminal law is only one mechanism of social control. Criminal law decides who is criminally liable for what crime and what the response to that crime should be. Alternately, torts are private wrongs for which a nongovernmental party sues the wrongdoer for monetary damages. Although torts are similar to crimes, and sometimes even have the same name as related crimes, they are treated differently and do not result in a conviction with societal condemnation.

Crimes can be classified or graded according to many schemes. The most common are felony or misdemeanor. Typically a crime is a felony if it is punishable by at least one year in a state prison. Misdemeanors are punishable by one year or less in a local jail. Some crimes cover behavior that is inherently evil or bad in itself. These are called crimes of moral turpitude. Murder is an example of such a crime. Conversely, crimes without moral turpitude are behaviors that are criminal only because the law says it is. Parking violations are examples of such crimes. Crimes can also be classified according to the subject or the value that is harmed. Examples would be crimes against person, property, public order, public morals, and the administration of justice.

The criminal law itself can be divided into two parts: the special part of the criminal law provides the definitions of various crimes; and the general part provides general principles that apply to all offenses. This would include *mens rea* provisions and accomplice liability provisions. The specific part of criminal law is where the definitions of crimes are found.

In order to determine what the criminal law is in any jurisdiction within the federal system (the states, the nation, or the District of Columbia), one would have to refer to several sources. Legislation is only one of several sources of criminal law. American criminal law is derived from English common law. Common law was judge-made law based on the common customs. Over time, English common law was supplemented or abolished by statutes (or codes), but some states still refer to common law as a source of criminal law. However, most criminal law is found in state codes and municipal codes. These codes have been greatly influenced by the Model Penal Code, which was completed in 1962. Nevertheless, judges continue to be a source of law by their interpretations of the constitution and statutes. Additionally, administrative agencies have been delegated the task of creating criminal laws and penalties.

The Constitution establishes a federal system for America. Power is shared and divided between the states and federal government. Thus, both the states and the federal government can pass criminal laws. We have fifty sets of state criminal law, the criminal law in the District of Columbia, and the criminal law of the federal government. Although there are some common basic concepts, there are many differences among these jurisdictions.

Criminal law is guided by considerations of the purposes of criminal punishment. Punishment has two goals: retribution and prevention. Retribution is the idea of an eye for an eye. Criminals should be blamed and pay their debt to society. Preventing further crime is the second goal. There are four kinds of prevention: general deterrence—which punishes someone to make an example of them; special deterrence—which punishes offenders to prevent them from committing more crimes; incapacitation—which prevents criminals from committing more crimes by locking them up; and rehabilitation—which prevents future crimes by changing or treating the individual offender. Although every society has justified criminal punishment based upon retribution or the four types of prevention, the degree of emphasis has varied in different eras.

Study Guide

In order to impose criminal liability upon an offender, the state generally has to prove its case to a jury (or a judge in a bench trial) beyond a reasonable doubt. The state has the burden of proof, because under American jurisprudence, the defendant has the presumption of innocence. The burden of proof is made up of a burden of production (putting on evidence) and the burden of persuasion (convincing the jury to a certain level). Under some circumstances, such as when the defendant raises an affirmative defense —such as an excuse or justification—some states switch the burden of proof to the defendant concerning those facts related to the defense (for example, his mental state when he raises the defense of insanity).

Although much of the focus of this book is on the formal law, the reader should be aware that informal discretionary decision-making by criminal justice practitioners exists at every stage of the criminal justice process and ultimately influences the outcome of the case.

The textbook uses the text-case method. It includes explanatory text and excerpts from court cases/opinions. Generally, only appellate courts write opinions. The party who appeals is called the appellant. The party whose victory in the court below is being challenged is called the appellee.

When reading case opinions or excerpts, students need to be able to find the various parts of the cases. Only the majority opinion establishes law and the precedent. There may also be concurring opinions and dissenting opinions. These may provide well-reasoned alternatives to the majority opinion which may, at some later time, become the law of the land. Two of the most important parts of the case are the holding and the rationale. The holding is the legal rule announced by the court that decides the case. The rationale is the reasons underlying the holding.

Finally, the reader should be able to find court cases by using the opinion citation system. To do this, one needs to know the components of a legal citation, including the name of the case, the volume, reporter, page, and year of publication. There are a wide variety of publications and reporters for different jurisdictions.

Chapter 1: Criminal Law and Criminal Punishment: An Overview

Practice Test Bank

MULTIPLE CHOICE

1. A tort is a _____.
   a. private wrong
   b. type of crime
   c. type of pastry
   d. specific monetary punishment

2. Which of the following is a correct statement about felonies and misdemeanors?
   a. Historically, the distinction between felonies and misdemeanors was important, but today there is no need for such a classification.
   b. The criminal procedure is the same for both felonies and misdemeanors.
   c. The legal consequences for felony convictions may last long after the punishment for the conviction.
   d. Misdemeanors are generally less serious or blameworthy crimes.

3. One primary distinction between a crime and a tort is _____.
   a. the tort is brought by a government official acting on behalf of the citizens of that jurisdiction
   b. the crime is brought by a government official acting on behalf of the citizens of that jurisdiction
   c. the individual found responsible for a tort can receive many forms of punishment including fines, incarceration, and community service
   d. crimes, but not torts, harm the community as a whole

4. An eye for an eye approach to punishment is consistent with _____.
   a. general deterrence
   b. special deterrence
   c. incapacitation
   d. retribution

5. Retribution logically requires that the criminal be _____.
   a. blameworthy or culpable
   b. capable of change and wanting to change
   c. a potential re-offender or threat to society
   d. predictably dangerous or potentially dangerous

6. The idea of _____ involves confinement, surgical alteration, or execution to prevent further crimes by that defendant.
   a. rehabilitation
   b. special deterrence
   c. incapacitation
   d. retribution

7. The part of the criminal law that provides the elements of various particular crimes is called the _____ part.
   a. specific
   b. special
   c. specious
   d. spurious

8. In most jurisdictions, a felony is defined as a crime that is punishable by incarceration of at least _____ year(s) in a prison.
   a. one
   b. two
   c. three
   d. five

9. Murder and rape are examples of _____.
   a. crimes of moral turpitude
   b. crimes of non moral turpitude
   c. incorporatum
   d. crimes of regulation

10. Which of the following statements is most accurate regarding the criminal law in the U.S.?
    a. There is very little variation between jurisdictions because all states have adopted most of the Model Penal Code.
    b. There is very little variation between jurisdictions because all jurisdictions must conform to the U.S. Constitution and the U.S. Supreme Court decision.
    c. For a number of reasons, there is significant variation among jurisdictions in the U.S.
    d. Because of the Eighth Amendment, there are some differences between jurisdictions.

11. Under the federal system, government power is allocated between _____.
    a. state (and local) governments and the federal government
    b. the federal government and the United Nations
    c. state and local governments
    d. state government and the United Nations

12. In the U.S. today, most criminal law is _____ law.
    a. federal
    b. state
    c. county
    d. international

13. American criminal law has its origin in English _____.
    a. civil law
    b. Code law
    c. Common law
    d. Royal decrees

14. Today, at least half of the states have _____.
    a. retained common-law crimes as their only crimes
    b. abolished common-law crimes
    c. recognized common-law, statutory, and international crimes
    d. abolished their penal/criminal/crime codes

15. A code state is one which has _____.
    a. retained common-law crimes as their only crimes
    b. abolished common-law crimes
    c. recognized common-law, statutory, and international crimes
    d. abolished their penal/criminal/crime codes

16. Most states and the federal government have _____ levels of appellate courts.
    a. two
    b. three
    c. four
    d. five

17. In a court case/opinion, the legal rule that decides the case is called the _____.
    a. issue
    b. holding
    c. judgment
    d. reasoning

18. The established law of the case and the precedent is established in the _____ opinion.
    a. dominant
    b. concurring
    c. majority
    d. plurality

19. In the citation, 428 U.S. 364 (1976), 428 represents _____.
    a. the volume number
    b. the reporter
    c. the page number upon which the case begins
    d. the number of pages the decision is

20. Administrative law is _____.
    a. judge-made law
    b. law enacted by legislators
    c. law enacted by municipalities
    d. agency-made law

21. Punitive damages are _____.
    a. monetary damages designed to punish a civil defendant
    b. punishment which includes incarceration
    c. monetary damages designed to make the civil plaintiff whole
    d. like restitution and help cover the cost of treatment for the plaintiff

22. _____ means that the state in a criminal case must bring forth evidence to show that the defendant committed the act.
    a. Burden of proof
    b. Burden of persuasion
    c. Preponderance of evidence
    d. Presumption of proof

23. In some jurisdictions, defendants have the burden of production when presenting affirmative defenses. They may also have _____.
    a. the corpus delicti defense
    b. the ultimate burden of proof
    c. to prove their case beyond a reasonable doubt
    d. the burden of persuasion to convince the jury

24. The Model Penal Code was drafted by the _____.
    a. American Law Institute
    b. Center for Legal Codification
    c. American Bar Association
    d. Committee for Equal Justice under the Law

25. Ordinances are laws enacted by _____.
    a. state legislators
    b. Federal Congress
    c. municipalities
    d. judges through their case interpretations

26. Placing a tax on cigarettes in order to discourage cigarette smoking is an example of a _____.
    a. crime
    b. non-criminal wrong
    c. license
    d. regulation

27. Conduct that unjustifiably and inexcusably inflicts or threatens harm to an individual or public interest is the definition of _____.
    a. a tort
    b. a contract
    c. criminal liability
    d. a regulation

28. _____ occurs at every step in the criminal justice process.
    a. Retroactive decision making
    b. Discretionary decision making
    c. Pro forma decision making
    d. Discriminatory decision making

29. Which of the following is the best example of criminal punishment?
    a. a mental patient confined indefinitely to a padded cell in a state hospital
    b. a sentence of 30 hours of community service for a minor theft charge
    c. an award of one million dollars in punitive damages for a wrongful death act
    d. shock treatment to help condition a person not to be aroused sexually by the sight of young children

30. One of the greatest weaknesses with retribution theory is that _____.
    a. many offenders do not make rational choices
    b. many offenders have addictions
    c. it is difficult to determine what is just deserts (how much punishment is just)
    d. it is forward looking

TRUE/FALSE

1. Prior decisions that are relevant to deciding the current case are called precedents.
    a. true
    b. false

2. Discretionary decision making is a formal process within the criminal justice system.
    a. true
    b. false

3. The burden of production requires the party who carries the burden to persuade the jury either by a preponderance of the evidence or beyond a reasonable doubt.
    a. true
    b. false

4. The second set of numbers in a case/opinion citation is the date of the decision.
    a. true
    b. false

5. The first set of numbers in a case citation is the page number on which the case begins.
    a. true
    b. false

6. Most criminal laws in the U.S. are state laws.
    a. true
    b. false

7. Rehabilitation and prevention are prospective (looking to prevent future crime).
    a. true
    b. false

8. Principles of accomplice liability are part of the special part of the criminal law.
    a. true
    b. false

9. The highest level of proof—the one required in a criminal case—is preponderance of the evidence.
    a. true
    b. false

10. The federal government and most states utilize common-law crimes exclusively.
    a. true
    b. false

11. An example of discretionary decision making is a police officer instructing an underage drinker to pour out his beer rather than issue a "minor in possession" citation.
    a. true
    b. false

12. Ordinances may conflict with state law.
    a. true
    b. false

13. The constitution limits the ability of agencies to create criminal laws and punishments.
    a. true
    b. false

14. The American criminal law is based on the common law of Spain.
    a. true
    b. false

15. Punishing an individual to make an example of him and deter others from committing more crimes is called specific deterrence.
    a. true
    b. false

16. The elements of the crimes of rape or murder would be found in the special part of the criminal law.
    a. true
    b. false

17. Misdemeanors are crimes punishable by more than one year incarceration in a local jail.
    a. true
    b. false

18. The elements of burglary are set forth in the special part of criminal law.
    a. true
    b. false

19. Code jurisdictions are those that have kept common-law offenses.
    a. true
    b. false

20. Definitions of defenses and terminology used in criminal statutes are found in the general part of criminal law.
    a. true
    b. false

21. The Model Penal Code has been followed by all fifty states, but not by the federal government.
    a. true
    b. false

22. The presumption of innocence means that the state has the burden to prove that the defendant committed the crime.
    a. true
    b. false

23. Since the 1980s, rehabilitation and treatment have been emphasized as the primary criminal punishment.
    a. true
    b. false

Study Guide

24. A regulation is the government placing a burden on a behavior to discourage it, without necessarily punishing the behavior.
   a. true
   b. false

25. A license is a user fee intended to discourage behavior.
   a. true
   b. false

FILL-IN-THE-BLANK

1. The _____ consists of the numbers, letters, and punctuation that follow the title of a case in the excerpts or in the bibliography at the end of the book.

2. The party who appeals an adverse judgment or decision is called the _____.

3. A _____ is a private wrong for which a party can be sued.

4. The burden of proof as it applies to the state includes both the burden of _____ and the burden of _____.

5. _____ represents the number of prisoners per 100,000 people in the general population.

6. _____ are violations of state and federal agency rules.

7. A _____ is a private party who brings a civil suit such as a personal injury action.

8. Monetary awards against a private party to punish them for wrongdoing are _____.

9. When an appellate court agrees with the decision of the court immediately below it, we say it has _____ the lower court decision.

10. When a case is _____, it is sent back down to a lower court for further proceedings, in accordance with the appellate court's decision.

11. The _____ part of the criminal law specifies principles that apply to all crimes.

12. Larceny, arson, burglary, and theft are classified as crimes against _____.

18

13. Judge-made law, originally based on the common customs or traditions of the people, is called the _____ law.

14. Today, most new crimes are created by the legislature by passing _____.

15. _____ is when someone is blameworthy and society decides to express its condemnation through a criminal conviction.

ESSAY

1. Describe the main sources of criminal law. Give examples of each.

2. Discuss the evolution from common law system of criminal law to the predominantly code system of criminal law.

3. Describe and compare the power of judges, legislators, and administrative agencies to make criminal law.

Study Guide

4. Describe the goals of punishment and trace the trends in punishment.

5. How does the presumption of innocence relate to the burden of proof, the burden of production and the burden of persuasion?

CHAPTER 1 ANSWER KEY

Multiple Choice

1. a. See pg. 8, LO 1
2. c. See pg. 11, LO 1
3. b. See pg. 8, LO 4
4. d. See pg. 22, LO 4
5. a. See pg. 23, LO 4
6. c. See pg. 24, LO 4
7. b. See pg. 12, LO 2
8. a. See pg. 11, LO 1
9. a. See pg.11 LO 1
10. c. See pg. 19, LO 3
11. a. See pg. 19 LO 3
12. b. See pg. 13, LO 3
13. c. See pgs. 13-14, LO 3
14. b. See pg. 14, LO 3
15. b. See pg. 14, LO 3
16. a. See pg. 32, LO 3
17. b. See pg. 34, LO 7
18. c. See pg. 34, LO 7
19. a. See pg. 35, LO 7
20. d. See pg. 13, LO 3
21. a. See pg. 10, LO 4
22. a. See pg. 29, LO 5
23. d. See pg. 30, LO 5
24. a. See pg. 16, LO 3
25. c. See pg. 17, LO 3
26. d. See pg. 4, LO 3
27. c. See pg. 6, LO 1
28. b. See pgs. 30-31, LO 6
29. b. See pg. 22, LO 4
30. c. See pg. 24, LO 4

True/False

1. T. See pg.14 , LO 7
2. F. See pgs. 30-31, LO 6
3. F. See pg. 30, LO 5
4. F. See pg. 35, LO 7
5. F. See pg. 35, LO 7
6. T. See pg. 13, LO 4
7. T. See pg. 24, LO 4
8. F. See pg. 12, LO 3
9. F. See pg. 29, LO 5
10. F. See pg. 13, LO 3
11. T. See pg. 31, LO 6
12. F. See pg. 18, LO 3
13. T. See pg. 19, LO 3
14. F. See pg. 14, LO 3
15. F. See pg. 24, LO 4
16. T. See pg. 12, LO 2
17. F. See pg. 11, LO. 1
18. T. See pg. 12, LO 2
19. F. See pg. 14, LO 3
20. T. See pg. 12, LO
21. F. See pg. 17, LO 3
22. T. See pg. 29, LO 5
23. F. See pg. 29, LO 4
24. T. See pg. 4, LO 3
25. F. See pg. 4, LO 4

Study Guide

Fill-in-the-Blank

1. case citation. See pg. 35, LO 7
2. appellant. See pg. 33, LO 7
3. tort. See pg. 8, LO 1
4. production, persuasion. See pg. 30, LO 5
5. Rate of imprisonment. See pg. 20, LO 4
6. Administrative crimes. See pg. 19, LO 3
7. plaintiff. See pg. 8, LO 4
8. punitive damages. See pg. 10, LO 4
9. affirmed. See pg. 34, LO 7
10. remanded. See pg. 34, LO 7
11. general. See pg. 12, LO 2
12. property. See pg. 7, LO 2
13. common. See pg. 13, LO 3
14. statutes or codes. See pg. 16, LO
15. Culpable. See pg. 23, LO 1

Essays

1. Describe the main sources of criminal law. Give examples of each.

    There are five main sources of criminal law: the constitution (both State and Federal), case law (judge made law), codes/statutes (legislatively made law), administrative law (agency made law), and common law (law which developed over time deriving from English Common law). Although constitution doesn't specify many crimes (the U.S. Constitution only lists treason), it does govern the other sources of law (see chapter two, constitutional limits on criminal law). Codes, statutes, and ordinances are the primary source of criminal law, and case law is often the court's interpretation of those codes. Administrative ordinances detail certain behaviors (particularly violations) that carry criminal penalties and are therefore a source of criminal law (think of driving offenses, or fish and wildlife offenses). Finally, common law has historically provided most of the criminal law (definitions of crime based upon custom and usage in a community), but has largely been supplanted with codes. LO 3

2. Discuss the evolution from common law system of criminal law to the predominantly code system of criminal law.

    The earliest forms of English criminal law involved custom and tradition within small communities. Although the law was not written, there was a common understanding of what types of behaviors and circumstances were necessary to commit certain crimes. (We often say, "at common law, the elements of Crime X were A, B, C, and Y"). As times changed, these elements and circumstances changed. Court decisions also expanded and refined what these laws meant. As America developed and state and federal law-makers became more involved (embroiled) in concerns about criminal law, there was a shift from relying on tradition to relying on codes or statutes as the primary basis of criminal law. Much of the codification of the criminal law (putting the law of crimes into statutes) came about not as a rejection of the common law, but a restatement or affirmation of the common law principles, filling in gaps or defining concepts left ambiguous with the common law. In other areas, codification allowed legislators to "get with the times" and deal with emerging concerns and modern sentiments (consider the changes in rape laws discussed in chapter 10). The Model Penal Code was the result of the examination of common law and the discussions about what was working, what wasn't, and what the best approach was. The Model Penal Code, which has not been followed in its entirety by any state, allowed states to codify their existing law and to have similar discussions. Most states have abolished common law crimes, and to some extent chosen to adopt to a greater and lesser degree provisions of the MPC. Even when a state has completely "abolished the common law," it may have preserved it by codification, allowed it to remain as a source of definitions where terms were left undefined. LO 3

3. Describe and compare the power of judges, legislators, and administrative agencies to make criminal law.

   Case law (judge made law) is one of the greatest sources of criminal law. Although there has always been a concern about judge made law being antidemocratic (law making should be done by elected individuals representing the populous), judges have always had to fill in the gaps left open with common law and criminal statutes. Interpreting and defining what the statutes mean is arguably law making. As you read through the cases in this text, you will see that the court has to decide whether certain behavior is, for example, pre-meditated. The decision of the court in those cases becomes law for the next judges having to decide similar cases (the concept of precedent and stare decisis and why judges issue written opinions for the cases they review). Legislators (local, state, and federal) all have different titles, but perform similar duties. They enact new laws (statutes and ordinances), modify existing laws, and abolish old laws. Among those laws is the body of law known as criminal law, and when legislators perform their duties they are said to be "codifying" the criminal law. Most criminal law is a product of legislation. Administrative agencies make administrative law which sometimes has criminal penalties attached. For example, Departments of Motor Vehicles or Fish and Game will enact administrative rules—a breach of which results in criminal or quasi criminal penalties (fines, incarceration, etc). LO 3

4. Describe the goals of punishment and trace the trends in punishment.

Two primary answers (schools of thought) have emerged responding to the question "why do we punish criminals?". The first answer has been, "because they deserve it"—or retribution. The other answer has been, "so we can stop more crime"—or prevention. Prevention has four types: general deterrence (punishing the criminal to make an example of him and thus preventing crime by others), special deterrence (punishing the criminal to teach him a lesson and preventing his further criminal activity), incapacitation (preventing crime by making it impossible for the offender to commit crimes against society—through incarceration, surgery, or execution), and rehabilitation (treating or changing the offender so that they won't want to or need to offend). Because there are strong advocates and critics supporting each of these justifications for punishment, neither side has ever had a "corner on the market." Indeed, one can see that historically these approached have waxed and waned cyclically. The current trend in punishment was, until recently, retribution and incarceration. This is evidenced by mandatory minimum sentencing and "three-strikes" sentencing schemes that emerged in the late 1980s and have proliferated in the 1990s. (Their popularity may however be on the decrease due to their high costs and the slumping economy.) LO 4

5. How does the presumption of innocence relate to the burden of proof, the burden of production and the burden of persuasion?

The presumption of innocence means that the state (prosecution) has to put on evidence (burden of production) to convince the jury or judge (burden of persuasion) that the defendant committed the act (standard is beyond a reasonable doubt). The defendant has no obligation to prove that he is not guilty, because he is presumed to be not guilty. Sometimes the defendant has the burden to put on some evidence—when there is an affirmative defense. The burden of production is switched to the defendant in these cases because they are claiming some special circumstance (for example, if they had an alibi or were claiming they were insane). The defendant doesn't have to put on much evidence, but has to give the state notice that they are raising an affirmative defense, and then introduce some credible evidence. The burden then reverts to the state to put on enough more evidence to disprove the defense. The ultimate burden of proof as to the defendant's guilt as to all the elements of the crime, always remains with the state. LO 5

Chapter 2
Constitutional Limits on Criminal Law

LEARNING OBJECTIVES

1. To understand and appreciate the reasons for the limits on criminal law and criminal punishment in the U.S. constitutional democracy

2. To understand the principle of legality and the importance of its relationship to the limits of criminal law and punishment.

3. To appreciate the nature and importance of retroactive criminal law making.

4. To know the criteria for identifying vague laws, and understand and appreciate their constitutional significance and the consequences.

5. To know and understand and appreciate the limits placed on the criminal law and criminal punishment by the specific provisions in the Bill of Rights

6. To understand and appreciate the constitutional significance and consequences of principle of proportionality in criminal punishment.

7. To understand the importance of the right to trial by jury in the process of sentencing convicted offenders.

KEY TERMS AND CONCEPTS

- **constitutional democracy**—a type of government in which the majority of the people cannot make some action to be a crime if the constitution protects it as a fundamental right; p. 40

- **rule of law**—the notion that no one person can ever be above the law and that the law applies to every person; p. 40

- **ex post facto law**—laws passed after the occurrence of the conduct constituting the crime; p. 41

- **void-for-vagueness doctrine**—the principle that a statute violates due process if it doesn't clearly define crime and punishment in advance; p. 42

- **fair notice (in the void for vagueness doctrine)**—the requirement that the law be specific enough to put a reasonable person on fair notice of what is permitted and what is prohibited; p. 42

- **equal protection of the laws**—the constitutional requirement that the government must, at a minimum, have a rational basis for treating individuals differently. Some classes of individuals may not be treated differently unless the government has a compelling state interest in treating them differently; p. 46

- **expressive conduct (in First Amendment)**—actions that communicate ideas and feelings; for example, flag burning; p. 47

- **void-for-overbreadth doctrine**—the principle that a statute is unconstitutional if its definition of undesirable behavior includes conduct protected under the U.S. Constitution; p. 48

- **bench trial**—trials without juries, in which judges find the facts; p. 48

- **fundamental right to right to privacy**—a right that bans "all governmental invasions of the sanctity of a man's home and the privacies of life;" p. 52

- **Second Amendment**—the Amendment to the U.S. Constitution that protects the rights of individuals to possess firearms; p. 56

- **barbaric punishments**—punishment no longer considered acceptable; p. 59

- **cruel and unusual punishment**—Eighth Amendment protection against punishment that is either disproportionate or barbaric; p. 60

- **principle of proportionality**—a principle of law stating that the punishment must be proportional to the crime committed; p. 60

- **three-strikes-and-you're-out laws**—controversial mandatory minimum sentencing legislation for repeat offenders; p. 67

- **mandatory minimum sentences**—sentencing scheme which requires judges to impose non-discretionary minimum amount of prison time that all offenders have to serve; p. 67

- **fixed (determinate) sentencing**—sentences imposed by the judge which fix the term of imprisonment at the time of sentencing based upon the seriousness of the crime; p. 70

- **sentencing guidelines**—a type of fixed sentencing which establishes a range of penalties from which the judge chooses a specific sentence within the range based upon several factos (seriousness of the crime, prior criminal history of the offender, etc); p. 70

- *Apprendi* **rule**—from Apprendi v. New Jersey. This rule requires that before a judge can issue a harsher sentence than one in the sentencing guidelines (a departure sentence) the jury has to determine that the facts justifying the departure are proven beyond a reasonable doubt; p. 72

- **abuse-of-discretion standard**—an adjudicator's failure to exercise sound, reasonable, and legal decision making; p. 75

CHAPTER OUTLINE

I. Constitutional Limits on Criminal Law
   A. Constitutional democracy—The Constitution limits what the government can make criminal and directs how legislation should be enacted to protect individual's rights.
   B. Rule of Law—System of law in which no person or government is above the law.
   C. **Principle of Legality**
      1. First principle of criminal law
      2. No one can be convicted of, or punished for, a crime unless the law defined the crime and prescribed the punishment before they engaged in the behavior that was defined as a crime.
      3. Retroactive criminal law making is abhorrent.
         a. Knowing what the law commands gives people the chance to obey the law.
         b. The opportunity to obey the law fosters autonomy and human dignity.
         c. The ban on retroactive criminal law making regulates officials and fosters rule of law.

II. The Ban on *Ex Post Facto* Laws
   A. The principle "no crime without law; no punishment without law" (meaning no retroactive lawmaking) is so fundamental that it is embodied within the U.S. Constitution. Article 1 Section 9 prohibits legislatures from passing *ex post facto* laws.
   B. **Kinds of *Ex Post Facto* Laws**
      1. Statues that criminalize innocent acts after they are committed
      2. Statutes which increase the punishment for a crime after it was committed—*Garner v. Jones* (2000)
      3. Statutes which take away a defense that was available to the defendant when the crime was committed
   C. **The Purpose of the Ban on *Ex Post Facto* Laws**
      1. Give fair warnings to private individuals
      2. Prevent arbitrary government action

III. Void-for-Vagueness Doctrine
   A. Void-for-Vagueness: Laws which are too vague violate a person's rights to due process. Vague laws fail to warn a person of what the law is, or allow officials to arbitrarily decide what the law means, thus they deprive individuals of their right to life, liberty, or property.

B. **The Aims of the Void-for-Vagueness Doctrine**
   1. Failure to give fair warning to individuals as to what the law prohibits
   2. Allow arbitrary and discriminatory application of the law—*Lanzetta v. New Jersey*
C. **Defining Vagueness**
   1. What is fair notice?
      a. "Would an ordinary, reasonable person know that what he was doing was criminal?"
   2. Minimal guidelines to govern law enforcement
      a. Controlling law enforcement has recently been given more priority in the vagueness analysis than whether fair notice is provided.
   3. Presumption of constitutionality requires challengers to prove the law is vague rather than the government having to prove that it is not too vague.
D. *Case: State v. Metzger*

IV. Equal Protection of the Laws
A. The 14th Amendment prohibits states from denying a person equal protection of law. States don't have to treat everybody the same. Statutes can in fact treat classes of persons differently, but whether the statute will pass constitutional muster depends on what the classification is, how narrowly the statute is crafted, and how badly and why the state needs to treat the people in the class differently.
B. Race-based classifications—Courts must look at statute with strict scrutiny. Thus, such classifications always violate the constitution.
C. Gender-based classifications—Courts must look at statute with heightened scrutiny. State must show a "fair and substantial relationship between the classification and a legitimate state end."
D. Other classifications—Courts must show that there is a rational basis between the classification and the state's need to treat those falling in that classification differently.

V. The Bill of Rights and Criminal Law—The Bill of Rights bans defining certain kinds of behavior as criminal.

VI. Free Speech—First Amendment to U.S. Constitution
A. Application
   1. Speech is broad in scope, including expressive conduct and giving money to candidates
   2. Applies to federal government and to states
   3. Free speech is a fundamental right with preferred status (states need compelling interest to limit it).
   4. Some types of speech are not protected, and the government can make time, place, and manner restrictions on them.
      a. Obscenity

    b. Profanity
    c. Libel and slander
    d. Fighting words
    e. Clear and present danger
  B. Void-for-Overbreadth Doctrine—When a statute prohibits something that the constitution protects, the statute is said to be overbroad. The concern is that people will refrain from doing or saying things they have a lawful right to do and say because they are afraid they will be prosecuted. The concern then becomes that the overbroad statute will have a chilling effect on people's behavior.
    1. *R.A.V. v. City of St. Paul*
  C. *Case: People v. Rokicki*
  D. *Case: Barns v. Glen Theater, Inc et. al.*
  E. *Case: Texas v. Johnson*

VII. The Right to Privacy
  A. Application
    1. Right to privacy is found within the "penumbra" of the Constitution, not in any specific clause or Amendment. State constitutions may have specific provisions regarding the right to privacy.
    2. Right to privacy bans "government invasions into sanctity of home and privacies of life."
    3. Fundamental right—Each state has to show compelling state interest in order to justify invading this right.
  B. *Case: Griswold v. Connecticut*
  C. *Case: Stanley v. Georgia*
  D. *Case: Lawrence v. Texas*

VIII. The Right to Bear Arms
  A. Second Amendment—2008 first successful challenge to gun legislation
  B. *Case: District of Columbia v. Heller*
    a. The core of the Second Amendment is the right of law-abiding, responsible citizens to use arms in defense of hearth and home.
    b. Relatively narrow, but important decision nonetheless

IX. The Constitution and Criminal Sentencing
  A. **Barbaric Punishments**—Punishments which are no longer acceptable in a civilized society; thus, as society evolves, what has been considered barbaric, has likewise changed.
    1. Death itself isn't cruel and unusual, but if it involves unnecessary mutilation of the body or pain, it is cruel.
    2. *Case: In re Kemmler*

Study Guide

B. **Disproportionate Punishments**
    1. Principle of Proportionality—The punishment should fit the crime. Very harsh punishments, which are completely out of line with the severity of the crime, violate the principle of proportionality.
    2. Federal (*Weems*) and state (*Robinson*) ban on disproportional punishment.

C. **The Death Penalty: "Death is Different"**
    1. Death penalty for crime less than murder
    2. *Case: Kennedy v. Louisiana* – Court overturned death sentence for defendant convicted of raping a child less than 12 years old. Court pointed to national consensus against death penalty for crimes less than murder.

D. **The Death Penalty for the Mentally Retarded**
    1. *Case: Atkins v. Virginia* (2002). The court noted a consistent and pervasive change in public opinion against executing retarded offenders and held that it was now cruel and unusual punishment to execute retarded offenders. Also, retarded offenders aren't as blameworthy (culpable) or subject to deterrence as others.

E. **The Death Penalty for Juveniles**
    1. *Case: Roper v. Simmons* (2004). The court overruled earlier opinions and decided that due to "evolving standards of decency in a civilized society," it was now cruel and unusual punishment to execute offenders who committed their crimes before turning 18 years old.

F. **Sentences of Imprisonment**
    1. Lack of consensus on whether prison sentences have to be proportionate to the crime committed (*Solem v. Helm*)
    2. Mandatory Minimum—Three Strikes sentences
        a. Disproportionality issue is applicable to mandatory minimum and three strikes type of sentences.
        b. Controversial
            i. Pro—Help restore credibility of the criminal justice system, deter crime
            ii. Con—Harsh penalties won't have effect on crime, costly
        c. Sentences are popular
        d. *Case: Ewing v. California*
    3. Mandatory Minimum Sentences

G. **The Right to "Trial" by Jury**
    1. *Case: Apprendi v. New Jersey* – decision that for the court to do an upward departure from the presumed guideline sentence, a jury must find beyond a reasonable doubt the factors justifying that sentence enhancement.
    2. *Case: Blakely v. Washington*—Washington sentencing guidelines overturned to the extent that they allowed judge to increase sentence beyond guideline without jury finding.
    3. *Case: U.S. v. Booker*—*Apprendi* rule applied to U.S. Sentencing Guidelines, guidelines are now advisory and not mandatory
    4. *Case: Gall v. United States*—involved downward departure not increase

CHAPTER SUMMARY

Because the United States is a constitutional democracy, there are limits to the power of state and federal governments to create crimes. These limitations are found within the U.S. Constitution and the individual state constitutions. The rule of law means that no person is above the law. The principle of legality is the centerpiece of criminal law; it provides that no behavior is criminal unless there is already a law banning it and that no one will be punished unless there is already a law setting forth what the punishment is. Retroactive criminal law making is abhorrent to our system of law.

The purposes of banning *ex post facto* and vague criminal statutes are to give fair warning to individuals as to what the law prohibits and to prevent arbitrary enforcement by public officials. The constitutional basis for banning laws so vague that reasonable private individuals and public officials can't understand them is that such laws deprive individuals of life, liberty, or property without due process of law.

The U.S. Constitution doesn't guarantee that criminal laws treat everybody exactly alike; it does command that classifying people or behavior differently be reasonable (or have a rational basis). Classifications based on gender are subject to a heightened scrutiny by the court and the state must show a substantial relationship to the legitimate state interest. Classifications based upon race or ethnicity are subject to strict scrutiny (the highest level of scrutiny) and are generally always unconstitutional.

The Bill of Rights also limits the type of behavior that can be criminalized. Under the First Amendment to the U.S. Constitution, the guarantee of free speech is a fundamental right. Government action infringing on rights that are deemed fundamental must be shown to be more than reasonable. The action must be justified by showing that it furthers a compelling governmental interest. According to the U.S. Supreme Court, some kinds of non-verbal, expressive conduct are speech; some words aren't "speech," and some speech isn't protected by the guarantee of free speech. Obscenity and fighting words are examples of speech not protected by the First Amendment. Additionally, law makers need to take care when criminalizing behavior that they do not write a law so broadly that it bans protected expression (the doctrine of overbreadth). Overbroad statutes may have a chilling effect and cause people to avoid engaging in behaviors that are constitutionally protected.

The word privacy doesn't appear in the U.S. Constitution, but the U.S. Supreme Court has indicated in one case that it lies within the "penumbra" of the Constitution—meaning that it is implicit in several clauses of the Bill of Rights (the first ten Amendments to the U.S. Constitution). Many states do have a specific provision in their constitutions protecting the right to privacy of their citizens. The U.S. Supreme Court has dealt with privacy issues in matters concerning family life, reproduction, and child rearing. Recently the court examined whether statutes criminalizing consensual homosexual conduct between adults violated the right to privacy. In deciding that it did, the court in *Lawrence v. Texas* (2003) overruled an earlier 1986 decision.

The Second Amendment protects the right to bear arms. The Amendment was poorly worded, and there have been few U.S. Supreme Court cases interpreting the amendment, notwithstanding fairly vocal gun rights and gun control activists. The first successful challenge based upon the Second Amendment came in 2008, and the Court struck down a broad D.C. statute banning possession of handguns and requiring that firearms in the home be nonfunctional. Although it is an important case, the holding is rather limited.

The U.S. Supreme Court has interpreted the ban on cruel and unusual punishments to include barbaric punishments and punishments disproportionate to crimes. The death penalty is valid if certain constitutional rules are followed. Recently the Court has looked to the changing standards and sentiments of a civilized community in determining that executing retarded individuals and individuals who committed their crimes before they turned 18 years old both violate the ban on cruel and unusual punishment. Additionally, the Court has determined that three-strikes types of legislation is not disproportionate and withstands an Eighth Amendment cruel and unusual punishment challenge. Finally, the Court has recently determined that imposition of the death penalty for the rape of a child victim was disproportionate punishment.

Many states and the federal government had established sentencing guidelines for judges. In *Apprendi v. New Jersey*, the Court found that judges could not give a higher sentence than that specified in the guideline unless a jury had been convinced beyond a reasonable doubt of the factors upon which the "upward departure" was based. *Apprendi* lead to other decisions, and the Court ultimately threw out the sentencing guidelines to the extent that they are anything more than advisory (judges need to consider but don't have to follow the guidelines). The *Apprendi* rule still controls but is limited to upward departures, and the Gall decision seems to imply that reasonableness of the sentence may be the salient factor, and that appellate courts should defer to the lower courts (and only overturn if the lower court abused its discretion).

Practice Test Bank

MULTIPLE CHOICE

1. The U.S. is a _____.
    a. constitutional monarchy
    b. pure democracy
    c. parliamentary style government
    d. constitutional democracy

2. Damages to reputation in the form of spoken words are known as _____.
    a. libel
    b. slander
    c. profanity
    d. obscenity

3. Which of the following would violate the ban on *ex post facto* laws?
    a. retroactive criminal statute
    b. vague statute giving too much power to government
    c. statute broadly regulating protective speech
    d. providing death penalty for petty theft

4. The primary considerations in analysis of laws under the void-for-vagueness doctrine are _____.
    a. retroactivity and potential for punishing innocent people
    b. legislative encroachment on the judiciary and legislative tyranny
    c. infringement of First and Seventh Amendment rights
    d. reasonably fair notice and potential for arbitrary or discriminatory enforcement

5. In a constitutional democracy, _____.
    a. the will of the majority is the supreme law
    b. the power of the majority and government are limited by the Constitution
    c. the legislature has the final say on the meaning of the Constitution
    d. the Constitution can be amended just like any statute

6. The _____ Amendment requires that states provide equal protection of laws.
    a. First
    b. Sixth
    c. Eighth
    d. Fourteenth

Study Guide

7. The _____ Amendment requires the states provide due process of laws.
   a. First
   b. Eighth
   c. Fourteenth
   d. Fifteenth

8. Except when dealing with fundamental rights and classifications based on race, ethnicity, gender, etc., the government can meet an equal protection challenge to a law by _____.
   a. passing the strict scrutiny test
   b. meeting the requirement of heightened scrutiny
   c. showing that the law has a rational basis
   d. showing that the law furthers a compelling government interest

9. The First Amendment offers protection from government for _____.
   a. some expressive conduct as well as some spoken or written words
   b. every form of spoken or written word
   c. every form of expressive conduct
   d. some spoken or written words but no expressive conduct

10. The First Amendment protects which of the following?
    a. obscenity
    b. profanity
    c. expressive conduct
    d. slander

11. Statutes that ban some forms of unprotected speech, but which _____ the exercise of some protected speech, may be unconstitutional under the void-for-overbreadth doctrine.
    a. chill or deter
    b. can lead to arbitrary enforcement against
    c. promote or facilitate
    d. condone or ratify

12. In *People v. Rokicki* (1999), the defendant argued he was being unconstitutionally punished for his beliefs. The Illinois Supreme Court stated that the defendant's First Amendment challenge to the hate crime law was _____.
    a. invalid because he allowed his beliefs to motivate unreasonable conduct
    b. upheld because he was being punished because of his beliefs
    c. invalid because his beliefs were totally irrelevant to the case
    d. upheld because his conduct did not go beyond mere expression

13. In *Texas v. Johnson* (1989), the Court held that burning an American flag as part of a political protest could _____.
    a. be punished because it involved conduct
    b. be punished because the American flag is a unique symbol
    c. not be punished because it was protected expressive conduct
    d. not be punished because it was pure speech

14. Even though the word "_____" does not appear anywhere in the U.S. Constitution, the U.S. Supreme Court has held that there is such a fundamental right.
    a. liberty
    b. privacy
    c. property
    d. attainder

15. The idea that we cannot punish behavior unless there was already a law forbidding it is called _____.
    a. the doctrine of overbreadth
    b. the void for vagueness principle
    c. the principle of legality
    d. the principle of proportionality

16. The ban on cruel and unusual punishment is found in the _____ Amendment.
    a. Fifth
    b. Sixth
    c. Seventh
    d. Eighth

17. In *Kennedy v. Louisiana*, the court held that the death penalty is disproportionate when the crime involves _____.
    a. an adult killing a child
    b. an adult raping of a child
    c. a child killing another child
    d. a child raping another child

18. In *Stanley v. Georgia* (1969), the Court held that _____.
    a. a prosecution for mere possession of pornography in one's own home violates a fundamental right to be free from unwanted governmental intrusion into one's privacy
    b. a prosecution for homosexual conduct violates a fundamental right to be free from unwanted governmental intrusion into one's privacy
    c. a prosecution for pornography is constitutional in that obscenity is not within the area of constitutionally protected speech or press
    d. a prosecution for pornography violates equal protection of laws

19. The case of *Griswold v. Connecticut* (1965) involved _____.
    a. the use of contraceptives by a married couple
    b. the inter-racial marriage of a couple
    c. the right to free speech
    d. the right to be free from cruel and unusual punishment

20. The case of *Roper v. Simmons* (2004) involved _____.
    a. the application of the death penalty for a mentally retarded offender
    b. the application of the death penalty for a crime of rape
    c. the application of the death penalty for a juvenile offender
    d. the application of the electric chair as a method of execution under the death penalty

21. Barbaric punishment are those punishments which _____.
    a. violate international law
    b. are considered no longer acceptable to a civilized society
    c. involve imposing death to the offender
    d. are less severe than cruel and unusual punishment

22. Which of the following would be deemed to violate the principle of proportionality?
    a. imposing the death penalty for a particularly heinous murder
    b. imposing the death penalty for spitting on the sidewalk
    c. impose a fine for a violation
    d. impose a fine for a status offense

23. In the cases following *Apprendi v. New Jersey* the court _____.
    a. established that jurors need to take part in all felony sentencing
    b. established that jurors need to take part in all sentencing—regardless of the seriousness of the crime
    c. established that jurors need to take part in sentencing in which the judge wishes to give a sentence harsher than the guideline sentence
    d. established that jurors need to take part in sentencing if it involves imposition of the death penalty

24. The void-for-overbreadth doctrine prohibits _____.
    a. vague laws
    b. laws which prohibit constitutionally protected speech
    c. laws which retroactively make behavior a crime
    d. laws which have no limits on the arbitrariness and discretion of police officers

25. Laws regulating the purchase, ownership and possession of guns may run afoul of _____.
    a. Article I, Section 9 of the U.S. Constitution
    b. the First Amendment to the U.S. Constitution
    c. the Second Amendment to the U.S. Constitution
    d. state constitutions but not the federal constitution.

26. The rule of law and principle of legality require that people be punished only _____.
    a. for violating properly enacted laws
    b. if they had some culpable *mens rea*
    c. if they personally did the criminal act
    d. if their acts harm society

27. Which of the following methods of execution is not cruel and unusual punishment?
    a. crucifixion
    b. beheading
    c. drawing and quartering
    d. lethal injection

28. Which of the following scenarios raises issues of disproportionate punishment?
    a. a statute imposing a 20 year sentence for a third shoplifting offense
    b. a statute allowing for a mandatory minimum sentence for robbery
    c. a statute making homelessness punishable by 30 days jail
    d. a statute requiring a shoplifter wear a placard stating, "I am a thief."

29. The _____ Amendment provides for the right to associate and assemble with those of your choosing.
    a. First
    b. Fourth
    c. Fifth
    d. Fourteenth

30. The _____ case dealt with the state's ability to limit nude dancing.
    a. *Weems v. United States*
    b. *Gitlow v. New York*
    c. *Barnes v. Glen Theatre, Inc. et. al.*
    d. *People v. Rockiki*

Study Guide

TRUE/FALSE

1. Laws governing hate crimes, such as cross burnings, will always run afoul of the First Amendment's free speech clause because they involve expressive conduct.
   a. true
   b. false

2. The ban on *ex post facto* laws is designed to prevent excessively vague laws.
   a. true
   b. false

3. The void-for-vagueness doctrine totally prohibits any vagueness or uncertainty in laws.
   a. true
   b. false

4. Statues that criminalize innocent acts after they're committed violate the ban against *ex post facto* laws.
   a. true
   b. false

5. Laws involving gender classifications are tested under the rational basis test.
   a. true
   b. false

6. Yelling "fire" in a crowded movie theater is an example of non-protected speech known as clear and present danger.
   a. true
   b. false

7. The U.S. Supreme Court has held that states may not prohibit nude dancing.
   a. true
   b. false

8. Fighting words are not protected by the First Amendment.
   a. true
   b. false

9. The constitutional right to equal protection of laws means that the government cannot treat people differently.
   a. true
   b. false

10. According to the U.S. Supreme Court, beheading would not be considered cruel and unusual punishment.
    a. true
    b. false

11. According to the U.S. Supreme Court, imposing any jail sentence for a status offense, such as being a drug addict, would be cruel and unusual punishment.
    a. true
    b. false

12. The U.S. Supreme Court has disallowed the use of the death penalty for the rape of an adult victim.
    a. true
    b. false

13. After the *District of Columbia v. Heller* decision it became very clear that local, state and federal legislatures have a carte blanche (no restrictions) in crafting very expansive gun control laws.
    a. true
    b. false

14. The Sixth Amendment prohibits cruel and unusual punishment.
    a. true
    b. false

15. Executing people who are mentally retarded has been held as a violation to the ban on cruel and unusual punishment.
    a. true
    b. false

16. In *Atkins v. Virginia*, the U.S. Supreme Court held that imposing the death penalty on people who committed murder while a juvenile violates the ban on cruel and unusual punishment.
    a. true
    b. false

17. In deciding whether executing juvenile offenders violated the ban on cruel and unusual punishment, the court looked to evolving standards of decency.
    a. true
    b. false

18. Lengthy imprisonment sentences have generally been found to violate the principle of proportionality.
    a. true
    b. false

19. Statutes against hate crimes violate the First Amendment.
    a. true
    b. false

20. Broadly written laws that have an impact on protected speech and expression are invalid if they are deemed overbroad.
    a. true
    b. false

21. Freedom of speech and expression are fundamental rights.
    a. true
    b. false

22. Under equal protection, racial classifications are subject to strict scrutiny.
    a. true
    b. false

23. Under equal protection, classifications based on age are subject to strict scrutiny.
    a. true
    b. false

24. After *Apprendi v. New Jersey,* jurors must be involved in making factual determinations any time a judge departs from the sentencing guidelines.
    a. true
    b. false

25. There is a general consensus that a length of imprisonment which is disproportionate to the type and manner of crime which was committed violates the ban on cruel and unusual punishment.
    a. true
    b. false

FILL-IN-THE-BLANK

1. The Eighth Amendment principle of _____ requires that punishment fit the crime.

2. _____ is offensive, sexually explicit material which is not protected by the First Amendment.

3. Making a statement through acts or symbols is called _____ conduct.

4. Government classifications on the basis of race are subject to _____ by the courts.

Chapter 2: Constitutional Limits on Criminal Law

5. The Equal Protection Clause and the Due Process Clause are found in the _____ Amendment.

6. The American form of government is described as a _____ democracy.

7. The doctrine which dictates that laws provide notice to individuals as to what behavior constitutes a crime is the _____ doctrine.

8. The doctrine which states that laws can't prohibit constitutionally protected behavior is the _____ doctrine.

9. Laws which limit speech are subject to strict scrutiny because they may have a _____ effect on a person's desire to speak freely.

10. The void-for-vagueness doctrine addresses the evil of _____ and discriminatory practices in criminal justice administration.

11. The constitutional right to privacy is found within the _____ of the Constitution.

12. There are two types of cruel and unusual punishment under the Eighth Amendment: _____ punishment and _____ punishment.

13. After the case of *U.S. v. Booker*, sentencing guidelines are _____ and judges may impose sentences that are reasonable in light of all the circumstances.

14. Words that are likely to provoke the average person to retaliation and cause a breach of the peace are known as _____ words.

15. Damages to reputation expressed in print, writing, pictures, or signs are known as _____, whereas damages to reputation expressed in spoken words are known as _____.

ESSAY

1. Discuss the role of the Constitution in limiting criminal law.

Study Guide

2. Discuss how the Equal Protection clause of the 14th Amendment limits the type of criminal laws that can be passed.

3. How does the principle of legality conflict with retroactive law making?

4. Assume that a census worker is killed and the word "fed" is scrawled onto his back. Discuss the *People v. Rokicki* and *R.A.V. v. City of St. Paul* cases and cases mentioned in *Rokicki* to determine whether the killing could/should be prosecuted under a hate crime statutes identical to the one in *Rockiki*.

5, Discuss under what circumstances imposition of the death penalty will be deemed cruel and unusual under the 8th Amendment to the U.S. Constitution.

CHAPTER 2 ANSWER KEY

Multiple Choice

1. d, See pg. 40, LO 1
2. b, See pg. 47, LO 5
3. a, See pg. 41, LO 3
4. d, See pg. 42, LO 4
5. b, See pg. 40, LO 1
6. d, See pg. 46, LO 5
7. c, See pg. 42, LO 5
8. c, See pg. 46, LO 5
9. a, See pg. 47, LO 5
10. c, See pg. 47, LO 5
11. a, See pg. 48, LO 5
12. a, See pgs. 49-50, LO 5
13. c, See pgs. 51-52, LO 5
14. b, See pg. 52, LO 5
15. c, See pg. 40, LO 2
16. d, See pg. 58, LO 6
17. b, See pg. 61, LO 6
18. a, See pg. 55, LO 5
19. a, See pg. 53, LO 5
20. c, See pg. 66, LO 6
21. b, See pg. 59, LO 6
22. b, See pg. 60, LO 6
23. c, See pg. 72, LO 7
24. b, See pg. 48, LO 5
25. c, See pg. 56, LO 5
26. a, See pg. 40, LO 2
27. d, See pg. 60, LO 5
28. c, See pg. 60, LO 6
29. a, See pg. 46, LO 5
30. c, See pg. 51, LO

True/False

1. F, See pg. 49, LO 5
2. F, See pg. 41, LO 3,4
3. F, See pg. 43, LO 4
4. T, See pg. 41, LO 3
5. F, See pg. 46, LO 5
6. T, See pg. 48, LO 5
7. F, See pg. 51, LO 5
8. T, See pg. 47, LO 5
9. F, See pg. 46, LO 5
10. F, See pg. 60, LO 6
11. T, See pg. 60, LO 5
12. T, See pg. 60, LO 5
13. F, See pg. 57, LO 5
14. F, See pg. 72, LO 6
15. T, See pg. 64, LO 6
16. F, See pg. 64, LO 6
17. T, See pg. 65, LO 6
18. F, See pg. 66, LO 6
19. F, See pg. 49, LO 5
20. T, See pg. 48, LO 5

21. T, See pg. 47, LO 5
22. T, See pg. 46, LO 5
23. F, See pg. 46, LO 5
24. F, See pg. 72, LO 7
25. F, See pg. 66, LO 6

Fill-in-the-Blank

1. proportionality, See pg. 60, LO 6
2. Obscenity, See pg. 47, LO 5
3. expressive, See pg. 47, LO 5
4. strict scrutiny, See pg. 46, LO 5
5. Fourteenth, See pg. 46, LO 5
6. constitutional, See pg. 40, LO 1
7. void-for-vagueness, See pg. 42, LO 4
8. void-for-overbreadth, See pg. 48, LO 5
9. chilling, See pg. 48, LO 5
10. arbitrary, See pg. 42, LO 4
11. penumbra, See pg. 53, LO 5
12. barbarian; disproportionate, See pg. 59, LO 6
13. advisory. See pg. 73, LO 7
14. fighting, See pg. 47, LO 5
15. libel; slander, See pg. 47, LO 5

Essay

1. Discuss the role of the Constitution in limiting criminal law.

   The U.S. Constitution constrains what can be criminalized. For example, legislators cannot pas ex post facto laws. It also guides legislators in how they write criminal laws. For instance, the due process requirement of the Fourteenth Amendment has been interpreted to mean that Congress should not pass vague statutes or statutes that criminalize conduct which is constitutionally protected (doctrine of overbreadth). The Bill of Rights (first ten Amendments to the Constitution) also sets forth some guarantees and personal rights that may conflict with legislation, and to the extent that there is conflict, the rights set forth in the Constitution trump and the criminal law gives way. LO 1, 5

2. Discuss how the Equal Protection clause of the Fourteenth Amendment limits the type of criminal laws that can be passed.

Although the Fourteenth Amendment guarantees equal protection of law, that is not a general requirement that government treat everyone the same. For example, some states treat minors differently than adults (think about minor in possession laws), and yet, these statutes are constantly upheld as not violating the Fourteenth Amendment. It all boils down to who is being treated differently (classification or group of individuals) and why (state's reason for treating them differently. Most classifications, including those based upon age, certain types of employment, and prior criminal history, are said to be "non-suspect" classifications, and as long as the state can show that there is a rational basis for treating individuals differently than others, the Court won't find a Equal Protection violation. For example, habitual offenders can be treated differently than first time offenders. Generally, the state will point to its police powers and interest in maintaining the public health and safety of its citizens. Other classifications are deemed "suspect classifications." These include race and ethnicity. In order to justify treating individuals differently because of race, the Court will require the state prove that it has a compelling state interest. Additionally, the court must employ strict scrutiny to these types of laws as they affect fundamental rights. In essence, the states have not been able to justify race-based classifications. Finally, statutes treating men and women differently will be subject to "heightened scrutiny" meaning that the state will have to prove that there is a fair and substantial relationship between gender and a legitimate state end. An example of an unsuccessful attack on a criminal law that treated males differently than females is Michal M. v. Superior Court of Sonoma County. LO 1, 5

3. How does the principle of legality conflict with retroactive law making?

The principle of legality, at its core, is a ban on retroactive law making. The principle of legality states that there cannot be a crime without a law, and there cannot be criminal punishment without law. When a person does a behavior that society finds reprehensible or blameworthy, then society is free to either prosecute the individual for that behavior if there is already a law proscribing it, or it may decide to enact a law which will then apply to others who engage in similar behavior. Society cannot enact a law and then apply it retroactively to the person. Article I, Section 9 of the Constitution, the ban on ex post facto laws, is the embodiment of the principle of legality. LO 2

4. Assume that a census worker is killed and the word "fed" is scrawled onto his back. Discuss the *People v. Rokicki* and *R.A.V. v. City of St. Paul* cases and cases mentioned in *Rokicki* to determine whether the killing could/should be prosecuted under a hate crime statutes identical to the one in *Rockiki*.

Hate crime statutes implicate the First Amendment protections on the right to free speech. The First Amendment does not, however, provide limitless protection to all speech and clearly the government can regulate some speech (obscenity, profanity, libel and slander, fighting words, and speech that presents a clear and present danger). Hate crime statutes, have to be careful though because there is the danger that while prohibiting conduct, they may also prohibit speech. If so, they run afoul of the void-for-overbreadth doctrine. While we can prohibit certain conduct, the law should not regulate content. The legislation in R.A.V. was challenged as void for overbreadth and for its chilling effect on speech content (it was directed at using symbols in a way to arouse anger or alarm in others based upon race, creed, religion, and gender would be guilty of disorderly conduct. The RAV hate crime law was found to be unconstitutional and to violate the First Amendment because it was content based (allowed those who were proponents of tolerance to evade penalty while those who were opposed to tolerance to violate the statute.) Conversely, in Rokicki, the court found the Illinois hate crime statute not to violate the First Amendment as it was directed at conduct rather than content (Rokicki's behavior was unquestionably covered by the statute). The court found that he was being punished not because he held an unpopular view but because he allowed those views to trigger his conduct. The Court also upheld the hate crime statute based upon the U.S. Supreme Court's decision in Miller which allowed harsher penalties for bias motivated offenses.

Under the facts in this scenario, the census worker killer probably would not be liable for a hate crime if the statute was the same as the Illinois/Rokicki statue because being an employee of the federal government is not found within the types of group identification the bias motivation is directed against (not race, creed, religion, sexual preference, physical or mental disability). If the statute included employment affiliation, then perhaps a prosecution for a hate crime (in addition to the murder charge) might be appropriate. Additionally (and thinking back to chapter 1), it is most likely that the motive or anti-government bias may be an aggravating factor in the killer's sentencing for murder. LO 5

5. Discuss under what circumstances imposition of the death penalty will be deemed cruel and unusual under the Eighth Amendment to the U.S. Constitution.

The Eighth Amendment protection against cruel and unusual punishment has been interpreted to mean that individuals will not be punished with barbaric methods nor will the punishment be disproportionate to the crime. Punishment won't be considered cruel if it is merely the extinguishment of life. In order to not be cruel, death should be both instantaneous and painless, and it cannot involve unnecessary mutilation of the body. Beheading and crucifixion would be cruel but lethal injection is not (some types of "cut down" procedures to find veins into which the injection will be given may be).

Death penalty has recently been held to be disproportionate for a crime which does not result in the death of the victim. Kennedy v. Louisiana overturned a capital murder statute in Louisiana which allowed capital punishment for the rape of a child victim under the age of 12. The Court has also said that capital punishment is disproportionate penalty for certain types of offenders convicted of murder. Atkins v. Virginia held that application of the death penalty to mentally retarded murders violates the cruel and unusual punishment clause. Roper v. Simmons similarly held that application of the death penalty to offenders who were less than 18 years old at the time they committed the murder is cruel and unusual as it violates evolving standards of decency. LO 6

Chapter 3
The General Principles of Criminal Liability: *Actus Reus*

LEARNING OBJECTIVES

- To be able to identify the elements of, and to explain why, the voluntary act is the first principle of criminal liability.

- To be able to define, distinguish between, and understand the importance of the elements of, criminal conduct and criminal liability and therefore punishment

- To understand and appreciate the importance of the requirement of a voluntary act.

- To identify the circumstances when, and to be able to explain why, status is treated, sometimes, as an affirmative act.

- To be able to understand how the general principle of *actus reus* includes a voluntary act and how it is viewed by the constitution.

- To identify the circumstances when, and to be able to explain why, failures to act are treated as affirmative acts.

- To understand and identify the circumstances when, and to be able to explain why, possession is treated as an act.

KEY TERMS AND CONCEPTS

- **criminal conduct**—acts triggered by criminal intent; p. 81

- **criminal liability**—actus reus, mens rea, concurrence, causation, and harmful result, which are the basis for the elements of crime the prosecution has to prove beyond a reasonable doubt; p. 82

- **elements of a crime**—the parts of a crime that the prosecution must prove beyond a reasonable doubt, such as *actus reus, mens rea,* concurrence, causation, and bad result; p. 82

- *actus reus*—the criminal act or the physical element in criminal liability; p.82

- *mens rea*—the state of mind the prosecution has to prove beyond a reasonable doubt; criminal intent from an evil mind; the mental element in crime, including purpose, knowledge, recklessness, and negligence; p. 82

- *corpus delecti*—"the body of the crime", it refers to the elements (components) of a crime; p. 83

- **attendant circumstances element**—a circumstance connected to an act, an intent, and/or a result required to make an act criminal; p. 82

- **concurrence**—the requirement that *actus reus* must join with *mens rea* to produce criminal conduct or that conduct must cause a harmful result; p. 83

- **conduct crimes**—crimes requiring a criminal act triggered by criminal intent; p. 84

- **criminal acts**—voluntary bodily movements that constitute the action element of a crime; p. 84

- **bad result crimes (result crimes)**—serious crimes that include causing a criminal harm in addition to the conduct itself (for example, criminal homicide); p. 84

- **manifest criminality**—the requirement in law that intentions have to turn into criminal deeds to be punishable; p. 85

- **status**—who we are, as opposed to what we do; a condition that's not an action can't substitute for action as an element in crime; p. 86

- **one-voluntary-act-is-enough**—standard in the MPC, followed by most states, that provides as long as there is one voluntary act, it does not matter that the other acts surrounding the crime may be involuntarily; p. 86

- **criminal omissions**—two forms: 1) mere failure to act or 2) failure to intervene in order to prevent a serious harm; p. 91

- **failure to report (criminal omission)**—one type of omission *actus reus*; p. 91

- **failure to intervene (criminal omission)**—one type of omission *actus reus*; p. 91

- **legal duty**—liability only for duties imposed by contract, statute, or "special relationships;" p. 91

- **"Good Samaritan" doctrine**—the doctrine that imposes a legal duty to render or summon aid for imperiled strangers; p. 93

- **American bystander rule**—there's no legal duty to rescue or call for help to aid someone who's in danger, even if helping poses no risk whatsoever to the potential rescuer; p. 93

- **legal fiction**—treating something as a fact that's not a fact, if there's a good reason for doing so; p. 97

- **actual possession**—physical possession; on the possessor's person; p. 98

- **constructive possession**—legal possession or custody of an item or substance; p. 98

- **knowing possession**—awareness of physical possession; p. 99

- **mere possession**—physical possession; p. 99

CHAPTER OUTLINE

I. The Elements of Criminal Liability
   A. There are a number of general principles of criminal liability. The voluntary act is the first requirement.
      1. Criminal conduct defined
      2. Criminal liability defined
   B. The government must prove every element of the crime beyond a reasonable doubt.
      1. Criminal act—All crimes must have at a minimum a criminal act
      2. Criminal intent—Some minor crimes don't have a criminal intent
      3. Concurrence—When the criminal intent triggers the criminal act
      4. Attendant circumstances—Required particularly when the crime doesn't mention
         a. *Mens rea* (criminal intent) or bad result
      5. Bad result (causing a criminal harm)—Some crimes don't require a bad result
   C. Two types of crimes lead to criminal liability.
      1. Conduct crimes require proving three elements of crimes.
         a. *Actus reus* (criminal act)
         b. *Mens rea* (criminal intent)
         c. Concurrence (criminal act triggered by criminal intent)
      2. Result Crimes require proving five elements of crimes.
         a. *Actus reus*
         b. *Mens rea*
         c. Concurrence
            (1) *Actus reus* and *mens rea* produce criminal conduct.
            (2) The criminal conduct results in harm.
         d. Causation (must prove the criminal conduct produced criminal harm as defined in the criminal statute)
         e. Resulting harm (the specific result defined in the criminal code)
   D. Corpus Delicti means body of the crime (not necessarily body of the victim) and it is the elements that the state has to prove.

II. The Voluntary Act (*Actus Reus*): The First Principle of Liability
A. Three elements of criminal conduct: conduct that is without justification and without excuse.
B. Every crime involves a criminal act, referred to as the *actus reus*. *Actus reus* is the first principle of criminal liability.
C. We punish people for what they do, not who they are.
D. We punish people for what they do, not what they think.
  1. It is impossible to prove a mental attitude by itself.
  2. Thoughts don't hurt anyone.
  3. It is hard to separate daydreaming and fantasy from intent.
  4. Punishing thoughts is impractical, inequitable, and unjust.
  5. Manifest criminality leaves no doubt the criminal nature of the act.
D. **Voluntary Acts**: Reasoning for the voluntary act requirement
  1. Criminal law punishes people.
  2. Criminal law can't punish without blame.
  3. There is no blame without responsibility.
  4. There is no responsibility without a voluntary act (free will).
  5. *Case: Brown v. State*
  6. *Case: King v. Cogdon*
  7. *Case: People v. Decina*
  8. *Case: State v. Jerrett*
D. **Status as a criminal act**
  1. Act is what we do; status is who we are.
  2. Status is created in two ways.
      a. Voluntary act (first use of alcohol or other drug)
      b. Inherent (race, ethnicity, sex, age)
  3. *Actus Reus* and the U.S. Constitution
      a. Punishment for status violates U.S. Constitution, Amendment VIII (cruel and unusual punishment), by the same reasoning a voluntary act is required by the principle of *actus reus*.
      b. *Case: Robinson v. California*
      c. *Case: Powell v. Texas*

III. Omissions—Failure to act as a criminal act
A. Two types of criminal omissions
  1. Failure to report (accident, income tax)
  2. Failure to intervene (call for help or rescue)
B. It's wrong (but not always a crime) to stand by while bad things happen.
  1. Moral and legal duties differ.
  2. Failure to act is a criminal act only when there's a legal duty to act, created by:
      a. Statute
      b. Contract
      c. Special relationship
  3. Criminal liability exists only when both of the following are true:
      a. There's a legal duty to act.
      b. The legal duty is performed unreasonably.

  4. Failure to perform moral duties does not qualify as a criminal omission.
  5. Two approaches to creating and carrying out legal duties toward strangers in trouble:
    a. Good Samaritan doctrine—legal duty to help or summon help for strangers in danger
    b. American bystander rule (most states)—no legal duty to rescue or summon help for strangers
  6. *Case: Commonwealth v. Pestinakas*
  7. *Case: People v. Oliver*
  8. *Case: State v. Miranda*
  9. *Story: Kitty Genovese Story*

IV. Possession
 A. Possession is a passive state, not a positive act.
 B. Legal fiction makes it an act for good policy reasons.
  1. Reduce crime
  2. Many times possession is the result of a voluntary act.
 C. Two aspects of possession
  1. Control of items and substances
    a. Actual (substance or item on the person)
    b. Constructive (control the stuff but not on the person)
  2. Awareness of control
    a. Knowing possession (the person knows they possess the material in question)
    b. Mere possession (the material in question is physically on the person, but they don't know it)
 D. Kinds of possession
  1. Control: actual and constructive
  2. Awareness: knowing and mere
  3. *Case: Porter v. State*
  4. *Case: People v. E.C.*

CHAPTER SUMMARY

The prosecution is required to prove every element of the crime beyond a reasonable doubt. One basic principle of criminal liability is the requirement of a criminal act, which the prosecution has to prove beyond a reasonable doubt.

Two types of crime based on their elements are crimes of criminal conduct and crimes of criminal conduct causing criminal harms. Crimes of criminal conduct have a mental state and an act triggered by the mental state. The concurrence element requires that the act be caused or triggered by the intent (*mens rea*). Intending to commit a crime is not a crime because it hasn't ripened into a criminal act (*actus reus*). Crimes of criminal conduct causing harm have the additional elements of causation and harm. The act must cause the harm.

The *actus reus* can be a positive act (commission) or omission to act. A criminal act has to be a voluntary bodily movement because we can't blame people for their involuntary acts. Actions refer to what we *do*; status or condition refers to who or what we *are*. Some conditions we're born with; and others we produce by our acts. Making a disease a crime violates the cruel and unusual punishment clause of the Eighth Amendment to the U.S. Constitution. It's a criminal act to stand by and do nothing when there's a legal duty to act. A legal duty to act can be imposed by civil or criminal statutes, the common law, a contract, or a special relationship. *Actus reus* does not include a failure to do what one may have a "moral duty" to do.

There are two types of criminal omissions: failure to report and failure to intervene. Criminal omissions create criminal liability only when a legal duty is not reasonably performed.

Possession is a passive state, but it can qualify as a criminal act when properly defined by law. There are a number of aspects or possible elements of possession crimes: 1) physical control of an item; 2) awareness of physical control of some item; and 3) awareness of the nature of the item (whether it is contraband or not). Actual possession means the item is on your person or within your reach. Constructive possession means the item is under your control but not on your person or within your reach. Things you leave at your home, by putting them in your safe (for which you have the combination), are constructively possessed. Mere possession means you have possession of it, and know you have possession, but don't know the nature of the item (that it is contraband). Knowing possession means that you knowingly possess the item and know that the item is contraband. Most states require proof that the possessor knew the item was contraband before a conviction can be obtained.

Practice Test Bank

MULTIPLE CHOICE

1. To obtain a conviction, the prosecution must prove every element of the offense beyond _____.
    a. probable cause
    b. a reasonable suspicion
    c. clear and convincing evidence
    d. a reasonable doubt

2. The two main types of crimes are _____.
    a. criminal conduct crimes and bad result crimes
    b. criminal liability crimes and without fault crimes
    c. criminal action crimes and criminal omission crimes
    d. crimes with attendant circumstances and crimes without liability.

3. The essence of the principle of *actus reus* is _____.
    a. intention
    b. act
    c. concurrence
    d. contingency

4. The principle of *mens rea* involves _____.
    a. intent
    b. act
    c. concurrence
    d. harm

5. The requirement of manifest criminality before there is punishment means that _____.
    a. intent alone, without an act, is not a crime
    b. an act alone, without intent, is not a crime
    c. harm alone, without causation, is not a crime
    d. causation alone, without harm, is not a crime

6. To be criminal, an act must be _____.
    a. objective
    b. peremptory
    c. voluntary
    d. the cause of the harm

7. In *Powell v. Texas* (1968), the Court held that under the Eighth Amendment, an alcoholic _____.
   a. could not be guilty of any crime committed while intoxicated
   b. was not entitled to a constitutional defense of chronic alcoholism
   c. could not be guilty of public intoxication
   d. was not capable of a voluntary act while intoxicated

8. In *Robinson v. California* (1962), the Court specifically held that under the Eighth Amendment, government could not make it a crime to be _____.
   a. addicted to the use of narcotics
   b. a hypochondriac
   c. a compulsive gambler
   d. a nymphomaniac

9. Under the Eighth Amendment, government cannot punish someone for a/n _____.
   a. status, disease, or condition
   b. crime that has no *mens rea* element
   c. act that is not involuntary
   d. crime that is the result of a psychological compulsion

10. Acts committed during somnambulism or automatism cannot be criminal because the acts _____.
    a. are not reflexive
    b. do not indicate the personality of the offender
    c. are not voluntary
    d. are not spontaneous

11. In the crime of Driving While Intoxicated, "while intoxicated" is _____.
    a. the voluntary act
    b. the intention
    c. the attendant circumstance
    d. the result

12. The element of concurrence means that the _____.
    a. act must trigger the intent
    b. harm must flow from intent
    c. intent must trigger the act
    d. harm must flow from the act

13. As compared to crimes of criminal conduct, bad result crimes have two additional elements, _____.
    a. concurrence and victimization
    b. causation and harm
    c. conspicuity and damage
    d. contiguity and result

14. The three elements of crimes of criminal conduct are *actus reus*, *mens rea,* and _____.
    a. conduct
    b. concurrence
    c. consistence
    d. contagion

15. In terms of *actus reus*, an omission is a _____.
    a. duty
    b. mistake
    c. failure to act
    d. failure to think

16. A legal duty to act is an example of a criminal element called _____.
    a. (attendant) circumstances
    b. *mens rea*
    c. *actus reus*
    d. harm

17. Under the Good Samaritan doctrine, a person has a legal duty to _____.
    a. report all crimes to the police
    b. investigate crimes they witness
    c. render or summon aid for people in danger
    d. help the poor avoid economic crimes

18. A legal fiction is a legal rule that _____.
    a. assumes the existence of fact that does not exist
    b. distributes the burden of proof
    c. defines the role of the jury in fact-finding
    d. can be overcome by evidence

19. Legally, possession is deemed to be a type of _____.
    a. *mens rea*
    b. harm
    c. act
    d. concurrence

20. A person who is carrying an item in their pocket, purse, or backpack is in _____ possession of the container and items therein.
    a. constructive
    b. fictional
    c. derivative
    d. actual

21. To be guilty of possession of contraband, most states require that the prosecution prove that the defendant knew _____.
    a. the quantity of the item possessed
    b. the nature of the item possessed
    c. that the item was going to be sold for profit
    d. that the person who gave it to him/her had no right to possess it

22. In contrast to the Good Samaritan doctrine, the American bystander rule imposes _____.
    a. less duty to help complete strangers
    b. no duty to help one's own children
    c. more duty to assist others
    d. duties only when felonies are involved

23. The two main types of criminal omissions are failure to _____.
    a. report and intervene
    b. act and think
    c. prevent and conclude
    d. act subjectively and objectively

24. A person leaves their heroin at home locked in a safe to which he or she has the combination. The person then goes to the train station. While at the train station the person has _____ possession of the heroin.
    a. fractional
    b. joint
    c. constructive
    d. actual

25. A person who does not know the nature of an item they possess has _____ possession of that item.
    a. fictional
    b. constructive
    c. mere
    d. actual

26. An omission to act is a crime, only if there is a _____ duty to act.
    a. fictional
    b. moral
    c. actual
    d. legal

Study Guide

27. The requirement that there be an act element prevents government from punishing people _____.
    a. for bad thoughts only
    b. for their conduct
    c. for the harm they cause
    d. who lack concurrence

28. Which of the following is NOT a way that legal duties are created?
    a. Statutes
    b. Criminal Omissions
    c. Contracts
    d. Special Relationships

29. The people who failed to take action to help Kitty Genovese were not guilty of any crime because they _____.
    a. could not be sure the police would arrive in time
    b. knew the attacker was armed
    c. did not know the identity of the attacker
    d. had no legal duty to aid her or call the police

30. A legal duty can arise from statutes, contracts, and _____.
    a. special relationships
    b. manumissions
    c. forfeitures
    d. discretion

TRUE/FALSE

1. The *actus reus* is the mental element of a crime.
    a. true
    b. false

2. The concurrence element means that the mental element must trigger the harm.
    a. true
    b. false

3. The prosecution must prove every element of the crime beyond a reasonable doubt to get a conviction.
    a. true
    b. false

4. The voluntary act is the first principle of criminal liability because all crimes require a voluntary act at a minimum whereas some crimes don't require the other elements.
   a. true
   b. false

5. To be guilty of a criminal harm offense, the defendant must have caused the harm.
   a. true
   b. false

6. Crimes of criminal conduct have no concurrence element.
   a. true
   b. false

7. The term *actus reus* means evil act.
   a. true
   b. false

8. Under the Model Penal Code, to be guilty of an omission to act, the act must be one that the defendant was physically capable of performing.
   a. true
   b. false

9. Bodily movements made while unconscious are termed automatism.
   a. true
   b. false

10. A reflex or spasm is a voluntary act.
    a. true
    b. false

11. In *Robinson v. California,* the U.S. Supreme Court held that governments may omit the *actus reus* element when defining crimes.
    a. true
    b. false

12. In *Powell v. Texas*, the Court held that the government cannot punish an alcoholic for any crimes committed while intoxicated.
    a. true
    b. false

13. Government cannot punish a person solely for their status, condition, or disease.
    a. true
    b. false

14. A failure to act is termed an omission.
    a. true
    b. false

15. A failure to act can be a crime only if there is a legal duty to do the act.
    a. true
    b. false

16. All moral duties are also legal duties.
    a. true
    b. false

17. The Good Samaritan doctrine imposes more duties to assist than does the American bystander rule.
    a. true
    b. false

18. A contract cannot create a legal duty to act.
    a. true
    b. false

19. Most states punish mere possession of contraband.
    a. true
    b. false

20. If an item is in a defendant's pocket, he is in actual possession of that item.
    a. true
    b. false

21. The concept of manifest criminality requires that the defendant's acts cause harm.
    a. true
    b. false

22. A legal fiction is something that is always true.
    a. true
    b. false

23. The mere presence of the accused on shared premises where contraband is found is, by itself, not enough to prove ownership or possession.
    a. true
    b. false

24. Knowing possession means that the person knows such possession is illegal.
    a. true
    b. false

25. Criminal conduct is conduct that is without justification and without excuse.
    a. true
    b. false

FILL-IN-THE-BLANK

1. Another term for bodily movements while unconscious is _____.

2. The _____ is the act element of the crime.

3. The _____ is the mental element of the crime.

4. The _____ element requires that the mental element trigger the act.

5. If a person commits an act during a state of automatism, the act is probably not a crime because the act is not _____.

6. The prosecution must prove every _____ of the crime beyond a reasonable doubt.

7. A failure to act is called a/n _____.

8. A failure to act is not a crime unless there is a/n _____ duty to do the act.

9. Persons have a broad duty to assist others under the _____ rule.

10. Under the _____ rule, people have little or no duty to assist strangers in peril.

11. In _____, the Court held that a person could not be punished for being a drug addict.

12. Possessing an item without knowing the nature of that item is called _____ possession.

13. Although it may be a legal fiction, possession is deemed to be a form of _____.

14. Before it can be a crime, most states require that possession be _____ rather than just mere possession.

15. If a person leaves an item at home and goes elsewhere, they can still be in _____ possession of that item.

ESSAY

1. Explain why only voluntary acts are crimes. Be sure to provide examples.

2. Compare and contrast actual and constructive possession. Provide examples of each.

3. Compare and contrast knowing and mere possession. Provide examples of each.

4. Under what circumstances can an omission to act be deemed the *actus reus* of a crime? Be sure to provide examples.

5. Compare and contrast the Good Samaritan doctrine and the American bystander rule.

CHAPTER 3 ANSWER KEY

Multiple Choice

1. d. See pg. 82, LO 1
2. a. See pg. 84, LO 2
3. b. See pg. 82, LO 3
4. a. See pg. 82, LO 1
5. a. See pg. 85, LO 2
6. c. See pg. 87, LO 3
7. b. See pg. 90, LO 4
8. a. See pg. 89, LO 4
9. a. See pg. 90, LO 4
10. c. See pg. 86, LO 3
11. c. See pg. 83, LO 1
12. c. See pg. 83, LO 1, 2
13. b. See pg. 84, LO 1,2
14. b. See pg. 83, LO 2
15. c. See pg. 91, LO 6
16. a. See pg. 91, LO 6
17. c. See pg. 93, LO 6
18. a. See pg. 97, LO 7
19. c. See pg. 97, LO 7
20. d. See pg. 98, LO 7
21. b. See pg. 99, LO 7
22. a. See pg. 93, LO 6
23. a. See pg. 101, LO 6
24. c. See pg. 98, LO 7
25. c. See pg. 99, LO 7
26. d. See pg. 101, LO 6
27. a. See pg. 85, LO 2
28. b. See pg. 91, LO 7
29. d. See pgs. 96-97, LO 6
30. a. See pg. 91, LO 6

True/False

1. F. See pg. 82, LO 2
2. F. See pg. 83, LO 2
3. T. See pg. 82, LO 2
4. T. See pg. 82, LO 1
5. T. See pg. 84, LO 2
6. F. See pg. 83, LO 2
7. T. See pg. 82, LO
8. T. See pg. 94, LO 6
9. T. See pg. 86, LO 3
10. F. See pg. 87, LO 3
11. F. See pgs. 89-90, LO 4
12. F. See pg. 90, LO 5
13. T. See pg. 90, LO 5
14. T. See pg. 91, LO 6
15. T. See pg. 91, LO 6
16. F. See pg. 91, LO 6
17. T. See pg. 93, LO 6
18. F. See pg. 92, LO 6
19. F. See pg. 99, LO 7
20. T. See pg. 98, LO 7
21. F. See pg. 85, LO 2
22. F. See pg. 97, LO 7
23. T. See pgs. 99-100, LO 7
25. T. See pg. 81-82, LO
24. F. See pg. 99, LO 7

Fill-in-the-Blank

1. automatism. See pg. 86, LO 3
2. *actus reus*. See pg. 82, LO 2
3. *mens rea*. See pg. 83, LO 2
4. concurrence. See pg. 83, LO 2
5. voluntary. See pg. 86, LO 3
6. element. See pg. 82, LO 2
7. omission. See pg. 91, LO 6
8. legal. See pg. 91, LO 6
9. Good Samaritan. See pg. 93, LO 6
10. American bystander. See pg. 93, LO 6
11. *Robinson v. California*. See pg. 89, LO 5
12. mere. See pg. 99, LO 7
13. *actus reus*. See pg. 97, LO 7
14. knowing. See pg. 99, LO 7
15. constructive. See pg. 98, LO 7

Essay

1. Explain why only voluntary acts are crimes. Be sure to provide examples.

   Essentially, we only hold people who are blameworthy liable for their actions. In order to be blameworthy, the individual had to have some control over their actions; thus, the acts must be voluntary. Convulsions, acts done while under hypnosis, while asleep, or while unconscious are all deemed involuntary acts because the individual has no control over them. They are not the product of a voluntary act. The term voluntary, should not be confused with the mens rea of intentional, but should incorporate a conscious decision that causes a bodily movement. The MPC has broadened the scope of voluntary acts to include behavior that demonstrates one voluntary act even though it is surrounded by other involuntary acts. The example given is an individual who voluntarily gets in a car to drive knowing they are subject to fainting spells. Fainting is not a voluntary act, but getting in the car to drive is, so the MPC's "one-voluntary-act-is-enough" definition would cover this scenario. LO 3

Study Guide

2. Compare and contrast actual and constructive possession. Provide examples of each.

Actual possession means physical possession by one who knows what they possess. If Bob is carrying a wallet in his pants pocket which contains a baggie of illegal drugs and he knows he has the wallet/drugs, he is commits the voluntary act of actual possession. Constructive possession includes situations where the individual does not physically possess the item, but has the right and ability to control the item. If Bob gives Fred his backpack to hold while he goes on a carnival ride, and in the backpack there is a stash of marijuana, Bob is said to be in constructive possession of marijuana because he has the right and ability to control the backpack. LO 7

3. Compare and contrast knowing and mere possession. Provide examples of each.

Knowing possession applies to either actual or constructive possession and requires that the possessor is aware of what they possess. For example, in the scenario above, Fred is in actual possession of Bob's backpack, but may or may not knowingly possess the marijuana stash (depending on whether he is aware of the contents of the backpack). Likewise, Bob is in constructive possession of the backpack, but he may or may not have knowing possession (presumably he knows what is in his backpack, but there may be circumstances under which he does not.) Mere possession means that the person has actual or constructive possession of something, but does not realize what he possesses. If Fred does not know about the marijuana stash in the backpack, he only has mere, but not knowing possession. Most states require knowing possession for there to be criminal liability, but two states allow mere possession to be the basis of criminal liability. LO 7

4. Under what circumstances can an omission to act be deemed the *actus reus* of a crime? Be sure to provide examples.

Omission can only be the actus reus requirement when there is a legal duty to act. Legal duties can come from various sources: statutes, relationships, contracts. Criminal omissions stem from failure to report or failure to intervene. A criminal omission for failure to report may include the failure to file income tax returns. A criminal omission for failure to intervene would include a parent's failure to seek treatment for their child (based upon relationship). The case of People v. Oliver illustrates a criminal omission for failure to intervene based upon a relationship created by "assumption of care." She took the victim from a place where he could get treatment to her residence where he could not, thus establishing a special (although not formal) relationship. LO 6

5. Compare and contrast the Good Samaritan doctrine and the American bystander rule.

No criminal liability can be predicated upon an individual's moral duty to intervene. However, some states by statute, adopt the position that a person has a duty to aid a stranger in peril (if they can do so without risking harm to themselves). This approach is called the Good Samaritan Doctrine, and the few states which have adopted this approach impose a legal duty upon individuals to call for help for imperiled strangers. The American Bystander approach, which is followed by most states, imposes no duty to render aid—even if the "bystander risks nothing by helping." LO 6

Chapter 4
The General Principles of Criminal Liability:
Mens Rea, Concurrence, Causation, and Ignorance and Mistake

LEARNING OBJECTIVES

1. Understand and appreciate that most serious require criminal intent and a criminal act.

2. Understand the difference between general and specific intent.

3. Understand and appreciate the differences in culpability among the Model Penal Code's (MPC) four mental states—purposefully, knowingly, recklessly, and negligently.

4. Understand that criminal liability is sometimes imposed without fault.

5. Understand that the element of causation applies only to "bad result" crimes.

6. Understand that ignorance of facts and law can create a reasonable doubt that the prosecution has proved the element of criminal intent.

KEY TERMS AND CONCEPTS

- **culpability (blameworthiness)**—the idea that we can only punish people that we can blame, and we can only blame people that are responsible for what they do; p. 105

- **blameworthiness**—it is only fair to punish people for behavior which we can blame; p. 105

- **concurrence**—requirement that the criminal intent has to trigger the criminal act (in criminal conduct crimes) and criminal conduct has to cause a bad result (in bad result crimes); p. 106

- **cause in fact**—the objective determination that the defendant's act triggered a chain of events that ended as the bad result, such as death in homicide; p. 106

- **legal cause**—a subjective judgment as to whether it's fair and just to blame the defendant for the result; cause recognized by law to impose criminal liability; p. 106

- ***mens rea***—criminal intent, the mental attitude or state of mind needed for criminal behavior; p. 106

- **motive**—the reason why a defendant commits a crime; p.107

- **subjective fault**—fault that requires a "bad mind" in the actor; p.108

- **objective fault**—fault that requires no purposeful or conscious "bad mind" in the actor; it sets a standard of what the "average person should have known;" p.109

- **strict liability**—liability that requires neither subjective nor objective fault; p. 109

- **general intent**—intent to commit the *actus reus*—the act required in the definition of the crime; p. 109

- **specific intent**—the attitude represented by subjective fault, where there's a "bad" mind or will that triggers the act; the intent to do something beyond the *actus reus*; p. 110

- **general intent "plus"**—"general intent" refers to the intent to commit the *actus reus* of the crime; and "plus" refers to some "special mental element," in addition to the intent to commit the criminal act; p. 110

- **purpose**—the specific intent to act and/or cause a criminal harm; p. 112

- **knowledge**—consciously acting or causing a result; p. 112

- **recklessness**—the conscious creation of substantial and unjustifiable risk; p. 112

- **negligence**—the unconscious creation of substantial and unjustifiable risks; p. 113

- **purposely**—acts taken for the very aim of engaging in conduct or causing a criminal result; p. 113

- **principle of concurrence**—some mental fault has to trigger the *actus reus* in criminal conduct crimes and the cause in bad-result crimes; p. 123

- **causation**—the requirement that criminal conduct cause a harm defined in the criminal code; p. 124

- **factual cause**—conduct that, in fact, leads to a harmful result (another name for "but for causation"); p. 124

- **"but for" cause**—but for the actor's conduct, the result would not have occurred (another name for factual cause); p. 124

- **legal (proximate) cause**—a subjective judgment as to whether it's fair and just to blame the defendant for the result; cause recognized by law to impose criminal liability; p. 124

- **intervening cause**—the cause that either interrupts a chain of events or substantially contributes to a result; p. 125

- **proximate cause of a death**—a cause which in natural and continuous sequence produced the death, and the death wouldn't have happened without that cause; p. 126

- **superseding cause**—an intervening cause of harm which cuts off liability to the actor because it is independent from and not foreseeable to the actor's harm; p. 126

- **defense of excuse**—defense to criminal liability. Pertaining to this chapter, it means that actor was wrong but because of their mistake they are not liable for their behavior; p. 128

- **failure-of-proof defense**—classification of defenses which state that the state failed to prove beyond a reasonable doubt that the actor had the requisite mental state to commit the crime; p. 128

CHAPTER OUTLINE

I. The Principle of *Mens Rea*

Mens rea is the mental element of a crime that the prosecution must prove beyond a reasonable doubt. There are varying degrees of *mens rea*, and it is possible that a different *mens rea* is required for different elements of the crime (one for the voluntary act, one for the harm, and a different for causation). Thus, *mens rea* law is complicated and somewhat confusing.

    A. Serious crimes require both a criminal act (*actus reus*) and criminal intent (*mens rea*).

    B. **Proving "State of Mind"**—Proof of *mens rea*
        1. We can't see intent or measure it directly.
        2. We infer intent from actors' actions (circumstantial evidence).
        3. Confessions are the only direct evidence of *mens rea*.

    C. **Criminal Intent**—Four kinds of *mens rea* (criminal intent or blameworthy state of mind)
        1. *Mens rea* consists of four states of mind with different levels of culpability.
        2. Motive, although it may or may not be relevant, is not the same thing as *mens rea*. Also, motive may be an element of a crime (for example, the "attendant circumstance" in burglary).

3. Subjective fault, objective fault, and no-fault liability
    a. Subjective fault requires "bad mind" of the actor.
    b. Objective fault does not require "bad mind" but is present when a reasonable person would have known something that the actor claims he didn't know.
    c. Strict liability is when the law makes certain behavior a crime, even if the person didn't have any guilty mind.
4. **General Intent and Specific Intent** (not the MPC approach)
    a. General intent
        i. Intent to engage in the criminal act
        ii. *Case: State v. Hobbs*
    b. Specific intent—Sometimes limited to "subjective fault" (see below)
        i. Intent to cause a specific result; commonly defined as "general intent plus"
    c. General-Intent-Plus—the intent to commit actus reus plus some other mental element of a crime
    d. *Case: Harris v. State*
5. **The Model Penal Code's (MPC's) Mental Attitudes**—The four levels of culpability are:
    a. Purpose (or intentionally)—Acting on purpose and/or with the conscious object of causing harm
        i. *Case: State v. Stark*
    b. Knowledge—Acting knowingly but without the conscious purpose or object of causing harm
        i. *Case: State v. Jantzi*
    c. Recklessness—Acting with a conscious creation of a high risk of harm
        i. *Case: Koppersmith v. State*
    d. Negligence (or criminal negligence)—Acting with an unconscious creation of a high risk of harm
        i. *Case: Koppersmith v. State*

D. **Liability without Fault: Strict liability** offenses don't require culpability (i.e., *mens rea*)
    1. Justifications for strict liability
        a. The offenses are a danger to public health, safety, and morals.
        b. Penalties are limited to fines as the only punishment.
    2. Criticisms of strict liability
        a. It violates the basic idea of punishment for culpability.
        b. It could be expanded to include more serious crimes.
    3. *Case: State v. Loge*

II. Concurrence: The required relationship between intent and act
A. *Mens rea* triggers the criminal act.
B. Criminal conduct causes the criminal harm.

Study Guide

III. Causation: The required relationship between act and harm
   A. Applies only to crimes of criminal conduct causing criminal harm
   B. Two kinds of causation
      1. **Factual ("but for" or "except for") cause**
         a. Is an empirical question of fact
         b. "Except for" or "but for" an act by the defendant that triggered a chain of events, would this criminal harm have occurred?
         c. A necessary but not sufficient cause for proving causation
      2. **Legal (proximate) cause**
         a. Based on a subjective question of fairness: Should the defendant be blamed and punished for this injury or death? Is it fair to hold the defendant responsible?
         b. Two types of intervening acts in the chain between the triggering act of the defendant and the criminal harm:
            i. Coincidental intervening acts break the causal chain unless they're predictable or foreseeable.
            ii. Responsive intervening acts only break the causal chain if:
               (a) They're abnormal; or,
               (b) They're not predicable or foreseeable
            iii. Superseding causes—cut off liability, they are not predictable nor foreseeable.
      3. *Case: People v. Armitage*
      4. *Case: Velazquez v. State*
      5. *Case: People v. Kibbe*

IV. Ignorance and Mistake—Ignorance is not knowing what the facts are; mistakenness is not being correct in what you think you know are the facts or the law.
   A. Mistake is a defense when mistake prevents the formation of *mens rea*.
   B. Debate over whether mistake is a defense to criminal liability or a failure to prove criminal liability (because they lack the *mens rea* requirement)
   C. Mistake "doesn't work" with strict liability offenses (because they do not require a mental element, failure to show mental element means nothing)
   D. *Case: State v. Sexton*

CHAPTER SUMMARY

Most crimes have a *mens rea* or mental element that must be proven by the prosecution beyond a reasonable doubt. The basic idea is that it is not fair to punish someone unless they had some form of mental fault or blameworthiness.

The mental element can apply to or modify other elements of a crime, and thus, a crime can have more than one mental element. For instance, the *mens rea* can apply to the act, the harm, or the circumstances.

General intent means intent to do the criminal act. Specific intent means an intent that applies to any other element of the crime other than the criminal act. General-intent-plus crimes are those that require the intent to commit the criminal act, plus some other mental element.

There are many different types of intent or culpability in various jurisdictions. Many states follow the Model Penal Code approach of having only four types of culpability or *mens rea*: Purpose means it was the actor's conscious object; knowing means that the actor knew something was likely to happen or occur; recklessness means that the person was aware of a serious risk but went ahead and took that risk anyway, even though an objectively reasonable person would not have taken that risk; and negligence means the actor did not conform to the external, objective standard of what a reasonable person would have known or done in the same circumstances. Purpose and knowing are subjective mental states. Recklessness is both objective and subjective. Negligence is a totally objective standard.

A few crimes impose liability without fault because they do have a *mens rea* element. These strict liability crimes are controversial because they can punish persons who had no mental fault. A person could be punished for an accident. The court has allowed strict liability crimes when it is clear that the legislature intentionally omitted the *mens rea* requirement, when the public health and welfare is at stake, and when the offenses are relatively minor.

If a crime has a harm or result element, the prosecution must prove that the defendant caused the harm beyond a reasonable doubt. The prosecution must prove that the defendant's acts were both the cause in fact ("but for" cause) and the proximate or legal cause. Cause in fact is an empirical or factual issue. Proximate or legal cause involves the question of whether it is fair or just to make the defendant responsible for a harm that occurred in an unusual fashion. For instance, sometimes a defendant will act and set a chain of events in motion, but some other events will occur after the defendant's act and contribute to causation of the harm. In general, if this intervening cause was normal and foreseeable, the defendant will not be relieved of liability for the harm.

When a person is honestly mistaken as to the fact of something (and that mistake matters) it may be said that he or she lacks the required mental state about an element of a crime or that they have an excuse defense. Thus, there will generally be no criminal liability in the case of a mistaken fact. Some characterize mistake as a defense or excuse, others characterize it as a failure of proof. The mental element required by the statutes is important in determining whether a mistake will affect criminal liability. Mistake cannot be a defense to a strict liability offense because these offenses require no *mens rea*.

PRACTICE TEST BANK

MULTIPLE CHOICE

1. The mental element of a crime is called the _____.
    a. *actus reus*
    b. *mens rea*
    c. harm
    d. concurrence

2. In the absence of a confession, intent must generally be proven by _____ evidence.
    a. peremptory
    b. exclusive
    c. referential
    d. circumstantial

3. General intent is the intent to _____.
    a. do a criminal act
    b. cause a result
    c. cause the circumstances
    d. have the *mens rea*

4. John received a slingshot for his birthday. He wanted to practice his shot, and so he went out into the crowded sheets and let a stone fly. Although he didn't intend to hit any of the many people he saw, it hit Jill in the forehead and caused her death. John acted _____.
    a. intentionally
    b. knowingly
    c. recklessly
    d. negligently

5. A *mens rea* requirement that applies to anything other than the *actus reus* is called _____ intent.
    a. strict
    b. specific
    c. transferred
    d. general

6. The objective reasonable person standard is used in the definition of _____.
    a. negligence
    b. purposely
    c. knowingly
    d. transferred intent

7. The strongest objection to strict liability laws is that _____.
   a. they result in the punishment of people who are not blameworthy
   b. long periods of imprisonment are authorized for such offenses
   c. there is no strong public interest in preventing these crimes
   d. conviction of such offenses carries a heavy stigma equivalent to burglary or robbery

8. In the case of *State v. Stark,* the court held that Stark acted _____ in exposing several women to HIV.
   a. recklessly
   b. knowingly
   c. accidentally
   d. negligently

9. A defendant is criminally responsible for harm if the defendant's conduct was the _____.
   a. cause in fact and proximate cause
   b. "but for" cause of the harm
   c. natural result of the conduct
   d. intervening cause

10. *Mens rea* elements _____.
    a. apply only to the act element
    b. apply only to the harm element
    c. can apply to other *mens rea* elements
    d. can apply to any other element except *mens rea*

11. Which of the following is not a type of culpability in the Model Penal Code?
    a. purpose
    b. knowledge
    c. intention
    d. negligence

12. If it is not the defendant's conscious objective to cause the harm, but he is aware that the harm will occur, the defendant is said to have the *mens rea* termed _____.
    a. knowledge
    b. consciousness
    c. awareness
    d. complicity

13. Conscious risk creation is referred to as _____.
    a. purpose
    b. negligence
    c. recklessness
    d. perspicacity

14. If an actor does not behave like an objectively reasonable person would have under the same circumstances, the actor is _____.
    a. reckless
    b. feckless
    c. wanton
    d. negligent

15. Which of the following types of culpability is both objective and subjective?
    a. negligent
    b. reckless
    c. knowing
    d. purpose

16. Absence of knowledge about the facts surrounding an issue is called _____.
    a. mistake of fact
    b. ignorance of facts
    c. mistake of law
    d. ignorance of law

17. Factual cause is also referred to as a _____ cause.
    a. legal
    b. proximate
    c. but for
    d. distal

18. An event that occurs between the defendant's act and the harm and has a causal connection to the harm is called a/n _____ act or cause.
    a. intervening
    b. concurrent
    c. consecutive
    d. contingent

19. The prosecution must prove that the defendant caused the harm _____.
    a. by a preponderance of the evidence
    b. beyond a moral certainty
    c. by clear and convincing evidence
    d. beyond a reasonable doubt

20. One definition of the term "concurrence" requires that the criminal intent _____.
    a. cause the act
    b. cause the harm
    c. cause the *mens rea*
    d. be the proximate cause of the circumstances

21. A bartender serves 18-year-old Jim a beer thinking he is 21. Jim had produced a very professional looking fake identification. If the state has a statute saying that it is a crime to intentionally or knowingly serve anyone under 21 alcohol, the bartender will most likely be found _____.
    a. not guilty due to mistake
    b. guilty because the crime is a strict liability crime
    c. guilty because the mistake of fact wasn't reasonable
    d. not guilty due to lack of concurrence

22. In the Model Penal Code, the most blameworthy state of mind is _____.
    a. recklessness
    b. negligent
    c. purpose
    d. intention

23. An accidental injury can be a crime if the criminal statute is of the _____ type.
    a. strict liability
    b. capital
    c. vicarious liability
    d. mendacious

24. Concerning general intent crimes, _____.
    a. all states define general intent in the same terms
    b. general intent generally means the intent to engage in the particular act
    c. general intent generally means the intent to cause a particular result.
    d. they are less serious than specific intent crimes.

25. Legal or proximate cause issues involve the _____.
    a. empirical connection between the act and harm
    b. "but for" test
    c. "except for" test
    d. justice or fairness of making the defendant responsible for this harm

26. If a responsive, intervening act is normal and foreseeable, the defendant _____.
    a. is not responsible for the harm
    b. is responsible only for negligent offenses
    c. is responsible only for reckless harms
    d. is responsible for the harm

27. Mistake of fact cuts off liability to the actor because it is viewed as _____.
    a. a defense of excuse
    b. having the absence of a *mens rea*
    c. both a defense of excuse and the absence of *mens rea*
    d. neither a defense of excuse nor the absence of *mens rea*

28. A criminal statute is more likely to have more than one _____ element than it is to have more than one element of any other kind.
    a. intent
    b. act
    c. cause
    d. concurrence

29. U.S. Supreme Court Justice Oliver Wendell Holmes' statement that even a dog can distinguish between a kick and being stumbled over, highlights the importance of the _____ element of crimes.
    a. harm
    b. result
    c. concurrence
    d. intent

30. Being aware of a serious risk but taking it anyway is the form of intent termed _____.
    a. negligence
    b. recklessness
    c. knowledge
    d. purpose

TRUE/FALSE

1. In the absence of a confession, *mens rea* is usually proven by circumstantial evidence.
    a. true
    b. false

2. Different kinds of intent indicate different levels of blameworthiness.
    a. true
    b. false

3. Specific intent is intent to do the criminal act.
    a. true
    b. false

4. The four levels of culpability or intent in the Model Penal Code are purpose, knowledge, recklessness, and negligence.
    a. true
    b. false

5. Negligence is the most blameworthy form of intent.
   a. true
   b. false

6. Recklessness requires awareness of substantial and unjustifiable risks.
   a. true
   b. false

7. Negligence has both an objective and subjective component.
   a. true
   b. false

8. Strict liability crimes have no *actus reus* element.
   a. true
   b. false

9. In strict liability crimes, accidental injury can be criminal.
   a. true
   b. false

10. Proving criminal causation requires proving both factual and legal cause.
    a. true
    b. false

11. Intervening causes can never be proximate causes.
    a. true
    b. false

12. Specific intent is intent that is transferred to another victim.
    a. true
    b. false

13. The most blameworthy state of mind in the Model Penal Code is purpose.
    a. true
    b. false

14. Negligence involves conscious risk creation.
    a. true
    b. false

15. The issue of factual cause involves the "but for" test.
    a. true
    b. false

16. Negligence is a totally objective standard.
    a. true
    b. false

17. Questions of fairness and justice figure into the factual cause determination.
    a. true
    b. false

18. Factual cause is an empirical question.
    a. true
    b. false

19. A normal, foreseeable responsive intervening act will not prevent criminal liability for a crime.
    a. true
    b. false

20. An abnormal and unforeseeable intervening cause will generally not relieve the defendant of liability for causing the harm.
    a. true
    b. false

21. An earthquake could be an intervening cause.
    a. true
    b. false

22. Strict liability crimes always violate due process.
    a. true
    b. false

23. Premeditation, wickedly, and designedly are all example of *mens rea*.
    a. true
    b. false

24. A person can't evade liability by claiming mistake of fact to a strict liability crime.
    a. true
    b. false

25. The burden of proof on the causation issue is on the defendant.
    a. true
    b. false

Chapter 4: The General Principles of Criminal Liability:
Mens Rea, Concurrence, Causation, and Ignorance and Mistake

FILL-IN-THE-BLANK

1. The "except for" test is better known as the "_____" test.

2. Fairness and justice come into play in the legal or _____ test of causation.

3. The form of intent involving having a conscious objective is _____.

4. Negligence is a totally _____ standard.

5. _____ involves conscious risk creation.

6. _____ is intent to do the criminal act.

7. The mental element of the crime is called the _____.

8. _____ evidence proves a fact indirectly or by inference.

9. _____ is intent that applies to elements other than the act.

10. _____ is a defense to a crime if it prevents the formation of a culpable state of mind.

11. Regarding mens rea, burglary is an example of a _____ crime.

12. A crime without an intent element is called a _____ crime.

13. The most blameworthy form of intent in the Model Penal Code is _____.

14. The least blameworthy form of intent in the Model Penal Code is _____.

15. Proximate cause is also referred to as _____.

ESSAY

1. Compare and contrast specific and general intent. Be sure to provide examples.

2. Define and discuss strict liability crimes. What is the justification for such crimes? Be sure to provide examples.

3. What does the criminal law require in the way of a relationship between the act and intent? Why is this relationship important? Be sure to provide examples.

4. Compare and contrast factual causation and legal causation. Why must the defendant be both the factual and legal/proximate cause of the harm in order for him to have liability? When will intervening variables cut off liability? Give examples.

5. List and define the four types of *mens rea* found in the Model Penal Code. Define each and give an example.

Chapter 4: The General Principles of Criminal Liability:
Mens Rea, Concurrence, Causation, and Ignorance and Mistake

CHAPTER 4 ANSWER KEY

Multiple Choice

1. b. See pg. 105, LO 1
2. d. See pg. 108, LO 1
3. a. See pg. 109, LO 2
4. c. See pg. 113, LO 3
5. b. See pg. 110, LO 2
6. a. See pg. 118, LO 3
7. a. See pg. 121, LO 4
8. b. See pg. 113, LO 3
9. a. See pg. 124, LO 5
10. d. See pg. 107, LO 1
11. c. See pg. 112, LO 3
12. a. See pg. 112, LO 3
13. c. See pg. 113, LO 3
14. d. See pg. 113, LO 3
15. b. See pg. 118, LO 3
16. b. See pg. 128, LO 6
17. c. See pg. 124, LO 5
18. a. See pg. 125, LO 5
19. d. See pg. 124, LO 5
20. a. See pg. 123, LO 1
21. a. See pg. 129, LO 6
22. c. See pg. 112, LO 3
23. a. See pg. 120, LO 4
24. b. See pg. 109, LO 2
25. d. See pg. 124, LO 5
26. d. See pg. 126, LO 5
27. c. See pg. 128, LO 6
28. a. See pg. 110, LO 1
29. d. See pg. 105, LO 1
30. b. See pg. 117, LO 3

True/False

1. T. See pg. 108, LO 1
2. T. See pg. 112, LO 1
3. F. See pg. 110, LO 2
4. T. See pg. 112, LO 3
5. F. See pg. 112, LO 3
6. T. See pg. 117, LO 3
7. F. See pg. 118, LO 3
8. F. See pg. 120, LO 4
9. T. See pg. 120, LO 4
10. T. See pg. 124, LO 5
11. F. See pg. 125, LO 5
23. T. See pg. 107, LO 3
24. T. See pg. 120, LO 4, 6
12. F. See pg. 110, LO 4
13. T. See pg. 112, LO 3
14. F. See pg. 118, LO 3
15. T. See pg. 124, LO 5
16. T. See pg. 118, LO 3
17. F. See pg. 124, LO 5
18. T. See pg. 124, LO 5
19. T. See pg. 126, LO 5
20. F. See pg. 126, LO 5
21. T. See pg. 125, LO5
22. F. See pgs. 120-121, LO 4
25. F. See pg. 124, LO 5

Fill-in-the-Blank

1. but for. See pg. 124, LO
2. proximate. See pg. 124, LO 5
3. purpose. See pg. 112, LO 3
4. objective . See pg. 118, LO 3
5. Recklessness. See pg. 117, LO 3
6. general intent. See pg. 109, LO 3
7. *mens rea*. See pg. 106, LO 1
8. circumstantial. See pg. 108, LO 1
9. specific intent. See pg. 110, LO 1
10. mistake of fact. See pg. 128, LO 2
11. general intent plus. See pg. 110, LO 2
12. strict liability. See pg. 120, LO 4
13. purpose . See pg. 112, LO 3
14. negligence. See pg. 112, LO 3
15. legal cause. See pg. 124, LO 5

Essays

1. Compare and contrast specific and general intent. Provide examples.

   The meaning of general intent differs, but generally, general intent means the intent to engage in the voluntary act/omission/or possession. Some jurisdictions define general intent as the intent to commit a crime with no specific time or victim in mind. Other jurisdictions define general intent as the same thing as mens rea—meaning all levels of criminal intent. Specific intent generally means that the person intends the actus reus of the crime, plus some other special element. It could also mean to specifically intend the harm done. In chapter nine, you will read that first degree murder is a specific intent crime. This means that the murderer has to intend to commit the act and intend that the person die. In chapter ten you will read that arson is a general intent crime. What that means is that the person needs to intend to light something afire, it does not require that the person intend to burn down the building. LO 2

2. Define and discuss strict liability crimes. What is the justification for such crimes?

A strict liability crime is one in which the legislators intentionally decided to omit the mens rea requirement. Generally strict liability crimes are said to be minor in nature (but this isn't always so), or involve heavily regulated areas (such as traffic infractions). Strict liability crimes are permissible when they make clear that they impose liability without fault, that they protect the public health and safety, and when the penalty is not too severe. It is, nevertheless, problematic to make behavior blameworthy when it is not intentional, knowing, reckless, or even negligent. LO 4

3. What does the criminal law require in the way of a relationship between the act and intent? Why is this relationship important? Be sure to provide examples.

The concurrence requirement of criminal law means that the criminal intent has to trigger the voluntary act. The relationship is important because we don't hold people blameworthy for accidents. They may be civilly liable and have to pay damages, but criminal law is about blameworthiness and societal condemnation. If, for example, I back over my neighbor (whom I dislike) while backing up out of my driveway, this will not be a criminal act, unless I acted with negligence (gross deviation from the standard of care of a reasonable person). My actions were not triggered by my criminal intent. On the other hand, if I think about the myriad of ways to be rid of my neighbor but do nothing, that too is not culpable behavior. My criminal intent did not trigger any action. Only when the actus reus and the mens rea come together at the same time is there a violation of the criminal law. LO 1

4. Compare and contrast factual causation and legal causation. Why must the defendant be both the factual and legal/proximate cause of the harm in order for him to have liability? When will intervening variables cut off liability? Give examples.

Behavior that sets in motion a chain of events which leads to a particular result is a factual cause. If you can answer yes to the question, "but for X, would Y not have occurred?" then you have a factual cause. For example, John is driving his car on a rainy night, and Sam is his passenger. John fails to negotiate the turn and drives off the road into a field. Sam hits his knee on the dashboard when the car comes to a stop. But for John's driving off the road, Sam would not have hurt his knee. John is the factual or but/for cause of Sam's injury.

Legal causation (also known as proximate cause) answers the question of fairness. Is it fair to hold someone responsible for the harm just because they initially set into motion a chain of events (were the factual cause? Many factors help determine fairness: was the harm foreseeable, did someone else contribute in a more substantial way to the harm, did the victim himself contribute to the harm?

These other factors are called intervening variables, and the ones that cut off liability are often referred to as superseding variables. For example, John is driving quickly on a rainy night when the roads are slippery, and Sam is his passenger. John fails to negotiate a turn and drives off the road into a field. Sam hits his knee and the ambulance responds and transports Sam. As the ambulance drives through town, another car plows into it and Sam is killed. Is it fair to hold John liable for Sam's death just because he started the sequence of events? Is it fairer to hold the driver of the car that plowed into the ambulance liable? Although not definitive, generally intervening variables will cut off liability when they are unforeseeable. Say for example, Sam is transported to the hospital for his injured leg and a crazed person enters the hospital room, shooting everyone in sight and killing Sam. It may be foreseeable that an ambulance might encounter drivers who can't stop for them, but completely unforeseeable that a person would shoot Sam in the hospital waiting room. LO 5

5. List and define the four types of mens rea required in the Model Penal Code. Give examples of each.

The highest level of mens rea under MPC § 2.02 is purposely. A person acts purposely when they act with a conscious objective to engage in the conduct or to cause a result. For example, John goes to the playground behind his house with a slingshot. He sees his enemy Sam and thinks to himself, I am going to kill him with this pebble. John picks up the pebble, puts it into the slingshot, aims at Sam, pulls the sling back, and lets it fly. The pebble hits Sam square in the forehead and Sam dies. John has acted purposely. He intended to engage in the conduct and he intended to cause the result.

The next highest level of mens rea is knowingly. A person acts knowingly if he is aware of the nature of his conduct (conduct crimes) and is aware that it is practically certain that his conduct will cause a certain result (bad result crime). For example, same as above, but John does not necessarily intend that Sam die. John is aware that he is shooting the slingshot, and is practically certain (because he is a good shot and has seen the results of slingshot wounds) that his conduct will cause Sam's death.

The next highest level of mens rea is recklessly. A person acts recklessly when he consciously disregards a substantial and unjustifiable risk by engaging in the behavior (conduct crime) and that a result will occur (bad result crime). For example, the same scenario as above, but John sees a group of kids on the playground (not Sam), he doesn't mean to hit any of them, isn't certain that he will even get with in the area, but does realize there is a risk that when he shoots the pebble off into their area that it could hit them and hurt them. Nevertheless, he lets it fly. One child is struck and dies.

The last level of mens rea is negligently. A person acts negligently when they act failing to be aware of the risk that their actions cause. In order for a negligent action to be criminal, the risk has to be substantial and such that a reasonable person would be aware that his conduct creates a risk. It has to be a "gross deviation from the standard of care of a reasonable person." For example, John is at the playground with the slingshot. He doesn't see the group of kids but he should have, or he doesn't aim the slingshot in their direction, but should have been aware that he was a really bad shot and needed to make sure that no one was around when he shot off pebbles. The difference between the reckless mens rea and the negligent mens rea is awareness of the risk. See Koppersmith case for an example. LO 3

Chapter 5
Defenses to Criminal Liability: Justifications

LEARNING OBJECTIVES

1. To understand that the law of self-defense is undergoing major transformation.

2. To understand that defendants are not criminally liable if their actions were justified under the circumstances.

3. To understand that defendants are not criminally liable if they were not responsible for their actions.

4. To understand the courts proceeding and justified and excused conduct.

5. To appreciate that self-defense limits the use of deadly force to those who reasonably believe they are faced with the choice to kill or be killed right now.

6. To know and understand the differences of the four elements of self-defense.

7. To appreciate the historic transformation of retreat and its shaping of the stand-your-ground rule and the retreat rule.

8. To understand that there is no duty to retreat from your own home to avoid using deadly force.

9. To appreciate that the "New Castle Doctrine" laws are transforming the law of self-defense.

10. To understand that the choice to commit a lesser crime to avoid an imminent threat of harm from a greater crime is justified.

11. To understand that the defense of consent represents the high value placed on individual autonomy in a free society.

KEY TERMS AND CONCEPTS

- **criminal conduct**—acts triggered by criminal intent; p. 135

- **justification defenses**—defendants admit they were responsible for their acts but claim what they did was right (justified) under the circumstances; p. 136

- **excuses defenses**—defendants admit what they did was *wrong* but claim that under the circumstances, they weren't *responsible* for what they did; p. 136

- **affirmative defenses**—defenses in which the defendant bears the burden of production; p. 136

- **burden of production**—the responsibility to introduce initial evidence to support a defense; p. 136

- **burden of persuasion**—the responsibility to convince the fact finder of the truth of the defense; p. 136

- **preponderance of the evidence**—more than 50 percent of the evidence proves justification or excuse; p. 136

- **perfect defenses**—defenses that lead to outright acquittal; p. 136

- **imperfect defenses**—defenses reducing, but not eliminating, criminal liability; p. 137

- **necessity**—general principle of an honest and reasonable belief; p. 143

- **initial aggressor**—someone who provokes an attack and therefore can't use force to defend himself against the attack provoked; p. 138

- **withdrawal exception**—if initial aggressors completely withdraw from the fights they provoke, they can claim the defense of self-defense; p. 138

- **imminent danger of attack**—element in self-defense that injury or death is going to happen right now; p. 138

- **stand-your-ground rule**—if you didn't start the fight, you can stand your ground and kill; p. 143

- **retreat rule**—you have to retreat but only if you reasonably believe that backing off won't unreasonably put you in danger of death or serious bodily harm; p. 143

- **castle exception**—exception to the retreat rule, it allows a person to stand their ground and not retreat and use deadly force to fend off an unprovoked attack; p. 143

- **Florida Personal Protection Law**—law passed in Florida in 2005 which became the model of many states' castle laws; p. 150

- **cohabitants**—cotenants, or all the individuals rightfully living in a dwelling; p. 144

- **curtilage**—the area immediately surrounding the home; p. 149

- **choice-of-evils defense (general principle of necessity)**—general principle of an honest and reasonable belief that it's necessary to commit a lesser crime (evil) to prevent the imminent danger of a greater crime (evil); p. 160

- **defense of consent**—a justification defense that says if mentally competent adults want to be crime victims, no paternalistic government should get in their way; p. 166

- **voluntary consent**—consent that is given as a product of free will; p. 167

- **knowing consent**—consent that is given knowing understanding what is being consented to; p. 167

CHAPTER OUTLINE

I. Types of Defenses
   A. Principles of justification and excuse
      1. Justification defenses—The defendant was responsible, but the act was justified.
      2. Excuse defenses—The defendant did it, but isn't responsible for his action.
   B. **Affirmative Defenses and Proving Them**
      1. In some jurisdictions, defendants have some responsibility to prove their affirmative defenses (burden of production).
      2. In some jurisdictions where the defendant bears the burden of production, they also bear the burden of persuasion by preponderance of evidence.
      3. In other jurisdictions, the government has some responsibility to disprove such defenses.
   C. Results of defendants' successful proof of defense
      1. Perfect defenses—An acquittal results.
      2. Imperfect defenses—Reduce the crime to a lesser offense.
      3. Mitigating circumstances—Reduce the penalty for the crime.

II. Self-Defense—Self-defense is a justification for the use of force.
   A. Elements
      1. **Unprovoked Attack**
         a. Self-defense not available to initial aggressor
         b. Total withdrawal by attacker an exception
         c. *Case: State v. Good*
      2. **Necessity, Proportionality, and Reasonable Belief**
         a. Necessity means imminent danger of attack
         b. Honest and reasonable belief in imminent danger of death or serious bodily injury
         c. Reasonable (not excessive) force to repel attack
         d. *Case: People v. Goetz*

B. The **retreat** doctrine may limit self-defense.
1. Historically, English common law required retreat to the wall; American 19th century transformation to no duty to retreat
   a. true man
2. Two rules
   a. Retreat rule: you have to retreat if escape is reasonable
   b. Stand your ground rule: if you didn't start the fight, you can stand your ground even if you could escape by retreating
3. Castle exception—retreat from/in home not required; you can stand your ground.
4. Domestic Violence—issue is whether retreat is required by cohabitants
   a. *Case: People v. Tomlins*
   b. *Case: State v. Shaw*
   c. *Case: State v. Thomas*

III. Defense of Others—The defense of others is a justification for the use of force.
   A. Who is included?
      1. Most states include individuals in a "special relationship".
      2. Some states include anyone in imminent danger of harm.
   B. The defense applies only to those who can claim the right to defend themselves.
   C. *Case: State v. Aguillard*

IV. In the Defense of Home and Property—The defense of home and property is a justification for the use of force.
   A. Rooted in ancient idea that our home is our castle
   B. Extension of the right of self-defense
   C. Limits to using deadly force vary by state
      1. Must have reasonable belief intruders intend to commit:
         a. Violent felonies against occupants
         b. Any felony
         c. Any offense
      2. Area covered
         a. Entry into occupied home
         b. Entry into curtilage

V. New Castle Laws
   A. Laws modeled on the Florida Personal Protection Laws (2005)
   B. Controversial
      1. Proponents: public reasserting their fundamental rights to defend themselves and property
      2. Opponents: these laws are license to kill—so long as you can reasonably claim you were in fear, you can use deadly force against someone

C. **Law Enforcement Concerns**
   1. **officers use of force**—more scrutinized than civilians
      a. imbalance of power between civilian use of force and officer use of force
   2. **officer training** in response to castle doctrine expansions.
   3. **increased investigative burdens** to determine whether there is possibility of defense claims under new laws
   4. **law enforcement attitudes toward their performance**—As no retreat laws expand, the number of defendants invoking the castle exception will expand. Police will become lackadaisical in responding with increased claims of self-defense.
D. **Doubts that the Castle laws will deter crime**—May not be great public policy
   1. Citizens may feel safer because they have the right to defend themselves.
   2. Citizens may feel less safe because they won't know who is carrying a weapon.
E. **Why the Spread of Castle Laws Now**
   1. No empirical research, but there is speculation
      a. America's heightened concern about security
      b. Lack of police officer to protect the public
   2. Cases under the Castle law
      a. Galas—Florida
      b. Smiley, Jr—Florida
      c. Pannu-Mississippi
   3. *Case: State v. Harold Fish*

VI. **Choice of Evils (General Principle of Necessity)**-- The choice-of-evils defense is a justification defense.
   A. Basic idea—Immediate necessity justifies choosing to commit a lesser crime to avoid the harm of a greater crime.
   B. Elements
      1. Identify evils (usually in legislation)
      2. Rank evils (usually in legislation)
      3. Choose the lesser evil to avoid imminent harm from the greater evil.
   C. *Case: The Queen v. Dudley and Stephens*
   D. Model Penal Code's list of right choices
   E. *Case: People v. John Gray*
   F. *Case: State v. Ownbey*
   G. *Case: People v. Dover*
   H. *Case: State v. Celli*

VII. Consent—The defense of consent is a justification for some crimes.
   A. Justification—The value of individual autonomy in a free society
   B. Consent is not a defense, but there are four exceptions.
      1. No serious injury results from consent.
      2. Injury occurs during sporting events.
      3. Consent benefits the person who consents (patient consents to surgery).
      4. Consent is a defense to certain sex crimes.
   C. Exceptions are necessary to the defense but are not enough unless consent is also voluntary and knowing.
   D. *Case: State v. Shelley*
   E. *Case: State v, Hiott*
   F. *Case: State v. Brown*
   G. *Case: State v. Fransua*

CHAPTER SUMMARY

The two primary types of defenses include justification defenses and excuse defenses. Justifications free defendants from criminal liability because they prove the defendants aren't blameworthy. Their criminal acts were right or justified. An example is self-defense, which excuses free defendants from criminal liability because they prove the defendants aren't responsible for their acts. One example is the insanity defense.

When defendants raise affirmative defenses they generally have the burden of production; that is they must produce evidence to support their defense. Sometimes they also have the burden of persuasion, meaning they have to prove to the jury that they acted in accordance with the defense. Generally, when defendants meet the burden of production and persuasion they are exonerated (this means that the defense was a "perfect defense"), but sometimes defenses are imperfect defenses which only reduce the liability of the defendant.

Justification defenses are exceptions to the rule of law. They allow individuals to take the law into their own hands. According to the rule of law, the government has a monopoly on the use of force. Use of force by individuals must be justified by law.

Self-defense is a concession to necessity and is only justified when the force is reasonably and immediately necessary for defense. Deadly force is justified only when the necessity is unprovoked and the attack involves threatened death or serious bodily injury. The amount of force used must be the minimum amount reasonably necessary to defend against an imminent threat. The general rule is that a person must retreat if they can safely do so before using deadly force. This rule puts a premium on human life, even the life of an attacker. The castle exception and the rules regarding the defense of home clearly demonstrate that the ancient doctrine that homes are castles is still alive and well. In general, a person is not required to retreat from or in their own home before using deadly force.

New Castle laws have proliferated recently and seem to expand the right to use deadly force. Under these laws, individuals are allowed to use deadly force—without any duty to retreat—in order to protect themselves whenever they are in their home or a place they have a lawful right to be. These laws provide immunity from prosecution and civil action.

The right to defend others includes everyone from close family members to any stranger who needs immediate protection from attack. The same rules apply in self-defense.

The choice-of-evils defense is also based on necessity. This defense protects those who make the right choice in deciding to commit a lesser crime to avoid the imminent harm of a greater crime or social harm. The crime results in a net social good.

The general rule is that consent by the victim is not a defense. However, consent is a defense to some crimes in some circumstances. The consent must be knowing and voluntary. The value of individual autonomy (not necessity) is the heart of the defense of consent.

Practice Test Bank

MULTIPLE CHOICE

1. Which of the following is not one of the three types of legal defenses to crime?
    a. alibi
    b. justifications
    c. excuses
    d. mitigating circumstances

2. The current approach to self-defense requires that the defender _____.
    a. ward off future attacks by using a preemptive strike
    b. reasonably believe in the danger of an imminent attack
    c. use whatever amount of force the defender subjectively thinks is justified
    d. provoked the incident

3. In justification defenses, defendants admit they did the act but seek acquittal on the ground that their acts _____.
    a. were right
    b. were wrong, but they shouldn't be held responsible
    c. were not done purposely
    d. were done accidentally

4. The amount of force that the law allows to be used in self-defense is the minimum amount _____.
    a. reasonably excessive
    b. reasonably necessary
    c. unreasonably sufficient
    d. inversely proportionate

5. Under the castle exception to the retreat doctrine, the defender does not have to retreat before using defensive force if they _____.
    a. were the initial aggressor
    b. were verbally provoked by the attacker
    c. are attacked in their own home
    d. have already retreated once

6. The choice-of-evils defense is also known as the _____.
    a. public duty defense
    b. rational behavior defense
    c. principle or defense of necessity
    d. rational person test

7. In general, consent is _____.
   a. not a defense to crime
   b. a defense only to crimes resulting in death or serious bodily injury
   c. not a defense to intentional or purposeful crime
   d. a defense only if the conduct that causes injury has no benefit to society

8. The most famous English case involving choice-of-evils defense was _____.
   a. *The Queen v. Dunn and Bradstreet*
   b. *The Queen v. Bradley and Clemens*
   c. *The Queen v. Cooper and Lybrands*
   d. *The Queen v. Dudley and Stephens*

9. Self defense is available only against _____ attacks.
   a. unprovoked
   b. imminent danger
   c. provoked
   d. voluntary

10. A consent defense to a charge of assault is most likely to succeed when _____.
    a. the assaulter is weaker and smaller than the victim
    b. the assault occurs in a lawful sporting event
    c. the victim is already injured
    d. the consent is given after the assault

11. In order for the consent of the victim to be a valid defense, the consent must be _____.
    a. knowing and subjective
    b. voluntary and objective
    c. in writing
    d. voluntary and knowing

12. Which of the following is a step in the Model Penal Code approach to the choice-of-evils defense?
    a. compare the possible sentences for the two crimes involved
    b. rank the culpability involved in the two offenses at issue
    c. rank the harms
    d. choose the greater evil to avoid the lesser evil

13. To have a valid claim of using force to defend another person, the defendant must show that _____.
    a. the attacker also threatened to use force against the defender
    b. the person defended had a right to use force to defend themselves
    c. the use of force by the attacker against the victim was lawful
    d. the defender must be stronger than the person attacked

14. In *State v. Thomas* the issue the court had to decide was whether _____.
    a. Thomas needed to use force to defend herself from an imminent unlawful attack
    b. Thomas used reasonable amount of force in self-defense
    c. Thomas, as a cohabitant, had a duty to retreat under Ohio law
    d. Thomas initiated the unlawful contact and therefore could not claim self-defense

15. The Florida Personal Protection Law of 2009 does NOT _____.
    a. create a presumption that an occupant has reasonable fear of imminent peril of great bodily harm when another forcefully and unlawfully enters the dwelling
    b. create a presumption that an occupant has reasonable fear of imminent peril of great bodily harm when another forcefully or lawfully enters an occupied vehicle.
    c. create a presumption that a person who unlawfully enters a dwelling by force intends to commit an unlawful act of force or violence.
    d. create an obligation for retreat on an occupant whose home is unlawfully entered and limits the degree of force which can be used to non-deadly force.

16. The party that has the burden of persuasion on an issue must _____.
    a. prove the point or lose on the issue
    b. present some evidence to get the issue into the case
    c. inform the jury before trial that they will raise the issue
    d. present enough evidence to meet the burden of production

17. In *State v. Aguillard*, the defendant was unsuccessful in claiming the defense-of-others- defense because _____.
    a. the persons Aguillar was trying to defend were not part of his immediate family
    b. the persons Aguillar was trying to defend would not, under state law, been justified in using force to defend themselves—because abortion was legal in Louisiana
    c. Aguillar used an unreasonable amount of force in defense of the unborn
    d. the persons Aguillar was trying to defend could only use non-violent force to defend themselves

18. Most modern statutes limit the use of *deadly* force to cases where it is reasonable to believe intruders intend _____.
    a. to harm the property
    b. to commit crimes of violence against the occupants
    c. to commit a felony against the property
    d. to unlawfully enter the curtilage of the property

19. A defense in which defendants admit the act but claim they aren't legally responsible is called a/n _____.
    a. justification
    b. claim of right
    c. mitigating condition
    d. excuse

20. If the defendant establishes a perfect defense, the defendant _____.
    a. is committed to a mental hospital
    b. may still be convicted of a lesser offense
    c. is entitled to be found not guilty
    d. is entitled to a reduced sentence

21. A defendant is charged with murder but manages to get a conviction on manslaughter. This can occur if a defendant establishes certain types of _____.
    a. justifications
    b. excuses
    c. aggravating circumstances
    d. imperfect defenses

22. A person who violates the speed limit in order to get a critically injured person to the emergency room may claim which of the following defenses?
    a. duress
    b. necessity
    c. coercion
    d. statute of limitations

23. In most jurisdictions, the defendant's belief that self-defense was necessary must be sincere and _____.
    a. objectively reasonable
    b. subjectively unreasonable
    c. empirically accurate
    d. empirically verifiable

24. Defensive force may be used lawfully only if the danger is _____.
    a. foreseeable
    b. imminent
    c. mandatory
    d. contingent

25. The general rule is that self-defense is lawfully available only against ____ attacks.
    a. unprovoked
    b. justified
    c. legal
    d. excusable

26. Persons who are the initial, unprovoked aggressor can acquire a lawful right to defend themselves if they _____ from the fight they started.
    a. clearly desist
    b. irrevocably renounce themselves
    c. contingently abstain
    d. completely withdraw

27. The "true man rule," concerning the requirement that a person retreat before using force, is also known as the _____ rule.
    a. castle
    b. stand-your-ground
    c. reasonable retreat
    d. foreseeable desistance

28. A defense which requires the defendant to produce some evidence of the defense before the jury will be allowed to consider the defense is a/n _____.
    a. imperfect defense
    b. perfect defense
    c. statutory defense
    d. affirmative defense

29. Circumstances about the crime that may reduce the punishment are called _____ circumstances.
    a. contingent
    b. foreseeable
    c. mitigating
    d. compensatory

30. Justifications focus on the _____.
    a. personal accountability of the defendant
    b. the rightfulness of an otherwise criminal act
    c. legal responsibility of the defendant
    d. mitigating circumstances

TRUE/FALSE

1. A perfect defense leads to an acquittal.
    a. true
    b. false

2. It is never lawful to use force to protect property.
    a. true
    b. false

3. Preemptive strikes at a potential attacker are valid self-defense.
   a. true
   b. false

4. Consent is never a defense to any sex crime.
   a. true
   b. false

5. The choice-of-evils defense is also called the general principle of necessity.
   a. true
   b. false

6. The case of *State v. Shelley* shows that consent will always be a valid defense in a sporting contest.
   a. true
   b. false

7. Retaliation for past attacks or threats justifies defensive use of force.
   a. true
   b. false

8. There is no defense for using force against someone who is not attacking the actor but is attacking some other person.
   a. true
   b. false

9. Defendants prove most defenses beyond a reasonable doubt.
   a. true
   b. false

10. If the convicted defendant shows mitigating circumstances, they may be able to get a reduced sentence.
    a. true
    b. false

11. Necessity or choice-of-evils is not a valid defense if the state has already ranked the evils and specifically precluded the choice, such as the use of marijuana to alleviate pain.
    a. true
    b. false

12. In both excuses and justifications, the defendant admits doing the *actus reus*.
    a. true
    b. false

13. The burden of production is on the defendant for affirmative defenses.
    a. true
    b. false

14. Imperfect self-defense may, in some jurisdictions, reduce a murder to manslaughter.
    a. true
    b. false

15. The new castle laws have spread to many states in recent years.
    a. true
    b. false

16. In all states, a person must retreat from their home if they can safely do so before using deadly force.
    a. true
    b. false

17. A person cannot lawfully use force to prevent an anticipated attack.
    a. true
    b. false

18. No matter what may happen later, the initial attacker can never claim self-defense.
    a. true
    b. false

19. The Model Penal Code recognizes a choice-of-evils defense.
    a. true
    b. false

20. The choice-of-evils defense requires that the defendant has correctly identified and weighed the evils.
    a. true
    b. false

21. The choice-of-evils defense was available at common law.
    a. true
    b. false

22. The outside area immediately surrounding the home is called the curtilage.
    a. true
    b. false

23. At common law, the right to use deadly force to defend your own home was not recognized.
    a. true
    b. false

24. Most self defense statutes only require that the individual truly believed they were in imminent danger.
    a. true
    b. false

25. Consent is a defense to all crimes.
    a. true
    b. false

FILL-IN-THE-BLANK

1. Only the danger of a/n _____ attack justifies the use of force in self-defense.

2. Under the _____ exception to the retreat doctrine, one does not have to retreat in one's own home before using defensive force.

3. To have a valid claim of self-defense, the actor must have had an honest and _____ belief in the necessity of using force.

4. _____ is when an individual believes that injury or death is going to happen immediately.

5. The law regarding defense of homes is influenced by the common-law idea that a person's home is their _____.

6. The criminal law generally excludes the defense of _____, where serious injury is inflicted on the victim.

7. Running a stop sign to get a seriously ill person to the hospital would be an example of the _____ defense.

8. A/n _____ defense is one that reduces, but does not eliminate, criminal liability.

9. The duty to retreat before using deadly force is weakest when the person is attacked in their _____.

10. The lawn and/or other space immediately outside the home is called the _____.

11. The first castle doctrine passed in October 2005 and was called _____.

12. _____ circumstances are circumstances which may lead to a reduction in sentence.

13. The true man rule is also known as the _____ rule.

14. A/n _____ defense is one that, if established, requires a verdict of not guilty.

15. The burden of proof or _____ is a party's obligation to finally prove (or disprove) a defense or other matter.

ESSAY

1. Define, compare, and contrast justification and excuse defenses.

2. Discuss the elements of and limitations to the defense of consent.

Study Guide

3. Discuss the elements of and limitations to choice-of-evils defense.

4. Discuss the evolution of the New Castle Exceptions (to the retreat rule).

5. Discuss the elements of and limitations to a successful claim of self-defense.

CHAPTER 5 ANSWER KEY

Multiple Choice

1. d. See pg. 137, LO 4
2. b. See pg. 138, LO 5
3. a. See pg. 136, LO 2
4. b. See pg. 138, LO 5
5. c. See pg. 143, LO 8
6. c. See pg. 160, LO 11
7. a. See pg. 166, LO 12
8. d. See pg. 160, LO 11
9. a. See pg. 137, LO 6
10. b. See pg. 167, LO 12
11. d. See pg. 167, LO 12
12. b. See pg. 161, LO11
13. b. See pg. 148, LO6
14. c. See pg. 146, LO 9
15. d. See pgs. 150-152, LO 10
16. d. See pg. 136, LO 4
17. b. See pg. 148, LO 9
18. b. See pg. 149, LO 5
19. d. See pg. 136, LO 4
20. c. See pg. 136, LO 4
21. d. See pg. 137, LO 4
22. b. See pg. 161, LO 11
23. a. See pg. 138, LO 6
24. b. See pg. 138, LO 5
25. a. See pg. 138, LO 6
26. d. See pg. 138, LO 6
27. b. See pg. 143, LO 7
28. d. See pg. 136, LO 4
29. c. See pg. 137, LO 4
30. b. See pg. 136, LO 4

True/False

1. T. See pg. 136, LO 4
2. F. See pg. 148, LO 6
3. F. See pg. 137, LO 6
4. F. See pg. 167, LO 12
5. T. See pg. 160, LO 11
6. F. See pg. 168, LO 12
7. F. See pg. 137, LO 6
8. F. See pg. 148, LO 6
9. F. See pg. 136, LO 1
10. T. See pg. 137, LO 2
11. T. See pg. 161, LO 11
12. T. See pg. 136, LO 4
13. T. See pg. 136, LO 4
14. T. See pg. 137, LO 4
15. T. See pg. 154, LO 10
16. F. See pg. 143, LO 9
17. T. See pg. 137, LO 5
18. F. See pg. 138, LO 6
19. T. See pg. 161, LO 11
20. T. See pg. 161, LO 11
21. T. See pg. 160, LO 11
22. T. See pg. 149, LO 5
23. F. See pg. 143, LO 8
24. F. See pg. 139, LO 6
25. F. See pg. 167, LO 12

Study Guide

Fill-in-the-Blank

1. imminent. See pg. 138, LO 6
2. castle. See pg. 143, LO 10
3. reasonable. See pg. 138, LO 6
4. Imminent danger of attack. See pg. 138, LO 6
5. castle. See pg. 143, LO 10
6. consent. See pg. 167, LO 12
7. choice-of-evils. See pg. 161, LO 11
8. imperfect. See pg. 137, LO 4
9. home. See pg. 143, LO 5
10. curtilage. See pg. 149, LO 5
11. The Florida Personal Protection Law. See pg. 150, LO 10
12. Mitigating. See pg. 137, LO 4
13. stand-your-ground. See pg. 143, LO 7
14. perfect. See pg. 136, LO 4
15. persuasion. See pg. 136, LO 4

Essay

1. Define, compare, and contrast justification and excuse defenses.

   When a defendant claims a defense of justification, he argues that, although he is responsible for his actions, what he did was not wrong but in fact justified under the circumstances. When a defendant claims a defense of excuse, he argues, although what he did was wrong, he is not responsible for his behavior for whatever excuse he puts forth (insanity, age, intoxication, duress). Both justification and excuse are defenses which may be perfect defenses (completely exonerating the defendant) or imperfect defenses (which reduce, but do not exonerate, criminal liability). Justifications and excuses may be affirmative defenses that place a burden on the defendant to put forth some evidence of why he is either not responsible or not wrong. LO 4

Chapter 5: Defenses to Criminal Liability: Justifications

2. Discuss the elements of and limitations to the defense of consent.

The defense of consent embraces the notion of personal autonomy—that mentally competent adults should decide whether they want themselves to be violated, and that the government should not interfere. Obviously, at the core of the crime of rape is the lack of consent (see chapter eleven), but consent also justifies other behaviors as well. Most states allow the consent defense in four situations: when no serious injury results from the consensual crime, when the injury happens during a sporting event, when the conduct benefits the person who consented (surgery, for example), and when the consent is to sexual conduct. In order to raise a valid defense of consent the "victim" must have given both voluntary (unforced or threatened) consent and knowing consent (they knew what they were agreeing to). State v. Shelley shows some of the limits of the consent defense, even under circumstances where consent is recognized—sporting events. In Shelley the court found that the victim did not give implied consent to the injury that occurred during a basketball game. The court reasoned that the defendant's conduct exceeded what was considered within the rules of the sport. Consider the game of boxing: contenders consent to be hit repeatedly, but they do not consent to have their ears bitten off. LO 12

3. Discuss the elements of and limitations to choice-of-evils defense.

Choice of evils defense, also known as necessity, is a justification which allows a defendant to claim that what he did was not wrong under the circumstances because he made the right choice and chose the lesser of evils. The MPC and most states require the defendant successfully raising this defense to identify the evils, rank the evils, and choose the lesser of the evils. In essence, the defendant is claiming that they needed to violate the law in order to avoid a more serious harm. One limit to the choice of evils defense occurs when the legislature has already ranked and chosen the evil—a legislative preemption to the defense. This issue is seen in State v. Ownbey and People v. Gray et. al. LO 11

4. Discuss the evolution of the New Castle Exceptions (to the retreat rule).

Historically, the law of self-defense allowed the use of deadly force to meet unprovoked and unlawful use of deadly force against the defenders. Some states required an individual to retreat if they could do so safely before employing deadly force in self-defense. In those states requiring retreat, there generally was a "castle exception" which allowed individuals to stand their ground (refuse to retreat) in their own homes. Historically, the law of defense of property and habitation allowed individuals to use force to protect their property and habitation (homes) but they could not use deadly force to protect their property or homes. The question that arose from these general rules is what a person was supposed to do when their homes were invaded but it wasn't really clear what the intent of the intruder was. Was it to do the person harm, or was it merely to do the property/home harm? Although the text mentions that the new castle laws expanded the right to use deadly force in self-defense, (remember deadly force could always be used to repel unlawful, unprovoked, imminent deadly force), these laws really clarified by creating presumptions concerning the beliefs of the defender and the intent of the intruder. Also, they create civil and criminal immunity for anyone using force permitted by the law (they can't be prosecuted or sued). The text also notes that these laws broaden the legitimate circumstance where deadly force applies; they include intrusions into occupied vehicles. The laws have evolved in response to home invasions, carjackings, etc. LO 10

5. Discuss the elements of and limitations to a successful claim of self-defense.

The justification of self-defense allows an individual to use reasonable force, including deadly force, to repel the unlawful, unprovoked and imminent use of force by another. The defender has to honestly and reasonably believe they are faced with the choice of kill or be killed before they can use deadly force (force that likely to cause death). Excessive force is not allowed. The defender can only use force when needed to repel an imminent threat. It is not self-defense when a person takes pre-emptive action. It is not self-defense when a person uses force in retaliation. Both of those situations do not present the "imminent danger of attack" needed to be proved in a successful self-defense claim. The final requirement is that the defender did not provoke the attack. A person who is the initial aggressor in an incident can't then turn around and use force to defend against an individual who was only using force in self-defense. The exception to the "can't be the initial aggressor" rule is if the initial aggressor completely withdraws from the attack and then finds himself being attacked by the individual who initially was not the aggressor. The hallmark of self-defense is reasonableness. The behaviors of the person using the force will be measured in terms of what a reasonable person would have done or thought under the circumstances, not what this individual himself actually thought or believed. LO 4

Chapter 6
Defenses to Criminal Liability: Excuse

LEARNING OBJECTIVES

1. Understand that defendants who plead an excuse defense admit what they did was wrong but argue that, under the circumstances, they weren't responsible for their actions.

2. Understand that the defense of insanity excuses criminal liability when it seriously damages defendants' capacity to control their acts and/or capacity to reason and understand the wrongfulness of their conduct.

3. Appreciate that few defendants plead the insanity defense, and those who do, rarely succeed.

4. Understand that insanity is not the equivalent of mental disease or defect.

5. Understand how the right-wrong test focuses on defect in reason or cognition.

6. Understand how the volitional incapacity test focuses on defects in self-control or will.

7. Understand how the substantial capacity test focuses on reason *and* self-control.

8. Understand how the product-of-mental-illness test focuses on criminal acts resulting from mental disease.

9. Understand how current trends favor shifting the burden of proof for insanity to defendants.

10. Understand the difference between diminished capacity and diminished responsibility and appreciate how they apply only to homicide.

11. Understand how the different processes the law handles age and how juvenile court judges can use their discretion to transfer a juvenile to adult criminal court.

12. Understand that it is sometimes OK to excuse people who harm innocent people to save themselves.

13. Understand that voluntary intoxication is no excuse for committing a crime; involuntary intoxication is.

14. Understand that entrapment is used in all societies, even though it violates a basic purpose of government in free societies—to prevent crime, not to encourage it.

15. Understand why, despite immense criticism, syndrome excuses should be taken seriously.

KEY TERMS AND CONCEPTS

- **failure-of-proof theory**—the defendant disproves the prosecution's case by showing he or she couldn't have formed the state of mind required to prove the mental element of the crime; p. 176

- **insanity**—a legal term for a person who is excused from criminal liability because a mental disease or defect impairs his or her *mens rea*; p. 176

- **civil commitment**—involuntary confinement not based on criminal conviction; p. 178

- **right-wrong test (*M'Naghten* rule)**—test used in insanity defense to determine the defendant's capacity to either know right from wrong or to know the act is against the law; p. 181

- **volitional incapacity**—test to determine impairment of the will that makes it impossible to control the impulse to do wrong; p. 182

- **irresistible impulse test**—tests whether the will is so impaired that it makes it impossible for the person to control the impulse to do wrong; p. 183

- **substantial capacity test**—insanity due to mental disease or defect impairing the substantial capacity either to appreciate the wrongfulness of conduct or to conform behavior to the law; p. 182

- **product test (Durham rule)**—an insanity test to determine whether a crime was a product of mental disease or defect; p. 182

- **reason**—the mental capacity to distinguish right from wrong; p. 182

- **will**—free choice or decision; p. 182

- **M'Naghtan rule**—an insanity defense focused on whether a mental disease or defect impaired the defendants' reason so that they couldn't tell the difference between right and wrong; p. 182

- **mental disease**—disease of the mind, not equivalent to insanity; p. 182

- **mental defect**—mental retardation or brain damage severe enough to make it impossible to know what you're doing, or if you know, you don't know it's wrong; p. 182

- **irresistible impulse test**—test to determine impairment of the will that makes it impossible to control the impulse to do wrong; p. 183

- **two-stage (bifurcated) trial**—one phase of a trial to determine guilt, the other to determine punishment; p. 183

- **product-of-mental-illness test**—a test to determine whether a crime was a product of mental disease or defect; p. 188

- **diminished capacity**—mental capacity less than "normal" but more than "insane;" an attempt to prove that the defendant, incapable of the requisite intent of the crime charged, is innocent of that crime but may well be guilty of a lesser one; p. 189

- **diminished responsibility**—a defense of excuse in which the defendant argues, "What I did was wrong, but under the circumstances I'm *less* responsible;" p. 190

- **judicial waiver**—when a juvenile court judge uses their discretion to transfer a juvenile to adult criminal court; p. 191

- **defense of duress**—the excuse of being forced to commit a crime; p. 194

- **entrapment**—government actions that induce individuals to commit crimes that they otherwise wouldn't commit; p. 197

- **subjective test of entrapment**—focuses on the predisposition of defendants to commit crimes; p. 198

- **objective test of entrapment**—focuses on the actions that government agents take to induce individuals to commit crimes; p. 201

- **syndromes**—novel defenses of excuse based on symptoms of conditions, such as being a Vietnam vet suffering from post–traumatic stress disorder or having premenstrual symptoms; p. 201

Study Guide

CHAPTER OUTLINE

I. Excuses are a form of defense to a criminal charge.
　　A. Difference between justification and excuse
　　　　1. Justification—Admits responsibility, but, under the circumstances, claims it was the right thing
　　　　2. Excuse—Admits doing wrong, but, under the circumstances, claims not legally responsible
　　B. Two theories:
　　　　1. Excuse defenses excuse criminal conduct that the prosecution has proved beyond a reasonable doubt
　　　　2. Failure of proof theory of excuse—defendants raise reasonable doubt about the prosecutions case, particularly its failure to prove the mental element)

II. Insanity—Insanity is a defense based on a defendant's mental disease or defect.
　　A. Definition—The defendant was so mentally diseased, he couldn't know nature of acts or control actions.
　　B. A legal, but not a medical, concept
　　C. Rationale—can't blame people who aren't responsible
　　D. Few plead insanity; of those who do, few succeed.
　　E. Consequence of successful plea of insanity—civil commitment, not freedom
　　　　1. *Case: U.S. v. Hinckley*
　　F. **The Right-Wrong Test aka M'Naghten Rule**
　　　　1. Right-wrong test elements—depends on defendant's mental capacity to know right from wrong
　　　　　　a. Mental disease (psychosis) or mental defect (retardation) damaged reason at the time of the crime
　　　　　　b. The defendant didn't know (simple awareness)
　　　　　　　　(1) Nature of actions
　　　　　　　　(2) Right or wrong
　　　　　　　　　　(a) Legal wrong
　　　　　　　　　　(b) Moral wrong
　　　　2. *Case: People v. Schmidt*
　　　　3. *Case: State v. Odell*
　　G. **The Irresistible Impulse Test**
　　　　1. Irresistible impulse test elements
　　　　　　a. The defendant had a mental disease or defect at the time of the crime.
　　　　　　b. The defendant knew the nature of the act and knew it was wrong.
　　　　　　c. The mental disease or defect caused an impulse he couldn't control (volitional failure)
　　　　2. *Case: Hinkley*

H. **The Substantial Capacity Test**
   1. Substantial capacity test elements (Model Penal Code)
      a. The mental disease or defect damages either or both reason and will.
      b. The mental disease or defect causes
         (1) Substantial (not complete) lack of reason and control
         (2) Failure to appreciate (not just purely intellectual awareness of) nature or wrongfulness
         (3) Failure to conform behavior to law
   2. *Case: People v. Drew*
I. **The Product-of-Mental-Illness Test**
   1. Product-of-mental-illness test elements (Durham rule)
      a. Checks for both reason and will
      b. Acts that are a product of mental illness excuse criminal liability.
   2. New Hampshire and Maine (minus Maine)
J. The Burden of Proof
   1. States vary as to who has to prove insanity and to what level of certainty.
      a. Federal law prior to the Hinckley case, for example, required government to prove the defendant was not insane beyond a reasonable doubt.
      b. Federal law after the Hinckley case, requires defendants to prove they were insane by clear and convincing evidence.

III. **Diminished Capacity**—The diminished capacity defense negates intent.
   A. Mental disease or defect diminishes capacity but not enough to qualify as insanity defense
   B. Limited to diseases or defects that make it impossible to form the intent required to commit the crime
   C. Is not the same as diminished responsibility (a defense of excuse)
   D. In practice, both diminished capacity and the diminished responsibility defense apply only to homicide. Most states use them to reduce first degree to second degree murder (Some from murder to manslaughter).

IV. **Age**—Age is a defense or a basis for juvenile court jurisdiction.
   A. Immaturity excuses criminal liability, but statutes vary as to the age of capacity.
   B. Age of maturity varies, but three stages at common law and later:
      1. Early childhood—can't form criminal intent (irrebuttable presumption)
      2. Middle childhood—refutable presumption against capacity to form intent
      3. Adult—conclusive presumption of capacity to form intent
   C. Age can aggravate as well as excuse criminal responsibility.
   D. Age of capacity is different than the jurisdiction of the courts to try young offenders.

E. Young offenders in all jurisdictions may be subject to the jurisdiction of juvenile courts for certain offenses. Youthful offenders may also be waived into adult courts.
1. Judicial waivers—judges using discretion to transfer a juvenile to adult court
2. Prosecutorial waivers—prosecutor's discretion to file a case in adult court
3. Legislative waivers—legislators excluding juvenile court jurisdiction for certain offenses

F. *Case: State v. K.R.L.*
G. *Case: People v. Munoz*

V. Duress
A. **The Problem of Duress**
1. Duress is a defense involving a person being threatened if they don't commit a crime.
2. Should we excuse those who hurt others to save themselves?

B. **The Elements of Duress**
1. Threats amounting to duress: kinds of threats vary from killing to doing serious bodily harm
2. Immediacy of the threats: from instant to imminent threat
3. Crimes the defense applies to qualifying crimes vary from minor to serious (never for homicide).
4. Degree of belief regarding the threat: measurement of belief regarding threats varies as to objective or subjective.

VI. Intoxication—Intoxication may or may not be a defense.
A. Conflicting principles of accountability and causation
B. Voluntary is no excuse; involuntary is an excuse.
C. Statutes may provide that voluntary intoxication, which negates a *mens rea* element of a crime, may reduce culpability.
D. *Case: Burrows v. State*
E. *Case: State v. Hall*

VII. Entrapment is a defense based on the conduct of the police.
A. Definition—police inducting someone to commit a crime they wouldn't otherwise commit
B. Defense of entrapment is not of constitutional origin.
C. **The Subjective Test**—majority rule
1. Did criminal intent originate with the government?
2. Was the defendant predisposed to commit the crime?
3. *Case: Sherman v. U.S.*
3. *Case: Oliver v. State*
4. *Case: De Pasquale v. State*

D. The Objective Test—Minority rule
1. Did criminal intent originate with the government?
2. Would ordinary (reasonable), law-abiding people be tempted to commit the crime?
3. Dismiss even if the defendant is predisposed.

VIII. Syndromes—Syndrome defenses involve a variety of mental conditions.
A. Groups of symptoms (syndromes) impair mental capacity
B. Affects defendant's capacity to form specific intent
C. Expert testimony is used to inform the jury of the syndrome.
D. *Case: State v. Phipps*

CHAPTER SUMMARY

Defendants who plead excuses admit what they did was wrong but claim they weren't responsible because of mental abnormality or unusual circumstances.

The excuse of insanity is rarely used, rarely successful, and almost always leads to at least temporary civil commitment if successful. The defense of insanity stands for the proposition that we can't blame people who aren't responsible because of mental diseases or defects that impair their reason or will. Insanity is not the equivalent of mental disease or defect; rather, it is caused by mental disease or defect.

There are a number of tests of the insanity defense. The right-wrong (M'Naghten) test focuses on defects in reason. The product-of-mental-illness test (Durham rule) focuses on criminal acts resulting from (are the product of) mental disease. The irresistible impulse test focuses on defects in volition or self-control. The substantial capacity test (Model Penal Code) focuses on reason and self-control. Insanity is an affirmative defense in which the actual burden of proof varies, depending on the jurisdiction.

John Hinckley, who attempted to assassinate President Reagan, was found not guilty by reason of insanity. This verdict troubled many and may have been caused by the fact that the prosecution was required to prove that Hinckley was sane beyond a reasonable doubt. Subsequent federal legislation places the burden on the defendant to prove their insanity by clear and convincing evidence. Some states have also changed their law, placing the burden of proof on the defendant. The federal government shifted the burden of proof to the defendant by clear and convincing evidence and eliminated any volitional test of insanity.

Diminished capacity involves mental disease or defect that will not qualify for the insanity defense. It may reduce the degree of a crime, because it impairs the capacity to specific intent. If successful, it may reduce the crime to a lower level or complete acquittal because the required *mens rea* cannot be proven. The insanity defense leads to a special verdict.

Age can excuse criminal liability; it can also increase it. At common law, there was an irrebuttable presumption that a child under seven couldn't form criminal intent. Between seven and fourteen, there was a refutable presumption of incapacity to form intent. At age fourteen, children were presumed to be capable of forming intent. Many states follow some updated form of the common law. All jurisdictions now have juvenile courts and special laws for juveniles. Juveniles over a certain age who commit serious crimes can be tried in criminal courts as adults.

Duress can be an excuse when individuals are threatened and forced to commit a crime or be killed. In most states, duress is not a defense to murder.

At common law, and in most, if not all, states, voluntary intoxication was not a defense. While voluntary intoxication is not an excuse, involuntary intoxication is a defense.

Entrapment occurs when law enforcement officers actively induce, trick, or persuade individuals to commit crimes they otherwise wouldn't commit. There are two main types of entrapment defenses. The subjective version focuses on whether or not the defendant was predisposed to commit the crime anyway. The objective version focuses on whether the government action would cause a reasonable, law-abiding person to commit a crime.

Various types of syndromes or conditions such as post-traumatic stress disorder and premenstrual syndrome (PMS) have been tried as defenses. In general, they are not successful.

Practice Test Bank

MULTIPLE CHOICE

1. If diminished capacity evidence is utilized in an intentional homicide case, the result of accepting the evidence is _____.
   a. not guilty of any type of homicide
   b. reducing the homicide to a lower degree homicide
   c. not guilty by reason of insanity
   d. a verdict of not guilty by reason of diminished capacity

2. The only states that adopted the _____ rule (or product test) for the insanity defense were Maine and New Hampshire.
   a. Durham
   b. M'Naghten
   c. substantial capacity
   d. right-wrong

3. To establish the duress defense in most jurisdictions, it must be shown that the threat of harm against the defendant was _____.
   a. contingent
   b. foreseeable
   c. overt
   d. reasonably believed to be real

4. In the substantial capacity test, the traditional word "know" has been replaced by the word _____.
   a. understand
   b. comprehend
   c. appreciate
   d. aggrandize

5. The objective test of entrapment focuses on government action that _____.
   a. would cause a law-abiding person to commit a crime
   b. provides an opportunity for criminally inclined individuals to commit a crime
   c. would cause a predisposed person to commit a crime
   d. provides an opportunity for a predisposed person to commit a crime

6. Which of the following is not a valid legal excuse for crime?
   a. insanity
   b. voluntary intoxication
   c. entrapment
   d. duress

7. Only the excuse of _____, when raised as a successful defense, does not result in a complete acquittal and immediate release from custody.
    a. entrapment
    b. duress
    c. involuntary intoxication
    d. insanity

8. The M'Naghten test of insanity is referred to as the _____ test.
    a. right-wrong
    b. Durham
    c. McDonough
    d. product

9. The _____ test of insanity deals only with defendant's inability to control their conduct.
    a. product
    b. right-wrong
    c. M'Naghten
    d. irresistible impulse

10. The Model Penal Code's _____ test of insanity incorporates both the cognitive and volitional components of other tests.
    a. Durham
    b. M'Naghten
    c. product
    d. substantial capacity

11. The defense of diminished capacity is available _____.
    a. in most states for most offenses
    b. in most states only when the insanity defense is raised
    c. in most states, but for felonies only
    d. only in few states

12. Most jurisdictions utilize some form of the Model Penal Code's _____ test for their insanity defense.
    a. substantial capacity
    b. Durham
    c. irresistible impulse
    d. product

13. In the 1980s, many states and the federal government changed their _____ defenses, after the verdict in the trial of John Hinckley.
    a. duress
    b. diminished capacity
    c. entrapment
    d. insanity

14. The _____ test of insanity incorporates some of the ideas of both the right-wrong and irresistible impulse test.
    a. product
    b. Durham
    c. diminished capacity
    d. substantial capacity

15. The defense of diminished capacity _____.
    a. is the same as the right-wrong insanity test
    b. involves a claim that mental illness (but not quite insanity) kept the defendant from having the required intent
    c. asserts that the defendant's acts were involuntary
    d. is the same as diminished responsibility

16. At common law, there was an irrebuttable presumption that children under _____ could not form criminal intent.
    a. seven
    b. eight
    c. ten
    d. twelve

17. After the Hinckley insanity verdict, Congress changed the burden of proof for the federal insanity defense. The burden of proof is now on the defendant to prove insanity _____.
    a. by a preponderance of the evidence
    b. beyond a reasonable doubt
    c. by clear and convincing evidence
    d. beyond reasonable suspicion

18. Under the common law, when children reached the age of _____, they were presumed to be capable of criminal intent, just like adults.
    a. seven
    b. twelve
    c. fourteen
    d. seventeen

19. The subjective test of entrapment is an attempt to deal with _____.
    a. organized crime
    b. predisposed criminals
    c. government abuses
    d. young offenders

20. At common law, voluntary intoxication was a/n _____.
    a. justification
    b. defense
    c. mitigating factor
    d. aggravating factor

21. Combat soldiers and others subjected to extreme situations that later commit crimes sometimes attempt to use the _____ defense.
    a. PMS
    b. post-traumatic stress syndrome
    c. chronic fatigue syndrome
    d. traumatic automaton stress induced

22. The objective test of entrapment is so named because the test revolves around _____.
    a. subjective reactions to police conduct
    b. whether an objectively predisposed person would commit the crime
    c. how a hypothetical, reasonable person would react
    d. public attitudes toward the seriousness of the crime

23. When offenders raise age as a defense, they are claiming _____.
    a. they are too young to be tried in an adult court
    b. they are too young to have the capacity to be responsible for their behavior
    c. the prosecution must show that they are mature enough to be tried
    d. they are too old to be tried and incarcerated for their behavior

24. Which of the following tests of insanity is totally volitional?
    a. substantial capacity
    b. M'Naghten
    c. Durham
    d. irresistible impulse

25. The court does not have to consider the _____ when deciding to allow a waiver.
    a. seriousness of the offense
    b. sophistication and maturity of the juvenile
    c. precipitation by the victim
    d. threat the juvenile poses to public safety

26. Excuses tend to involve either _____ people or circumstances.
    a. mitigating
    b. codependent
    c. abnormal
    d. contingent

27. The hypothetical situation of a man who believes he's squeezing lemons but is really strangling his wife to death is an example of the _____ approach to insanity.
    a. subjective
    b. cognitive
    c. volitional
    d. objective

28. Under the Model Penal Code test of insanity, the defendant must lack _____ mental control.
    a. total
    b. complete
    c. partial
    d. substantial

29. Which of the following is an excuse, rather than a justification?
    a. duress
    b. necessity
    c. self-defense
    d. defense of others

30. In a majority of states, the defense of _____ cannot be used to a charge of murder.
    a. entrapment
    b. insanity
    c. duress
    d. involuntary intoxication

TRUE/FALSE

1. The cognition form of the insanity defense deals with the will or ability to control conduct.
    a. true
    b. false

2. Most jurisdictions utilize the subjective test of entrapment.
    a. true
    b. false

3. The irresistible impulse test is a cognitive type of insanity defense.
    a. true
    b. false

4. The Durham version of the insanity defense was first announced in a famous English case in 1843.
    a. true
    b. false

5. Many states use some version of the Model Penal Code substantial capacity test of insanity.
    a. true
    b. false

6. The substantial capacity test has both cognitive and volitional elements.
    a. true
    b. false

7. Most defendants who utilize the insanity defense at trial do so unsuccessfully.
    a. true
    b. false

8. Defendants usually succeed when they argue syndrome defenses such as PMS or post-traumatic stress disorder.
    a. true
    b. false

9. In criminal law, the insanity defense is a medical concept, not a legal one.
    a. true
    b. false

10. In all states and the federal courts, the prosecution must disprove insanity by a preponderance of the evidence.
    a. true
    b. false

11. At common law, voluntary intoxication was a defense.
    a. true
    b. false

12. Involuntary intoxication is a recognized defense in all states.
    a. true
    b. false

13. A defendant who succeeds with the diminished capacity defense will automatically be committed to a mental hospital.
    a. true
    b. false

14 At common law, a child under twelve years of age could not be guilty of a criminal offense.
    a. true
    b. false

15. In most states, the defense of duress cannot be used in murder prosecutions.
    a. true
    b. false

16. To have a successful duress defense, the defendant must retreat before using force if it can be done safely.
    a. true
    b. false

17. The predisposition of the defendant to commit the crime is relevant in the subjective test of entrapment.
    a. false
    b. true

18. Current federal statutes use the Durham test of insanity.
    a. true
    b. false

19. A defendant who has prior convictions for similar offenses would probably fare best in a jurisdiction that uses the objective test of entrapment.
    a. true
    b. false

20. Persons found not guilty by reason of insanity spend much less time in custody than do defendants convicted of the same offenses.
    a. true
    b. false

21. In an excuse, the defendant admits doing the act, but argues that the act was right or justified.
    a. true
    b. false

22. The John Hinckley trial and verdict stimulated considerable change in the law of insanity.
    a. true
    b. false

23. Under the irresistible impulse test, the defendant does not have to be suffering from a mental disease or defect.
    a. true
    b. false

24. The defense of insanity is limited to murder cases.
    a. true
    b. false

25. Since the late 1980s, most jurisdictions and the federal government have abolished the insanity defense.
    a. true
    b. false

Study Guide

FILL-IN-THE-BLANK

1. The defense of _____ is recognized in only a few states.

2. _____ intoxication is not a defense.

3. The M'Naghten test of insanity is also known as the _____ test.

4. At common law, a child under the age of _____ could not be guilty of a crime.

5. The diminished capacity defense relates to negating the _____ element of crimes.

6. The Durham or_____ test of insanity basically asks if the mental illness caused the crime.

7. Under the _____ test of entrapment, the government cannot introduce evidence of the defendant's prior convictions for similar offenses.

8. If government agents offer inducements to get persons to commit crimes, this could implicate the _____ defense.

9. To establish the insanity defense, it must be shown that the defendant suffered from a mental disease or _____.

10. In some states, a defendant who is not insane but is mentally ill may be able to use the defense of _____.

11. The _____ test of entrapment focuses on the predisposition of the defendant to commit the crime.

12. In federal courts, and in many states, the burden of proof on the insanity defense is on the _____.

13. At one time, the state of _____ had the diminished capacity defense but later abolished it because of public hostility.

14. At common law, a child was presumed capable of criminal intent upon reaching the age of _____.

15. Young offenders are typically dealt with in _____ court rather than adult criminal court.

ESSAY

1. Discuss the evolution of the excuse defense of age

2. How does the Model Penal Code's substantial capacity test differ from the M'Naghten test of insanity?

3. Compare and contrast the insanity and diminished capacity defenses.

4. Discuss the two major approaches to the entrapment defense

5. Compare and contrast the excuses of involuntary and voluntary intoxication.

CHAPTER 6 ANSWER KEY

Multiple Choice

1. b. See pg. 189, LO 10
2. a. See pgs. 188-189, LO 8
3. d. See pg. 195, LO 12
4. c. See pg. 185, LO 7
5. d. See pg. 201, LO 14
6. b. See pg. 196, LO 13
7. d. See pg. 178, LO 3
8. a. See pg. 182, LO 5
9. d. See pg. 183, LO 6
10. d. See pg. 184, LO 7
11. d. See pg. 190, LO 10
12. a. See pg. 182, LO 7
13. d. See pg. 184, LO 10
14. d. See pg. 184, LO 7
15. b. See pg. 190, LO 10

16. a. See pg. 190, LO 11
17. c. See pg. 189, LO 9
18. c. See pg. 190, LO 11
19. b. See pg. 198, LO 14
20. d. See pg. 196, LO 13
21. b. See pg. 202, LO 15
22. c. See pg. 201, LO 14
23. b. See pg. 190, LO 11
24. d. See pg. 182, LO 6
25. c. See pg. 191, LO 11
26. c. See pg. 176, LO 2
27. b. See pg. 182, LO 5
28. d. See pg. 184, LO 7
29. a See pg. 176, LO 12
30. c. See pg. 195, LO 12

True/False

1. F. See pg. 182, LO 5
2. T. See pg. 198, LO 14
3. F. See pg. 183, LO 6
4. F. See pg. 188, LO 8
5. T. See pg. 182, LO 7
6. T. See pg. 184, LO 7
7. T. See pg. 177, LO 3
8. F. See pg. 201, LO 15
9. F. See pg. 176, LO 4
10. F. See pg. 189, LO 9
11. F. See pg. 196, LO 13
22. T. See pgs. 188-189, LO 9
24. F. See pg. 178, LO 2, 3

12. T. See pg. 205, LO 13
13. F. See pgs. 189-190, LO 10
14. F. See pg. 190, LO 11
15. T. See pg. 195, LO 12
16. F. See pg. 195, LO 12
17. T. See pg. 198, LO 14
18. F. See pg. 188, LO 8, 9
19. T. See pg. 201, LO 14
20. F. See pg. 178, LO 3
21. F. See pg. 177, LO 1
22. T. See pgs. 188-189, LO 9
25. F. See pg. 189, LO 9

Study Guide

Fill-in-the-Blank

1. diminished capacity. See pg. 190, LO 10
2. Voluntary. See pg. 196, LO 13
3. right-wrong. See pg. 181, LO 7
4. seven. See pg. 190, LO 11
5. *mens rea*. See pg. 189, LO 10
6. product. See pg. 182, LO 8
7. objective. See pg. 201, LO 14
8. entrapment. See pg. 197, LO 14
9. defect. See pg. 182, LO 4
10. diminished capacity. See pg. 189, LO 10
11. subjective. See pg. 198, LO 14
12. defendant. See pg. 189, LO 9
13. California. See pg. 190, LO 10
14. fourteen. See pg. 190, LO 11
15. juvenile. See pg. 191, LO 11

Essays

1. Discuss the evolution of the excuse defense of age.

   At common law, children under the age of seven could not be criminally liable. Children who were between seven and fourteen years old were presumed to be too young to be criminally liable. The state could put forth evidence to rebut that presumption. Fourteen year olds were treated as adults. States now vary in the age of criminal capacity, and often the separate issue of court jurisdiction gets blended with the issue of when a child can have the capacity to commit a crime. They are separate questions. States vary as to the minimum age for capacity, and some states set no minimum age. The juvenile court/ adult court issue resolves where the proceeding will be held assuming that the child could have criminal capacity. LO 11

2. How does the Model Penal Code's substantial capacity test differ from the M'Naghten test of insanity?

The M'Naghten test of insanity (also known as the Right/Wrong test) states that a person is not guilty of a criminal act when, because of a mental disease or defect, he does not know the nature and quality of his actions or that what he was doing was wrong. There is some variations by states which have adopted this test as to whether "wrong" means legally wrong or morally wrong and whether "know" means to be simply aware (cognition) or whether it requires an appreciation of the significance of the action. The Model Penal Code's test was an effort to deal with the criticisms of the right/wrong test and the irresistible impulse test. Under this test, a defendant will not be guilty of a crime when because of a mental disease or defect he lacks a substantial capacity (not complete mental capacity) to either appreciate the criminality (grasp the significance that the act is wrongful) or to conform his behavior to the requirements of law (volitional aspect). In sum, the MPC test combines the right and wrong test with the irresistible impulse test and clears up some definitional issues. LO 5, 6, 7, 8

3. Compare and contrast the insanity and diminished capacity defenses.

Insanity is a legal term and is an affirmative defense based upon mental disease or defect which affects the defendant's ability to either know or control his behavior. If successful, a plea of insanity may result in a civil commitment of an offender rather than incarceration. Some states, however, use a guilty but mentally ill finding which nevertheless results in criminal liability for the defendant. The trend has been to shift the burden of production and persuasion to the defendant as to whether he was insane at the time of the offense. The defense of diminished capacity is not a complete defense and is most frequently limited to cases of homicide. When successful, the diminished capacity defense will mitigate the level of the crime, but not result in a not guilty verdict. So, for example, when charged with a first-degree murder, the offender may raise the excuse of diminished capacity (challenging the state's ability to prove the requisite mens rea of intentional, purposeful behavior) which would still result in a conviction for second degree murder or manslaughter (depending on state law's definitions of those crimes). Many states have abolished a diminished capacity defense, or when they allow it, allow the evidence as a factor in sentencing. LO 9, 10

4. Discuss the two major approaches to the entrapment defense.

The two main approaches to entrapment are the subjective test of entrapment which focuses on the predisposition of the defendant to commit the crime and the objective test of entrapment which focuses on the government's behavior. The subjective test of entrapment is employed by most of the states and all federal courts. In order to successfully raise this defense, the defendant has to prove that the government pressured him or her to commit crimes they would not have committed without the pressure (lack of predisposition). The subjective test focuses on where the criminal intent originated. If it originated with the defendant, there is no entrapment. Examples of cases in which the subjective test was used are: Sherman v. U.S, Oliver v. State, and DePasquale v. State. The Oliver case is a rare example of a successful use of the entrapment defense.

The minor approach is the objective test of entrapment. It is directed at unsavory police methods. If the intent originates with the government and their actions would tempt an ordinary law-abiding person to commit the crime, the court should dismiss the case even if this particular defendant was predisposed to commit the crime. The test is "objective" because it focuses on a reasonable law abiding citizen and the government's inducements...not the inclinations of the defendant in the case at hand. LO 14

5. Compare and contrast the excuses of involuntary and voluntary intoxication.

Generally, the excuse of involuntary intoxication is a complete defense whereas the excuse of voluntary intoxication, which is rarely allowed, acts only to lower the mens rea element and results in conviction on a lesser crime. Involuntary intoxication applies to those cases where an individual unwittingly and unwillingly consumes an intoxicating substance (alcohol, controlled substances, or any other type of substance which may result in an adverse physical reaction). The classic example is when someone slips something into the drink of another. Involuntary intoxication defense is not successful when the person voluntarily consumes the intoxicant but has a much different or greater reaction than anticipated. For example, if a person smoked marijuana to get high not knowing that it was laced with LSD which prompted a violent episode, they probably would not be able to successfully claim involuntary intoxication. Voluntary intoxication, when permitted by statute, allows a defendant to claim that he was too intoxicated to form the requisite mens rea of purposeful or knowing behavior. It may result in a conviction for a crime of recklessness or negligence, but it is not a complete defense. Moreover, even when statutes allow defendants to raise the voluntary intoxication defense, most juries are not sympathetic to it. LO 13

Chapter 7
Parties to Crime and Vicarious Liability

LEARNING OBJECTIVES

1. Appreciate that participants before and during the commission of crimes are guilty of the crime itself.

2. Understand how participants after the commission of crimes are guilty of a separate, less serious offense.

3. Understand that the core idea of accessory liability is that it's not as blameworthy to help someone else escape prosecution and punishment as it is to participate in the crime itself.

4. Understand that vicarious liability has to be created by statute.

5. Understand that vicarious liability can apply either to enterprise (mainly business) or to individuals.

KEY TERMS AND CONCEPTS

- **complicity**—the principle regarding parties to crime that establishes the conditions under which more than one person incurs liability before, during, and after committing crimes; when one person is liable for another person's crime; p. 208

- **vicarious liability**—the principle of liability for another based on relationship; p. 208

- **accomplices**—the parties liable as principals before and during a crime; p. 209

- **accessories**—the parties liable for separate, lesser offenses following a crime; p. 209

- **conspiracy**—agreeing to commit a crime; p. 209

- **Pinkerton rule**—the rule that conspiracy and the underlying crime are separate offenses; p. 209

- **mere presence rule**—a person's presence at the scene of a crime doesn't by itself satisfy the *actus reus* requirement of accomplice liability; p. 210

- *respondeat superior*—employers are legally liable for their employees' illegal acts; p. 221
- **parent responsibility laws**—statutes that make parents liable for their children's crimes.

CHAPTER OUTLINE

I. There are two types of liability for someone else's criminal act.
    A. Complicity—Parties-to-crime laws establish when a person can be held liable for the crimes of another.
    B. Vicarious liability laws establish which types of relationships can create criminal liability.

II. Parties to Crime
    A. There were four types of parties to crime at common law:
        1. Principals in the first degree actually commit the crime.
        2. Principles in the second degree are present when the crimes are committed.
        3. Accessories-before-the-fact
            a. Help before the crime is committed
            b. Are not present when the crime is committed
        4. Accessories-after-the-fact help after the crime is committed.
    B. Distinction important because at common law, the accomplices could not be prosecuted until the principal in the first degree was convicted
        1. All felonies were capital offenses (thus very serious penalty for someone who may not be quite so involved)
    C. As capital crimes decreased, the nature of accomplice liability was streamlined.

III. Participation before and during the commission of a crime—Accomplices are prosecuted for committing the crime itself (helping a murderer is murder).
    A. Distinguish between accomplice and conspiracy liability
        1. Pinkerton Rule—conspiracy is separate offense from crime agreed to
    B. **Accomplice *actus reus***
        1. Core idea—accomplice took some positive act to help commit a crime.
        2. Words can be accomplice *actus reus*.
        3. Mere Presence Rule--presence at the crime scene isn't enough unless there's a duty (parent to minor child)
            a. *Case: Bailey v. U.S.*
            b. *Case: State v. Walden*
        4. Actions after the crime can be relevant to prove *actus reus*.
        5. *Case: State v. Ulvinen*

C. **Accomplice *mens rea***
   1. Purpose clearly qualifies.
   2. Jurisdictions vary and sometimes are confused as to whether knowledge, recklessness, or negligence qualify.
   3. *Case: Backun v. U.S.*
   4. *Case: U.S. v. Peoni*

IV. Participation after the commission of a crime—Accessory
   1. A separate, lesser offense than accomplice liability
   2. Elements of accessory after the fact
      a. Accessory personally helped the person who committed the felony (*actus reus* element)
      b. Accessory knew a felony was committed (*mens rea* element)
      c. Accessory helped for the purpose of hindering prosecution (*mens rea* element)
      d. Someone other than the accessory actually committed a felony (circumstance element)
   3. *Case: State v. Chism*
   4. *Dunn v. Commonwealth*

V. Vicarious Liability.
   A. Vicarious liability makes one liable for the acts of another because of a relationship.
   B. **Corporate Liability**
      1. History: concern about corporate crime is not new; creature of federal law
         a. stems from U.S. Constitution's contract clause
         b. stems from U.S. Constitution's commerce clause giving Congress power to regulate interstate commerce
      2. Self-regulation of corporation for benefit of its shareholders
      3. Lessons of subprime crisis, collapse of corporate giants
      4. Respondeat Superior—legal and policy bases for vicarious corporate criminal liability
         a. corporate employees' acts are imputed to the corporation
         b. *Case: New York Central and Hudson River Railroad Company v. U.S.*
      5. *Case: U.S. v. Arthur Anderson, LLP v. U.S.*
   C. **Individual Vicarious Liability**—individuals vicariously liable for their agents' actions—employees' crimes committed within the scope of their employment but without the approval or knowledge of their employers.
      1. generally must be established by statute, not by courts (meaning there is no common-law vicarious liability)
         a. *Case: State v. Tomaino*
      2. Traffic violations—difficulty proving who parked the vehicle
         a. *Prima facie* case—presumes driver was the operator and is responsible

3. Parental responsibility—parents responsible for acts of children
   a. Distinguish traditional parental liability statutes which hold parents liable for failure to supervise their child (omission is the parents *actus reus*) with vicarious liability statutes which hold parents responsible for the acts committed by their child.
   b. *Case: the Alex Provenzino story*
   c. *Case: State v. Akers*

CHAPTER SUMMARY

A person can be criminally liable for the criminal acts of another. The doctrine of complicity (parties to crime) establishes when you can be held criminally liable for someone else's crimes. The doctrine of vicarious liability establishes what types of relationships can make you liable for someone else's crimes.

The common law on complicity was complex. A principal in the first degree was the person who actually committed the crime. Principals in the second degree were those who were present at the scene of the crime and aided the principal in the first degree. Such aid could take the form of being a lookout or driving the getaway car. Accessories-before-the-fact were those who were involved in the crime before it was committed and were not present when it was committed. An example would be a person who provides safe-cracking tools for the safecracker. Finally, an accessory-after-the-fact is one whose only aid comes after the crime was completed.

Today, the law has been simplified. Under the current approach, participants before and during the commission of crimes are guilty of the crime itself. These persons are liable as accomplices. Participants after the commission of crimes are guilty of a separate, less serious offense.

Liability as an accomplice is different from liability as a co-conspirator. Persons in a conspiracy to commit a crime can also be liable for both the conspiracy and the crimes of other conspirators. This flows from the Pinkerton rule. The crime in conspiracy is the agreement to commit the other crime.

The essence of accomplice *actus reus* is that the accomplice took some positive action to aid or assist in the commission of a crime actually committed by another. The *mens rea* of complicity varies, depending on the jurisdiction. It may be purpose, knowledge, recklessness, or negligence.

The core idea of accessory liability is that it's not as blameworthy to help someone else escape prosecution as it is to participate in the crime itself.

Vicarious liability transfers the *actus reus* and *mens rea* of an individual to another person or from more persons to an enterprise because of a relationship. Most vicarious liability involves business relationships such as employer-employee, manager-corporation relationships. However, it can also apply to other enterprises or between individuals. Vicarious liability of corporations is based upon federal and state statutes and has become increasingly important in light of recent financial collapse of corporate giants such as Enron. The court has used the doctrine of *respondeat superior* to extend vicarious liability to the corporations.

Individual vicarious liability involves making an individual responsible for the acts of other individuals: for instance, making owners of cars vicariously liable for operators' parking tickets. The liability is created because of the owner-operator relationship. Vicarious liability of parents based on the parent-child relationship grew out of public fear, frustration, and anger over juvenile crime. There is little case law on such statutes and some have been held unconstitutional.

Practice Test Bank

MULTIPLE CHOICE

1. The _____ rule or principle states that everyone who is involved in a crime, whether before, during, or after, may be responsible for that crime.
   a. vicarious liability
   b. complicity
   c. Pinkerton
   d. Wharton

2. Mr. A robs the bank. Mr. B waits outside with the getaway car. Under the common law, with regard to the bank robbery, Mr. B is a/n _____.
   a. principal in the first degree
   b. accessory-after-the-fact
   c. accessory-before-the-fact
   d. principal in the second degree

3. Mr. A commits a burglary. A few days before, he got the burglary tools from Mr. B., who has no other involvement in the burglary. Under the common law approach, Mr. B is a/n _____.
   a. accessory-before-the-fact
   b. accessory-after-the-fact
   c. principle in the third degree
   d. principal in the second degree

4. An agreement between two or more persons to commit a crime is a _____.
   a. solicitation
   b. conspiracy
   c. complicity crime
   d. vicarious liability offense

5. The current approach to complicity _____.
   a. maintains most of the common law distinctions
   b. eliminates the principle and accessory classifications of the common law
   c. retains the common law terminology of accessories before the fact
   d. retains the common law terminology of principal in the second degree

6. Accomplice liability _____.
   a. requires *actus reus* but not *mens rea*
   b. requires *mens rea* but no *actus reus*
   c. requires both *actus reus* and *mens rea*
   d. is a strict liability offense

7. The Pinkerton rule is applicable only to _____.
   a. accomplices
   b. the doctrine of complicity
   c. conspiracies
   d. accessories

8. Vicarious liability arises most frequently in employment or _____ relationships.
   a. personal
   b. producer-consumer
   c. family
   d. business

9. To convict a person of being an accessory-after-the-fact, the government must show that _____.
   a. the person intended to aid the criminal after the crime
   b. there was a conspiracy to aid after the crime that was entered into before the crime
   c. the Pinkerton rule applies
   d. the person provided aid to a person whom he knew had committed a misdemeanor

10. In general, merely being present at the scene of a crime _____.
    a. is sufficient to create accomplice liable
    b. is not sufficient to create accomplice liability
    c. is the *actus reus* of accomplice liability
    d. creates a presumption that there was a conspiracy to commit the crime

11. Corporate criminal law is the creature of _____.
    a. federal law
    b. state common law
    c. state codes
    d. administrative laws

12. In *State v. Akers*, the New Hampshire appellate court overturned the parents' vicarious liability conviction for acts of their children because the law _____.
    a. violated equal protection because it applied only to parents
    b. violated substantive due process by punishing parenthood
    c. was a bill of attainder
    d. was overbroad

13. Mere presence of the actor at the scene of a crime may create accomplice liability if _____.
    a. the actor has a duty to prevent the crime and fails to prevent or attempt to prevent it
    b. the actor secretly hopes the crime will be completed
    c. the actor knows the victim but does not intervene
    d. the actor knows the criminal but does not intervene

14. The case of *State v. Walden*, in which the defendant was charged for not preventing her one-year-old son from being beaten, illustrates _____.
    a. the exception to the mere presence rule
    b. the exception to the rule against accessories-after-the-fact
    c. the rule of vicarious liability
    d. the rule of accomplice liability

15. The rule that the conspiracy to commit a crime and the crimes committed pursuant to the conspiracy are separate offenses is called the _____ rule.
    a. Wharton
    b. Peoni
    c. Brady
    d. Pinkerton

16. The _____ of accomplice liability is frequently phrased in terms of aiding, abetting, or assisting another who commits a crime.
    a. *mens rea*
    b. *actus reus*
    c. circumstances
    d. concurrence

17. According to the U.S. Supreme Court in *Bailey v. U.S.* (1969), flight from the scene of a crime _____.
    a. by itself proves accomplice liability
    b. by itself proves guilty of the crime
    c. is not evidence of accomplice liability
    d. by itself cannot prove accomplice liability

18. In *State v. Ulvinen* (1983), the Minnesota appellate court held that _____ alone could not prove accomplice liability for murder.
    a. being related to the victim
    b. living in the same household as the victim
    c. passive approval of the crime
    d. refusing to cooperate with the police

19. The rule of the Peoni case requires that the accomplice not only intended to aid the offender and knew of the crime to be committed, but that the accomplice also intended or desired that _____.
    a. the crime be committed
    b. there be a conspiracy
    c. the actual offender not be caught
    d. the accomplice not be caught

20. The early decisions on accomplice liability held that the only *mens rea* required for accomplice liability was intent _____.
    a. to aid the offender knowing a crime would be committed
    b. to form a conspiracy
    c. that the offender commit the crime
    d. to benefit from the crime committed

21. Crimes involving being an accessory-after-the-fact typically have _____ *mens rea* element(s).
    a. one
    b. two
    c. three
    d. four

22. Most accessory-after-the-fact criminal statutes contain _____ circumstance element(s).
    a. no
    b. one
    c. two
    d. three

23. Unlike accomplice liability, vicarious liability does not require that the person being held vicariously liable _____.
    a. participate in the crime
    b. be aware of the circumstances
    c. be involved in a conspiracy
    d. not be involved in a conspiracy

24. Strict liability crimes have no _____.
    a. *actus reus* element
    b. voluntary act element
    c. legality requirement
    d. *mens rea* element

Study Guide

25. Vicarious liability is based on _____.
    a. benefiting from the crime
    b. being involved in the crime
    c. relationships
    d. personal *actus reus* and *mens rea*

26. Vicarious liability of individuals usually involves _____.
    a. homicides
    b. traffic tickets
    c. felonies
    d. conspiracies

27. _____ laws make parents liable for the crimes of their children, if the parents fail to supervise and control their children.
    a. Parental responsibility
    b. Vicarious parental liability
    c. Conspiracy
    d. Parental combination

28. Corporate liability is always a form of _____ liability.
    a. co-conspirator
    b. accomplice
    c. accessory
    d. vicarious

29. In *State v. Chism*, the court noted that Louisiana law differed from common law with regard to the required mens rea for accessory liability. It held that Louisiana law _____.
    a. required that Chism had to know that a completed felony had been committed.
    b. required that Chism had to have reasonable grounds to believe that a felony had been committed.
    c. required only that a felony be committed and Chism aid the offender after the fact—regardless of whether he knew about the felony
    d. required that Chism not only aid in helping the offender after the fact, but also take at least a minimal role in accomplishing the felony

30. In *State v. Tomaino* the court had to determine whether the owner was liable for the clerk renting pornographic material to a minor. The court found _____.
    a. the clerk was not responsible because the "victim" looked old enough to buy the video.
    b. the owner was not responsible because he had properly trained the clerk and he was therefore not reckless.
    c. that the pertinent Ohio statute required personal action so the owner could not be vicarious liable.
    d. that the owner was responsible because he failed to supervise the clerk and failed to post a sign warning of no underage rentals.

TRUE/FALSE

1. Complicity creates liability because of a relationship with the offender.
    a. true
    b. false

2. Vicarious liability hinges on providing aid or assistance to an offender.
    a. true
    b. false

3. At common law, the person who actually committed the crime is the principal in the first degree.
    a. true
    b. false

4. A co-conspirator could be an accessory-before-the-fact.
    a. true
    b. false

5. The Pinkerton rule states that accomplices are liable for all crimes committed by the persons they aid.
    a. true
    b. false

6. The doctrine of complicity establishes when one person can be criminally liable for the acts of another.
    a. true
    b. false

7. At common law, a person who knowingly harbored a felony fugitive to prevent the felon's capture would be an accessory-after-the-fact.
    a. true
    b. false

8. At common law, a person who acted as a lookout for another criminal would be a principal in the third degree.
    a. true
    b. false

9. A person who aids, abets, or assists another in committing a crime is an accomplice to that crime.
    a. true
    b. false

Study Guide

10. Flight from the scene of a crime is enough evidence to convict an individual of a crime or being an accomplice.
    a. true
    b. false

11. Mere presence at the scene of a crime is, all by itself, not enough to convict one of being an accomplice to that crime.
    a. true
    b. false

12. Barring some duty to the victim, passive approval of a crime is, by itself, enough to warrant conviction as an accomplice.
    a. true
    b. false

13. Early court decisions on accomplice liability did not require proof of intent to facilitate the crime, only proof of intent to aid the criminal.
    a. true
    b. false

14. The minority rule is that in addition to general intent, accomplice liability also requires intent that the crime be committed.
    a. true
    b. false

15. A person cannot be held liable as an accomplice for negligent or reckless acts.
    a. true
    b. false

16. Most accessory-after-the-fact statutes require that the defendant know the person they aided committed a felony.
    a. true
    b. false

17. According to the mere presence rule, presence at the scene of the crime, followed by flight, is enough action to satisfy the *actus reus* requirement of accomplice liability.
    a. true
    b. false

18. Words can qualify as accomplice actus reus.
    a. true
    b. false

19. Corporations cannot be vicariously liable for the acts of their employees.
    a. true
    b. false

20. The best way to control criminal behavior by a corporation is through self-regulation.
    a. true
    b. false

21. A person can be vicariously liable even though they personally did no act and had no criminal intent.
    a. true
    b. false

22. Corporations have no legal personality and therefore cannot be sued
    a. true
    b. false

23. Parental responsibility laws make parents liable if their children commit a crime because the parents failed to supervise or control their children.
    a. true
    b. false

24. Every law imposing vicarious criminal liability on parents for the acts of their children has been found to be constitutional.
    a. true
    b. false

25. The Court in *New York Central and Hudson River Railroad Company v. U.S.* was important because in it the court first held that a corporation could not be sued and held responsible its actions because it was not a person.
    a. true
    b. false

FILL-IN-THE-BLANK

1. Laws making parents liable for acts of offspring because of failure to control or supervise are called _____ laws.

2. At common law, persons who protected or harbored the felon after the felony was completed were called accessories-after-the-_____.

3. The doctrine of _____ sometimes makes persons liable for the acts of others.

4. _____ makes one liable for the acts of another because of the relationship to the other.

5. At common law, the person who actually committed the crime was termed a _____ in the first degree.

6. At common law, persons who assisted the criminal before the crime was committed were called _____.

7. At common law, persons involved in a crime who were present at the scene of the crime were termed _____.

8. In most jurisdictions today, participants before and/or during the crime are called _____.

9. An agreement to commit a crime is called a/n _____.

10. Under the _____ rule, conspirators can be convicted of both conspiracy and the crime committed.

11. The _____ is the governmental body that regulates corporations through its regulation of the stock market.

12. The doctrine of _____ holds that the acts of the servant are imputed to the master.

13. A well-established rule states that _____ at the scene of a crime is, alone, not enough to justify conviction as an accomplice.

14. Aiding, abetting, assisting, etc. are the *actus reus* of _____.

15. In many modern codes, a person who assists a criminal after the crime is called a/n _____.

ESSAY

1. Discuss the four parties to a crime under the common law. Provide an example of each.

2. Discuss the evolution of accomplice liability since common law.

3. Define, compare, and contrast accomplice and vicarious liability.

Study Guide

4. How does the government use vicarious liability to combat corporate crime.

5. What are the four elements of most accessory-after-the-fact statutes?

CHAPTER 7 ANSWER KEY

Multiple Choice

1. b. See pg. 208, LO 1
2. d. See pg. 208, LO 1
3. a. See pg. 208, LO 1
4. b. See pg. 209, LO 1
5. b. See pg. 208, LO 1, 3
6. c. See pg. 209, LO 3
7. c. See pg. 209, LO 1
8. d. See pg. 219, LO 4
9. a. See pg. 216, LO 2
10. b. See pg. 210, LO 1
11. a. See pg. 220, LO 5
12. b. See pg. 231, LO 5
13. a. See pg. 210, LO 1
14. a. See pg. 210, LO 1
15. d. See pg. 209, LO 2

16. b. See pg. 210, LO 1
17. d. See pg. 210, LO 3
18. c. See pg. 213, LO 3
19. a. See pg. 214, LO 3
20. a. See pg. 213, LO 2
21. b. See pg. 215, LO 3
22. b. See pg. 215, LO 3
23. a. See pg. 219, LO 4
24. d. See pg. 219, LO 4
25. c. See pg. 219, LO 4
26. b. See pg. 229, LO 5
27. a. See pg. 229, LO 5
28. d. See pg. 219, LO 5
29. b. See pg. 217, LO 2
30. c. See pg. 229, LO 5

True/False

1. F. See pg. 208, LO 1
2. F. See pg. 208, LO 5
3. T. See pg. 208, LO 1
4. T. See pgs. 208-209, LO 1
5. F. See pg. 209, LO 2
6. T. See pg. 208, LO 1
7. T. See pg. 208, LO 3
8. F. See pg. 208, LO 1
9. T. See pg. 210, LO 1
10. F. See pg. 210, LO 1

11. T. See pg. 210, LO 1
12. F. See pg. 213, LO 1
13. T. See pgs. 213-214, LO 1
14. T. See pg. 209, LO 1
15. F. See pg. 215, LO 1
16. T. See pgs. 215-216, LO 2
17. F. See pg. 210, LO 2
18. T. See pg. 210, LO 1
19. F. See pg. 219, LO 5
20. F. See pg. 221, LO 5

Study Guide

21. T. See pg. 208, LO 5
22. F. See pg. 221, LO 5
23. T. See pg. 229, LO 5
24. F. See pgs. 230-231, LO 5
25. F. See pg. 221, LO 5

Fill-in-the-Blank

1. parental responsibility. See pg. 229, LO 5
2. fact. See pg. 215, LO
3. complicity. See pg. 208, LO 1
4. Vicarious liability. See pg. 208, LO 5
5. principal. See pg. 208, LO 1
6. accessories-before-the-fact. See pg. 208, LO 1
7. principals in the second degree. See pg. 208, LO 1
8. accomplices. See pg. 208, LO 1
9. conspiracy. See pg. 209, LO 1
10. Pinkerton. See pg. 209, LO 1
11. Securities and Exchange Committee (SEC). See pg. 221, LO 5
12. *respondeat superior*. See pg. 221, LO 5
13. mere presence. See pg. 210, LO 1
14. accomplice liability. See pg. 210, LO 1
15. accessory. See pg. 215, LO 3

Essays

1. Discuss the four parties to a crime under the common law.

   At common law there were very specific laws of complicity. Because all felonies were capital offenses at common law, in order to prosecute individuals who helped in the commission of a crime, the main actor had to first be convicted. At common law, parties to a crime were either 1) a principal in the first degree (the person who committed the crime), 2) a principal in the second degree (person who was present when the crime was committed and helped commit it), 3) an accessory before the fact (persons not present when the crimes were committed but who helped beforehand), and 4) an accessory after the fact (persons who helped after the crime was committed). LO 1, 2

2. How are accomplices different than co-conspirators?

Both accomplice and conspiracy liability are based on the involvement of more than one person in a crime. Accomplices are individuals who aid another in the commission of a crime. Accomplice mens rea is a little murky, some states require the specific purpose of aiding the other and the purpose that the other commit the crime but other states require only knowingly helping someone, and do not require the intent that they commit the crime. See U.S. v. Peoni and Backum v. U.S.

Conspiracy on the other hand is the act of agreeing with another to commit a crime. The conspiracy mens rea is generally (see chapter eight) the specific intent to commit the criminal objective. A conspiracy can exist regardless of whether the agreed to crime is ever committed (some states require some overt act in furtherance of the criminal enterprise).

Accomplice liability requires the completion of the crime. Additionally, a person can render aid to another with the intent that they commit a crime—even without forming an agreement to do so (though this is a situation which is difficult to envision) LO 1, 2, 3

3. Define, compare, and contrast accomplice and vicarious liability.

Accomplice liability and vicarious liability both stem from the area of law dealing with who can be a party to a crime. Accomplice liability is based upon the actions and intentions of a person who either directly engages in the crime or helps another to commit a crime. Accessory after the fact is a part of the discussion of accomplice liability, and specifically targets those individuals who are directly responsible for helping another after the commission of a crime. The actus reus and mens rea of accomplice liability is personal to the actor. For example, when an individual did something and had some criminal intent.

Vicarious liability, on the other hand, involves holding persons (and corporations) responsible for the actions of others. The person being held responsible did not commit any act nor did they have any guilty mind, but because of their relationship to the actor, a policy decision was made to hold them responsible. Regarding corporate liability, a corporation can be held guilty of the crimes of its agents, so the actus reus and mens rea of the president, etc is transferred to the corporation. Individual vicarious liability occurs in the same way. An owner of a business who committed no voluntary act nor had any criminal intent can nevertheless be held responsible for the acts of his or her employee because of the employer-employee relationship.

Accomplice liability is based upon personal blameworthiness and therefore punishing aiders and abettors is seen as a justified societal response. Vicarious liability imposes criminal blameworthiness upon individuals who have not done anything blameworthy, and so it is more difficult to justify but will be imposed when statutes are clear that they intend to be vicarious liability statutes. LO 1,4,5

Study Guide

4. How does the government use vicarious liability to combat corporate crime?

Historically, the government has taken a hands-off approach to regulating corporations, relying instead on the marketplace, corporate self-discipline, and the pressure of the business community to cause corporations to act responsibly and follow the law. However, it has recently become quite clear that self-regulation has not been working. Blatant criminal acts by corporate agents for their own personal benefit and the benefit of the corporation have been exposed, and although Congress could be prescriptive in regulating corporate activity (based on the interstate commerce clause and the contracts clause), it has instead used vicarious liability and the doctrine of respondiat superior to seek criminal penalties for corporations for the acts of their officers. This is seen in its prosecution of Arthur Anderson, LLP and Enron Corp. LO 5

5. What are the four elements of most accessory-after-the-fact statutes?

Most accessory after the fact statutes have four elements: two mens rea elements, one actus reus element, and one circumstance element. The accessory after the fact personally aided the one who committed the crime, the accessory knew the felony was committed, the accessory aided the person who committed the crime for the purpose of hindering the prosecution of the person, and someone else committed the felony (not the accessory). The cases of State v. Chism and State v. Ulvinen both highlight accessory after the fact liability. The interesting twist in Ulvinen is that the mom's behavior was classic "accessory after the fact" behavior. She personally aided her son, she knew he had killed his wife, she helped him dismember her son's wife's body so as to destroy the evidence, and she was not the person who committed the killing, but the statute excluded parents from the list of people who could be charged for being an accessory after the fact. LO 2

Chapter 8
Inchoate Crimes:
Attempt, Conspiracy and Solicitation

LEARNING OBJECTIVES

1. Understand how inchoate offenses punish people for crimes they have started to commit but have not finished committing. Inchoate offenses require some action but not enough to complete the crime intended.

2. Appreciate the dilemma inchoate offenses present to free societies and know the three different ways the inchoate offenses are resolved.

3. Understand how liability for criminal attempt offenses is based on two rationales: preventing dangerous conduct and neutralizing dangerous people.

4. Understand that the *mens rea* of inchoate crimes is *always* the purpose or specific intent to commit a specific crime.

5. Understand that the *actus reus* of attempt is an action that's beyond mere preparation but not enough to complete the crime.

6. Understand the differences between legal impossibility as a defense to attempt liability and factual impossibility that is not.

7. Understand that voluntary and complete abandonment of an attempt in progress is a defense to attempt liability in about half the states. Be aware of the debate that accounts for this dichotomy

8. Understand that punishing conspiracy and solicitation to commit a crime is based on nipping in the bud the special danger of group criminality.

KEY TERMS AND CONCEPTS

- **criminal attempts**—intending to commit a crime and taking steps to complete it but something interrupts the completion of the crime's commission; p. 235

- **criminal conspiracy**—agreement between two or more persons to commit a crime; p. 235

- **criminal solicitation**—urging another person to commit a crime, even though the person doesn't respond to the urging; p. 235

- **inchoate offenses**—offenses based on crimes not yet completed; p. 235

- **offenses of general application**—describes the inchoate crimes, which are partly general and partly specific; p. 235

- **dangerous act rationale**—looking at how closely a defendant came to completing a crime; p. 237

- **dangerous person rationale**—looking at how fully a defendant developed a criminal purpose to commit a crime; p. 237

- **general attempt statute**—statute that defines the elements of attempt that apply to all crimes; p. 238

- **specific attempt statutes**—attempt statutes that define the elements of attempting to commit specific crimes; p. 238

- **attempt *mens rea***—specific intent to commit a crime that's never completed; p. 239

- **attempt *actus reus***—steps taken to complete a crime that's never actually completed; p. 241

- **last proximate act rule**—your acts brought you as close as possible to completing the crime; p. 241

- **proximity tests**—tests of dangerous conduct: physical proximity, dangerous proximity, and indispensable element; p. 242

- **dangerous proximity test to success test/physical proximity test**—looking at the seriousness of the offense intended; the closeness to completion of the crime; and the probability the conduct would actually have resulted in completion of the crime; p. 243

- **indispensable element test**—asks whether defendants have gotten control of everything they need to complete the crime; p. 243

- **unequivocality test/*res ipsa loquiter* test ("act speaks for itself")**—examines the likelihood the defendant won't complete the crime (attempt law); p. 243

- **probable desistance test**—a dangerous person test that focuses on how far defendants have gone, not on what's left for them to do to complete the crime; p. 244

- **"substantial steps" test/MPC test**—the Model Penal Code, substantial acts toward completion of a crime that strongly corroborate the actor's intent to commit the crime; p. 244

- **legal impossibility**—the defense that what the actor attempted was not a "crime;" p. 249

- **factual impossibility**—the defense that some extraneous factor made it impossible to complete a crime; p. 249

- **extraneous factor**—a condition beyond the attempter's control; p. 249

- **defense of voluntary abandonment**—the actor voluntarily and completely gives up his criminal purpose before completing the offense; p. 255

- **conspiracy**—agreeing to commit a crime; p. 258

- **conspiracy *actus reus*** —consists of two parts: 1) an agreement to commit a crime (in all states) and 2) an overt act in furtherance of the agreement (in about half the states); p. 259

- **overt act (in conspiracy)**—requirement of conspiracy *actus reus* of some act toward completing the crime in addition to the agreement; p. 260

- **conspiracy *mens rea*** —specific intent to commit a crime, or specific intent to commit a legal act by illegal means; p. 262

- **criminal objective**—the criminal goal of an agreement to commit a crime; p. 263

- **unilateral approach**—(in conspiracy) not all the conspirators need to agree to commit a crime to impose criminal liability (conspiracy *actus reus*); p. 263

- **wheel conspiracies**—one or more defendants participate in every transaction; p. 264

- **chain conspiracies**—participants at one end of the chain may know nothing of those at the other end, but every participant handles the same commodity at different points, such as manufacture, distribution, and sale; p. 264

- **solicitation**—trying to get someone to commit a crime; p. 265

- **solicitation *actus reus*** —urging another person to commit a crime; p. 266

- **solicitation *mens rea*** —intent to get another person to commit a crime; p. 267

CHAPTER OUTLINE

I. Inchoate crimes are incomplete crimes.
   A. Inchoate comes from the Latin "to begin."
   B. Inchoate crimes are separate crimes of starting but not finishing any other crime.
   C. Whether to make it a crime to start but not finish committing the crime poses a problem:
      1. Is the law punishing someone who has done no harm or setting someone free who is determined to do harm?
      2. Dilemma of criminal attempt law is resolved through three requirements:
         a. Requiring specific intent
         b. Requiring some action
         c. Punishing inchoate crimes less severely than completed crimes
   D. Three types of inchoate offenses:
      1. Attempt—trying to commit a crime
      2. Conspiracy—agreeing to commit a crime
      3. Solicitation—trying to get someone else to commit a crime
   E. All inchoate offenses are specific intent crimes.

II. Attempt—An attempt is a failed effort to complete a crime.
   A. **Attempt History**
      1. Began with "excessive leniency"
      2. In the 1500s and 1600s, modern attempt law began punishing attempts more seriously.
      3. By the 1800s, attempts to commit indictable offenses were misdemeanors.
   B. **Rationales** for criminal attempt law
      1. Dangerous act rationale—prevent harm from dangerous conduct (focuses on how close to completion the crime is)
      2. Dangerous person rationale—neutralize dangerous people (focuses on how developed the criminal purpose is)
      3. Both (1) and (2) look at actions taken to measure the danger.
   C. **Elements** of Attempt
      1. **Attempt m*ens rea***
         a. Purpose or specific intent always present
         b. No knowing, reckless, or negligent attempts
         c. *Case: People v. Kimball*
      2. **Attempt a*ctus reus***
         a. How much action is enough?
            i. Preparation isn't enough to qualify as the *actus reus* of attempt.
            ii. Toughest problem in criminal attempt is drawing a line between preparation and attempt.

b. There are several tests employed by states—and they are not necessarily mutually exclusive. Some are stricter than others (for example, the last proximate act rule is the strictest).
c. Tests to help draw the line between preparation and the act of attempt:
  i. Physical proximity test
    (a) Focus on
      (i) Dangerous conduct, not dangerous people
      (ii) What's left to do, not what's already done
    (b) Completion of all but the last act needed to accomplish the crime is surely enough, but so are acts falling short of this point.
  ii. Indispensable element test—defendants who've gotten control of everything they need to complete the crime
  iii. Dangerous proximity test (physical proximity test) — defendants have gotten dangerously close to completing the crime
  iv. Unequivocality (probable desistance) test—aka res ipsa loquiter tests (act speaks for itself)
    (a) Focus on dangerous persons, not dangerous conduct
    (b) Focus on what's already done, not what's left to do
    (c) Unequivocality test asks whether an ordinary person observing defendants' actions without knowing their intent would guess they were determined to commit the crime.
    (d) *Case: State v. Stewart*
  v. Probable desistance test
    (a) Dangerous person test that focuses on how far defendants have gotten, not what's left to do to complete the crime
    (b) Defendant got far enough that it is unlikely they will turn back
  vi. "Substantial steps" (Model Penal Code) test
    (a) Purpose—clarify and simplify other tests (proximity and unequivocality)
    (b) Distinguish more sharply between preparation and beginning to attempt to complete the crime
    (c) Base attempt law on neutralizing dangerous persons not just preventing dangerous conduct
    (d) Focus on dangerous persons
    (e) Focus on what's already done, not what's left to do
    (f) Definition—Substantial steps that "strongly corroborate" defendant's criminal purpose (list of things which "strongly corroborate")
    (g) *Case: Young v. State*
    (h) *Case: People v. Rizzo*
    (i) *Case: Commonwealth v. Peaslee*

D. **Impossibility** of completing the crime as a defense
    1. Legal impossibility is a defense to criminal attempt; factual impossibility is not.
    2. Legal impossibility
        a. Defendants intend to commit crimes, do everything they can to complete the crime, but what they intend and do isn't a crime.
        b. It is a defense
    3. Factual impossibility
        a. Defendants intend to commit a crime and take all the steps necessary to complete it, but a fact makes it impossible to complete.
        b. People bent on committing crimes shouldn't benefit from a stroke of luck—this isn't a defense.
    4. *Case: State v. Damms*
    5. *Case: State v. Robins*
    6. *Case: State v. Kordas*
E. **Voluntary Abandonment** of attempts as a defense
    1. Complete and voluntary abandonment of attempt is an affirmative defense in about half the states.
    2. Arguments in favor of the abandonment defense
        a. People who voluntarily and completely give up their criminal attempts aren't dangerous.
        b. We want to encourage people who are just about to hurt someone or their property to give up their plans.
    3. Argument against defense of abandonment—It encourages bad people to take the early steps in committing crimes because they know they won't be punished.
    4. *Case: LeBarron v. State*

III. **Conspiracy** is an agreement to commit a crime.
    A. Agreeing to commit crimes (criminal conspiracy) is further removed from completed crimes than trying to commit them (criminal attempt).
    B. Justifications for conspiracy law
        1. Works hand in hand with attempt to nip criminal purpose in the bud
        2. Strikes at the special danger of group criminal activity
    C. **Conspiracy** *actus reus*
        1. **Agreement** to commit a crime is the heart of the crime of conspiracy.
            a. Doesn't have to be in writing
            b. An unspoken understanding, inferred from facts and circumstances, is good enough to prove agreement.
            c. *Case: videotape of supporters of Dr. Spock*

2. About half the states require an **"overt act"** in addition to the act of agreement.
    a. Purpose—verify the firmness of the agreement
    b. Act doesn't have to amount to much; it can be of "very small significance"
    c. *Case: U.S. v. Garcia*

D. **Conspiracy** *mens rea*
1. Crime of purpose (specific intent)
2. Can mean intent to make the agreement or intent to achieve the criminal objective.

E. **Parties to conspiracy**
1. Traditional approach—two or more individuals agreeing to commit crimes
2. Unilateral approach—not all the conspirators had to agree to commit a crime as long as the defendant believes they did

F. **Large-scale conspiracies**
1. Wheel conspiracies: two sets of conspirators:
    a. Hub—conspirators who participate in all transactions
    b. Spokes—conspirators who only participate in one transaction
2. Chain conspiracies—participants at one end of the chain don't know anything of participants at the other end, but they all handle the same illegal commodity at different points (manufacture, distribution, sale).
    a. *Case: U.S. v. Bruno*

G. **Criminal objective** of conspiracy
1. Traditionally included everything from treason to disturbing the peace
2. Some effort to limit the reach of conspiracy
    a. Requires an overt act in addition to an act of agreement
    b. Applies to criminal objectives only
3. Model Penal Code adopted overt act requirement and half states follow mens rea includes purposeful conduct / specific intent to carry out the objective of the agreement.
4. RICO laws—intended for organized crime, but now are used against white-collar crime as well.

IV. **Solicitation** is asking or encouraging someone else to commit a crime.
A. Definition—The crime of trying to get someone else to commit a crime
B. Arguments against criminal solicitation law
1. The act of soliciting isn't dangerous enough to punish because an independent moral force (the person solicited) stands between the solicitation and its objective.
2. Solicitors aren't dangerous enough people and they prove it by needing someone else to do their dirty work.
C. Arguments for criminal solicitation law
1. Solicitation is another form of the danger of group criminality.
    2. Solicitors are smart masters at manipulating others to do their dirty work.

Study Guide

    D. **Solicitation *actus reus*** requires words that actually try to get someone to commit a crime (not just approve the commission of the crime).
    E. **Solicitation *mens rea*** requires purpose or specific intent to get someone to commit a specific crime.
    F. The **criminal objective of solicitation** varies from limiting it to violent felonies in some jurisdictions to including all crimes in other jurisdictions.
        1. *Case: State v. Cotton*

CHAPTER SUMMARY

Inchoate offenses involve punishing people for crimes they haven't completed. The term "inchoate" comes from the Latin meaning "to begin." Inchoate offenses require some action but not enough to finish the crime intended. Such offenses enable the police, courts, and corrections to intervene before the intended harm occurs. All of these offenses have both a general intent and a specific intent element. General intent is to do the act, say the words, make an agreement, etc. Specific intent is any intent other than general intent. In these crimes, the specific intent is to commit a crime above and beyond the inchoate offense. Inchoate crimes are generally punished separately and less severely than the completed offense.

Criminal liability for criminal attempt offenses is based on two rationales—first, preventing dangerous conduct, and second, neutralizing dangerous people. The *mens rea* of inchoate crimes is the specific intent to commit a complete crime.

The *actus reus* of attempt is an action that is beyond mere preparation but not actually completion of the crime. How much action is required to make one guilty of an attempt is hotly debated, and there are a number of approaches. A proximity approach focuses on how close the defendant gets to completing the crime. An unequivocality approach focuses on whether the defendant got far enough along that stopping is unlikely. The Model Penal Code test requires that the defendant have taken substantial steps and that such steps strongly corroborate the actor's criminal intent.

Legal impossibility is a defense to attempt liability. If the defendant did everything he or she wanted to do and it still wouldn't be a crime, then it is a valid defense. The principle of legality would seem to require this. Factual impossibility is not a defense. If certain factors unknown to the defendant would make it impossible to complete the crime, this is not a defense. In some jurisdictions voluntary and complete abandonment of an attempt in progress may be a defense to attempt liability.

Solicitation and conspiracy both involve more than one person. Punishing conspiracy and solicitation to commit a crime is based not only on preventing crime but also on the special danger of group criminality.

Criminal conspiracy is the crime of agreeing with one or more people to commit a crime. The *actus reus* of conspiracy is the agreement. Some jurisdictions also require that one of the co-conspirators commit some overt act in pursuance of the conspiracy. Conspiracy is a specific intent crime. In addition to intending to agree (general intent), they must also intend to commit the planned crime.

The traditional approach to conspiracy required that at least two people really and sincerely agree to commit a crime (bilateral approach). Under this approach, a person could not be guilty of conspiring with an undercover police officer that had no intent to agree or carry out a crime. Under the unilateral approach, there can be a conspiracy even though another party does not truly agree and doesn't even know some of the others involved.

Criminal solicitation is the crime of trying to get one or more persons to commit a crime. The *actus reus* is a solicitation, command, or encouragement to commit a crime. In addition to a general intent to ask or command, there must be a specific intent that the solicited crime be completed.

Practice Test Bank

MULTIPLE CHOICE

1. The term inchoate comes from the Latin verb which means "to _____."
    a. contemplate
    b. envision
    c. begin
    d. conspire

2. All inchoate crimes are _____ crimes.
    a. specific and general intent
    b. circumstances
    c. capital
    d. redemptive

3. As compared to the completed crime, inchoate crimes are _____.
    a. always misdemeanors
    b. punished the same as the completed crime
    c. more severely punished than the completed crime
    d. less severely punished than the completed crime

4. The rationales for attempt focus on two different types of danger: _____.
    a. group activity and inciting others
    b. dangerous persons and dangerous conduct
    c. imitation and stimulation of crime
    d. group activity and stimulation of crime

5. The indispensable element test of attempt *actus reus* focuses on whether the actor _____.
    a. is likely to give up the attempt
    b. had gotten control of everything necessary to complete the crime
    c. satisfies the *res ipsa loquitur* criterion
    d. is just one step away from completing the crime

6. The Latin term *res ipsa loquitur* means the _____.
    a. thing is inherently evil
    b. thought is the origin of the act
    c. act speaks for itself
    d. intent without action is no crime

7. The Model Penal Code test of attempt *actus reus* requires that the defendant take _____ toward completing the crime.
   a. irreversible action
   b. substantial steps
   c. the last proximate act
   d. the next-to-last proximate act

8. The second part of the Model Penal Code test of attempt *actus reus* also requires that the defendant's actions _____.
   a. go beyond any reasonable stopping point
   b. indicate that desistance is unlikely
   c. indicate that they are dangerously close to completing the offense
   d. strongly corroborate intent to commit the crime

9. In most states, and under the Model Penal Code, which of the following would not be an attempt?
   a. lying in wait for the victim to walk by
   b. reconnoitering the planned crime scene
   c. enticing the victim to the place where the crime is planned to occur
   d. beginning to gather the materials necessary for the crime

10. The defense of _____ impossibility involves actors doing everything they can to carry out the criminal intent, but the law doesn't criminalize what they did.
    a. factual
    b. virtual
    c. legal
    d. juristic

11. The defense of _____ impossibility involves the situation where some extraneous factor interrupts or prevents completion of the crime.
    a. factual
    b. virtual
    c. real
    d. legal

12. Which of the following is a recognized form of the impossibility defense to attempt?
    a. legal
    b. factual
    c. real
    d. virtual

13. According to the appellate court in *State v. Damms*, a defendant can be guilty of the crime of attempted murder because/even though the defendant admitted to police that he _____.
    a. believed the gun was loaded (even though it was in fact unloaded)
    b. believed his wife was already dead (even though she wasn't)
    c. believed the wounds would not be fatal (even though they were)
    d. believed the police would stop him before he pointed the gun at this wife

14. Which of the following would be a valid impossibility defense?
    a. The intended victim escapes before the defendant attacks the victim.
    b. The defendant is apprehended by the police before finishing the crime.
    c. The poison is not strong enough to kill the victim.
    d. What the defendant wants to do to the victim is not a crime.

15. To be a defense to attempt, the abandonment of the attempt must be _____.
    a. caused by an extraneous factor
    b. compelled
    c. voluntary
    d. caused by police intervention

16. About half the states have a second *actus reus* element for conspiracy. They require that _____.
    a. the conspirators take a substantial step toward the crime
    b. the conspirators move beyond mere preparation
    c. one of the conspirators attempt the crime
    d. one of the conspirators do an overt act pursuant to the conspiracy

17. Mr. X conspires with Mr. Y to commit a murder. Unbeknownst to Mr. X, Mr. Y is an undercover police officer that is only trying to build a case against Mr. X. Under the unilateral approach to conspiracy, _____.
    a. both Mr. X and Mr. Y are guilty of conspiracy
    b. Mr. X is not guilty of conspiracy because there is no real agreement
    c. Mr. X has an affirmative defense
    d. Mr. X is guilty of conspiracy

18. Chain conspiracies usually involve a _____.
    a. distributor who sells to numerous dealers
    b. smuggler who has a number of wholesale customers
    c. dealer who has multiple customers
    d. pipeline from a smuggler to a distributor to a wholesaler

19. Most modern conspiracy statutes _____.
    a. limit the objective to committing a crime
    b. include any objective which is contrary to public policy
    c. limit the objective to using unlawful means to do a lawful thing
    d. include any objective which is injurious to public health

20. The federal _____ Act is a specialized conspiracy law frequently utilized against organized crime.
    a. PACO
    b. RICO
    c. CHACO
    d. OCCA

21. Which of the following is not a typical element of solicitation statutes?
    a. general intent
    b. specific intent
    c. communicating some inducement
    d. communication must be to a particular person

22. A few states restrict the crime of solicitation to solicitation of _____.
    a. felonies
    b. misdemeanors
    c. capital felonies
    d. crimes which are *mala prohibita*

23. Which of the following is required to obtain a solicitation conviction?
    a. The person solicited must accept the offer.
    b. The solicitor must have specific intent.
    c. The solicitor and solicited must enter into a conspiracy.
    d. The person solicited must commit the crime.

24. At common law, the crime of attempt _____.
    a. did not exist
    b. had no specific intent element
    c. required some injury
    d. required that the defendant do the last proximate act

25. Physical proximity tests of attempt *actus reus* focus on _____.
    a. how close the defendant got to completing the crime
    b. whether a reasonable person would see that a crime is in progress
    c. whether the defendant is likely to cease the attempt
    d. how much of the defendant's intent is shown by action

26. The unequivocality test of attempt *actus reus* focuses on _____.
    a. whether the defendant is likely to give up the attempt
    b. how much remains to be done before completing the crime
    c. whether the defendant has taken substantial steps
    d. whether the defendant has started preparing for the crime

27. The Model Penal Code test of attempt *actus reus* focuses on _____.
    a. probable desistance and unequivocality
    b. steps taken by the defendant and unequivocality
    c. intent and steps taken by the defendant
    d. *res ipsa loquitur* and intent

28. According to the Model Penal Code, soliciting an innocent agent to commit the crime is _____.
    a. an attempted conspiracy
    b. an attempted solicitation
    c. an attempt
    d. a conspiracy

29. Unlike the early common law approach to attempt, the law today does not require _____.
    a. that any or partial harm be caused on inflicted
    b. any specific intent
    c. any general intent
    d. that there be any *actus reus*

30. At common law, an attempted capital offense such as robbery, murder, or burglary resulted in _____.
    a. execution
    b. sentencing to life in prison
    c. guilty of a non-capital felony
    d. guilty only of a misdemeanor

TRUE/FALSE

1. All inchoate offenses have a specific intent element.
    a. true
    b. false

2. Inchoate crimes are punished at the same level as the object or completed crime.
    a. true
    b. false

3. Attempt was not a crime at common law.
    a. true
    b. false

4. There are no such things as reckless, negligent, or strict liability attempts.
    a. true
    b. false

5. An attempt requires more than mere preparation to commit the crime.
   a. true
   b. false

6. The Model Penal Code definition of the *actus reus* of attempt is an example of the probable desistance approach.
   a. true
   b. false

7. Legal impossibility is a defense to the crime of attempt.
   a. true
   b. false

8. Factual impossibility is a valid defense to the crime of attempt.
   a. true
   b. false

9. The Model Penal Code *actus reus* of attempt involves substantial steps that strongly corroborate the actor's criminal purpose.
   a. true
   b. false

10. A person cannot be convicted of attempting to murder someone with a pistol if the pistol was, in fact, unloaded at the time.
    a. true
    b. false

11. To be a valid defense, the abandonment of an attempt must be voluntary.
    a. true
    b. false

12. In some jurisdictions, there are two act elements in the crime of conspiracy.
    a. true
    b. false

13. The offense of conspiracy is frequently criticized because of its vagueness.
    a. true
    b. false

14. The fact that one conspirator has been acquitted does not prevent the government from prosecuting the others for conspiracy.
    a. true
    b. false

15. In most modern conspiracy statutes, the criminal objective is usually limited to agreements to commit crimes.
    a. true
    b. false

16. RICO stands for Racketeer Influenced and Corrupt Organizations.
    a. true
    b. false

17. In some jurisdictions, the crime of solicitation is limited to solicitation to commit misdemeanors.
    a. true
    b. false

18. A solicitation that does not reach or is not heard by the intended recipient cannot be a crime.
    a. true
    b. false

19. To be criminal, a solicitation must be directed toward a specific individual.
    a. true
    b. false

20. The crime of solicitation is a strict liability crime.
    a. true
    b. false

21. In a wheel conspiracy, one or more defendants participate in every transaction.
    a. true
    b. false

22. A person can be guilty of conspiracy even though they do not know all of the others in the conspiracy.
    a. true
    b. false

23. The Model Penal Code definition of conspiracy includes an overt act element.
    a. true
    b. false

24. For the solicitor to be guilty of solicitation, the person solicited must accept the offer.
    a. true
    b. false

25. The primary purpose of requiring some overt act in some conspiracy statutes is to help identify who is involved in the conspiracy.
    a. true
    b. false

FILL-IN-THE-BLANK

1. Under the _____ test, an attempt has been committed when the person has gotten control of everything they need to complete the crime.

2. Abandonment is not a defense to attempt unless the abandonment is _____.

3. In some states, the second *actus reus* requirement is that there be a/n _____ act by one of the conspirators in pursuance of the conspiracy.

4. The term _____ means "the thing stands for itself."

5. _____ impossibility is not a valid defense to attempt.

6. The _____ test of attempt *actus reus* focuses on how close the defendant got to completing the crime.

7. Acts toward committing a crime that do not constitute an attempt are called _____.

8. In the _____ approach to conspiracy, a person can be guilty even though no one else in the conspiracy really agrees to commit the crime.

9. Under the _____ approach to attempt *actus reus*, the test is whether the acts confirm the intent.

10. _____ impossibility is a defense to attempt.

11. RICO means _____.

12. In a/n _____ conspiracy, one or more defendants participate in all transactions.

13. Of the inchoate offenses, only _____ is sometimes defined as having two act elements.

14. _____ can be thought of as the first half of a conspiracy.

15. The principle of _____ leads to the conclusion that legal impossibility is a defense to attempt.

ESSAY

1. Compare and contrast conspiracy, attempt and solicitation.

2. Discuss the various approaches to the *actus reus* of attempt. Provide an example of each.

3. Identify, compare and contrast the defenses to attempt liability.

4. Discuss the evolution of conspiracy law. How have these changes dealt with modern, large-scale conspiracies?

5. Compare and contrast the unilateral and bilateral approach to conspiracy.

CHAPTER 8 ANSWER KEY

Multiple Choice

1. c, See pg. 236, LO 1
2. a, See pg. 236, LO 4
3. d, See pg. 236, LO 2
4. b, See pg. 237, LO 3
5. b, See pg. 243, LO 5
6. c, See pg. 243, LO 5
7. b, See pg. 244, LO 5
8. d, See pg. 244, LO 5
9. d, See pg. 245, LO 5
10. c, See pg. 249, LO 6
11. a, See pg. 249, LO 6
12. a, See pg. 249, LO 6
13. a, See pg. 250, LO 6
14. d, See pg. 249, LO 6
15. c, See pg. 255, LO 7
16. d, See pg. 259, LO 8
17. d, See pg. 263, LO 8
18. d, See pg. 264, LO 8
19. a, See pg. 264, LO 8
20. b, See pg. 265, LO 8
21. d, See pg. 266, LO 8
22. a, See pg. 267, LO 8
23. b, See pg. 266, LO 8
24. c, See pg. 237, LO 4,5
25. a, See pg. 242, LO 5
26. c, See pg. 244, LO 5
27. c, See pg. 244, LO 5
28. c, See pg. 245, LO 8
29. a, See pg. 237, LO 4, 5
30. a, See pg. 237, LO 2

True/False

1. T, See pg. 236, LO 4
2. F, See pg. 236, LO 1
3. F, See pg. 237, LO 2
4. T, See pg. 239, LO 4
5. T, See pg. 241, LO 5
6. F, See pg. 244, LO 5
7. T, See pg. 249, LO 6
8. F, See pg. 249, LO 6
9. T, See pg. 244, LO 5
10. F, See pg. 250, LO 6
11. T, See pg. 255, LO 7
12. T, See pg. 259, LO 8
13. T, See pg. 263, LO 8
14. T, See pg. 263, LO 8
15. T, See pg. 259, LO 8
16. T, See pg. 265, LO 8
17. F, See pg. 267, LO 8
18. F, See pgs. 266-267, LO 8
19. F, See pg. 266, LO 8
20. F, See pg. 239, LO 8
21. T, See pg. 264, LO 8
22. T, See pg. 263, LO 8
23. T, See pg. 265, LO 8
24. F, See pg. 265, LO 8
25. F, See pg. 260, LO 8

Fill-in-the-Blank

1. indispensable element. See pg. 243, LO 5
2. voluntary. See pg. 255, LO 7
3. overt. See pg. 259, LO 8
4. *res ipsa loquitur*. See pg. 243, LO 5
5. Factual. See pg. 249, LO 6
6. physical proximity. See pg. 243, LO 5
7. mere preparation. See pg. 245, LO 5
8. unilateral. See pg. 263, LO 8
9. unequivocality. See pg. 243, LO 5
10. Legal. See pg. 249, LO 6
11. Racketeer Influenced and Corrupt Organizations. See pg. 265, LO 8
12. wheel. See pg. 264, LO 8
13. conspiracy. See pg. 259, LO 8
14. Solicitation. See pg. 265, LO 8
15. legality. See pg. 249, LO 6

Essay

1. Compare and contrast conspiracy, attempt and solicitation.

Conspiracy, attempt and solicitation are all inchoate (meaning incomplete) offenses. They are similar in that the mens rea attached for each is purposeful. The persons involved have to have the specific intent to commit the crime or cause the harm. Generally, there has to be some (overt) action on the part of the actors which indicates or manifests the true intent to commit the crime. These crimes differ in their actus reus components. For attempt, there is a variety of approaches determining when the criminal act has been satisfied (see question two). For conspiracy, the actus reus involves entering an agreement to commit a crime. And for solicitation, the actus reus involves requesting, soliciting, asking another to commit another crime. Other ways in which the crimes are different concerns whether the inchoate crime folds into the intended crime (called merger). With conspiracy, the agreement to commit the other crime is separate from the other crime (no merger—Pinkerton rule); with solicitation there is also a separate crime; with attempt, however, if the person completes the underlying crime, they are usually not charged with both the attempt and the completed crime. LO 1, 4, 5, 8

2. Discuss the various approaches to the *actus reus* of attempt. Provide an example of each.

The approaches to the actus reus requirement of attempt highlight two rationales about why we punish people who haven't completed the crime: because they commit dangerous acts, or because they are dangerous individuals. The dangerous act rational tries to prevent the harm from the dangerous conduct, so it focuses on how close the person got to completing the underlying crime. The approaches which fall into this category are proximity tests, including the physical proximity test, the dangerous proximity test, and the indispensible element test. The physical proximity/dangerous proximity to success tests ask whether defendants have come dangerously close to completing their crimes. The indispensible element test focuses on whether the actor has gathered everything they need to complete the crime. Other states have been more concerned with attempts reflecting dangerous people. Three tests that have grown out of the dangerous person rationale are the unequivocality test (res ipsa loquiter), the probable desistance test, and the substantial steps test (found in the MPC). The unequivocality tests asks whether an ordinary person who saw the acts without knowing the actors intent would conclude the actor was determined to commit a crime. This is also know as the stop film test. The probable desistence test focuses on how far defendants have gone and whether it is unlikely that they will turn back. Finally, the substantial steps test adopted by the MPC looks at whether there were substantial steps (ones which strongly corroborate the actor's purpose) taken toward completing the crime. All approaches tend to distinguish between mere preparation (not attempt) and the beginning of the attempt. Some states have preparation statutes which criminalize the acts of preparation. LO 5

3. Identify, compare and contrast the defenses to attempt liability.

There are two defenses to attempt liability: legal impossibility and voluntary abandonment. In any discussion of impossibility as a defense to a criminal attempt, the distinction between a factual impossibility (which is not a defense) and a legal impossibility (which is a defense) will be addressed. Factual impossibility exists when, if the facts were as the defendant believed them to be, the crime would have been committed. So, for example, if John goes to the hospital and enters Bob's room thinking Bob is asleep and shoots Bob intending to kill him, the crime would be criminal homicide if things were as John expected (an alive Bob who he shot and mortally wounded). If, however, moments before the shot and unbeknownst to John, Bob had died from the injuries which put him in the hospital, John will not be able to raise impossibility as a defense, and he should be convicted of attempted murder. If things were as he believed, he would have killed Bob. Legal impossibility is a defense to attempt, and is seen in the following example. Ruth believes it against the law to bring a certain type of cheese into the USA when she travels from Switzerland to visit her son. There is, however, no law prohibiting the importation of this cheese. So, even though she intends to commit cheese smuggling, if prosecuted, she will successfully raise the impossibility defense. It is legally impossible to commit the offense, even if everything was as she believed it to be. [Think about how impractical it would be for prosecutors to try to prosecute individuals for crimes that do not exist.] The State v. Damms case, however, shows how blurry the lines between factual and legal impossibility are. LO 6

The second defense to attempt is voluntary abandonment. In states which provide for this defense, an individual who has a true change of heart and willfully and voluntarily desists from his criminal plan can successfully defend against prosecution for attempt. The rationale is that such a person no longer presents a threat, and should be able to evade criminal liability. The issues generally surround whether the change of heart was sincere, stemming from the defendant himself, or whether it was prompted by an extraneous factor. The case of LeBarron shows that changes of heart prompted by extraneous factors do not qualify as voluntary abandonment (also known as renunciation). LO 7

4. Discuss the evolution of conspiracy law. How have these changes dealt with modern, large-scale conspiracies?

Conspiracy law involves two or more individuals agreeing to commit a crime. Both at common law and under modern statutes, there is some murkiness as to the required mens rea. Yes, as indicated above, all inchoate crimes have purposeful as their mens rea, but what is sometimes unclear is whether the individuals must specifically intend to agree or whether they must specifically intend to commit the crime (attain a specific criminal objective). Also unclear is whether a conspiracy exists when there is a difference of opinion as to the ultimate objective. Under modern law, most states have adopted the unilateral approach, so as long as one of the participants really intended to go through with the crime, it is still conspiracy—even though the other secretly did not intend to go through with it. Modern large-scale conspiracies are either wheel conspiracies (in which one or more individuals participate in every transaction—the hub of the conspiracy) or chain conspiracies (where participants at one end of the transaction have no connection with others at the other end of the transaction—for example, in a complex illegal drug trade operation). Conspiracy law generally holds that one co-conspirator is liable for all other acts of all other co-conspirators so long as they were committed during the course of and in furtherance of the conspiracy. This has far reaching implications for individuals involved with large-scale conspiracies: A Maine street dealer of methamphetamine would be liable for a murder committed in Mexico by someone transporting precursor drugs to a superlab. LO 4, 8

5. Compare and contrast the unilateral and bilateral approach to conspiracy.

Traditionally, two or more parties to a conspiracy had to have a meeting of minds as to the agreement. So, if a defendant agreed with an undercover officer to sell cocaine for money there would not be a conspiracy because the undercover officer's intent was not really to buy the cocaine (the crime of possession of cocaine) but rather to apprehend the other. This was called the bilateral approach. Under modern law, most states have adopted the unilateral approach, and so as long as one of the participants really intended to go through with the crime, it is still conspiracy—even though the other secretly did not intend to go through with it. LO 8

Chapter 9
Crimes Against Persons I: Murder and Manslaughter

LEARNING OBJECTIVES

1. Understand that criminal homicide is different from all other crimes because of the finality of its result: the death of the victim.

2. Appreciate that most of the law criminal homicide is about grading the seriousness of the offense. Grading murder into first and second degree is important because only first-degree murder qualify for the death penalty.

3. Appreciate that the meaning of "person" is integral to homicide law and understand how that presents problems at both ends of the life cycle.

4. Understand how degrees of murder developed through history and their relation to capital punishment

5. Understand how most criminal homicide statutes apply to corporations, but prosecutions are rare.

6. Understand that the heart of voluntary manslaughter is an intentional, sudden killing triggered by an adequate provocation.

7. Know that provocation is not an excuse for criminal homicide; it only reduces the seriousness of the crime and the punishment to allow for human frailty.

8. Know that the central elements in involuntary manslaughter are its *actus reus* (voluntary act or omission) and its *mens rea* (unintentional killing; causing the criminal harm of death.

9. Understand that criminal negligence homicide statutes cover a wide field, including the most common, unintentional deaths caused by operating vehicles and firearms, but also medicine, handling explosives, delivering dangerous drugs, allowing vicious animals to run free, failing to care for a sick child, and not providing fire exits in businesses.

KEY TERMS AND CONCEPTS

- **born-alive rule**—homicide law once said that to be a person, and therefore a homicide victim, a baby had to be "born alive" and capable of breathing and maintaining a heartbeat on its own; p. 275

Study Guide

- **feticide**—law defining when life begins for purposes of applying the law of criminal homicide; p. 277

- **euthanasia**—the act or practice of causing or hastening the death of a person who is suffering from an incurable or terminal disease or condition, especially a painful one; p. 278

- **presumption of bodily integrity**—the principle of personal autonomy presumes that every individual controls the integrity of their own body; p. 280

- **murder**—intentionally causing the death of another person with "malice aforethought;" p. 282

- **manslaughter**—unlawful killing of another person without malice aforethought; p. 282

- **justifiable homicide**—killing in self-defense, capital punishment, and police use of deadly force; p. 284

- **excusable homicide**—accidental killings done by someone "not of sound memory and discretion" (insane and immature); p. 284

- **criminal homicide**—a homicide that's neither justified nor excused; p. 284

- **malice aforethought**—killing on purpose after planning it; p. 285

- **depraved-heart murder**—extremely reckless killing; p. 285

- **intent-to-cause-serious-bodily-injury**—murder when death results following acts triggered by the intent to inflict serious bodily injury short of death; p. 286

- **express malice aforethought**—intentional killings planned in advance; p. 286

- **implied malice aforethought**—killings that weren't intentional or planned but still resulted from the intention to do harm; p. 286

- **murder *actus reus***—causing the death of a person; p. 287

- **murder *mens rea***—the purposeful, knowing, reckless, or negligent killing of a person; p. 288

- **first-degree murder**—premeditated, deliberate killings and other particularly heinous capital murders; p. 289

- **capital cases**—death penalty cases in death penalty states and "mandatory life sentence without parole" cases in non-death penalty states; p. 290

- **bifurcation**—a mandate that the death penalty decision be made in two phases: a trial to determine guilt and a second separate proceeding, after a finding of guilt, to consider the aggravating factors for, and mitigating factors against, capital punishment; p. 290

- **criteria for decision (in death penalty cases)**—must be limited by the criteria established and announced *before* the decision to sentence the defendant to death but includes aggravating factors for and mitigating factors against imposing death; p. 290

- **specific intent plus real premeditation deliberation**—the law looks at three areas to determine whether a killing was premeditated and deliberate: signs of planning, motive, and deliberate method in the killing; p. 293

- **equivalent-of-specific-intent definition**—some courts define a willful, premeditated, deliberate killing as the same as specific intent, which may render the difference between first- and second-degree murder meaningless; p. 293

- **second-degree murder**—a catchall offense including killings that are neither manslaughter nor first-degree murder; unintentional killings; p. 301

- **felony murder**—unintentional deaths that occur during the commission of felonies; p. 303

- **voluntary manslaughter**—intentional killing done in the "heat of passion;" p. 313

- **adequate provocation (voluntary manslaughter)**—the circumstance element in voluntary manslaughter that is the trigger that sets off the sudden killing of another person; acts that qualify as reducing murder to manslaughter; p. 313

- **objective test of cooling-off-time (voluntary manslaughter)**—in voluntary manslaughter, the element of whether, in similar circumstances, a reasonable person would have had time to cool off; p. 314

- **last-straw rule/long smoldering or slow burn rule**—a smoldering resentment or pent-up rage resulting from earlier insults or humiliating events, culminating in a triggering event that, by itself, might be insufficient to provoke the deadly act; p. 315

- **extreme mental or emotional disturbance (voluntary manslaughter)**—a defense that reduces criminal homicide to manslaughter if emotional disturbance provides a reasonable explanation for the defendant's actions; p. 315

- **common law paramour rule**—a husband who caught his wife in the act of adultery had adequate provocation to kill and could reduce criminal homicide to voluntary manslaughter; p. 316

- **involuntary manslaughter**—criminal homicides caused either by recklessness or gross negligence and resulting in the unconscious creation of substantial and unjustifiable risks; p. 320

- **criminal negligence manslaughter**—includes the mental elements of both recklessness and negligence; p. 320

- **unlawful act manslaughter**—sometimes called "misdemeanor manslaughter," it's involuntary manslaughter based on deaths that take place during the commission of another crime; p. 323

- **malum prohibitum crime**—a crime not inherently bad or evil but merely prohibited; p. 315

CHAPTER OUTLINE

I. Criminal Homicide in Context
    A. Criminal homicide is relatively rare.
    B. Criminal homicide is the most serious of all felonies known to our law.
    C. Criminal homicide is divided into two categories: murder and manslaughter.
    D. How we classify a killing determines what punishment should be inflicted upon the offender.

II. The Meaning of "Person" or "Human Being" - Defining the beginning and end of life is controversial and differs among jurisdictions (some include fetal murder and brain death).
    A. **When does life begin**? Homicide law has generally followed a born-alive rule.
        1. Born-alive rule
            a. *Case: People v. Chavez* (exception to the rule)
            b. *Case: Keeler v. Superior Court*
            c. *Case: State v. Cotton*
        2. Feticide
    B. **When does life end**?
        1. The determination that life has ended has evolved from the cessation of the heart beating, the lungs breathing, to "brain death"
        2. The development of artificial life support has complicated homicide law and introduced legal, ethical, and moral complications.
        3. *Case: State v. Fiero*

    C. Doctor-Assisted Suicide
        1. Euthenasia and **Kinds of Euthanasia**
        2. **Arguments Against Doctor Assisted Suicide**
            a. Intrinsic immorality
            b. Slippery slope
        3. **Arguments in Favor of Doctor-assisted Suicide**
            a. Arguments against pain and for compassion
            b. **Constitutional right to doctor-assisted suicide**
                i. *Case: Washington v. Glucksberg*
                ii. *Case: Gonzalez v. Oregon*
        4. **Doctor-assisted Suicide and the Criminal Law**
        5. **Public Opinion and Doctor-assisted Suicide**

III. Murder
    A. The History of Murder Law
        1. English common-law murder recognized three forms of homicide
            a. Justifiable homicide
            b. Excusable homicide
            c. Criminal homicide
        2. Murder defined by Coke in the early 1600s—"When a person of sound memory and discretion, unlawffuly [sic] killeth any reasonable creature in being and under the king's peace, with malice aforethought, either express or implied."
        3. Blackstone's definition, 1796
            a. Person of sound memory and discretion
            b. Unlawfully (without justification)
            c. Killeth (many forms)
            d. Reasonable creature (someone already born alive)
            e. Under king's peace (basically anyone except an enemy during war)
            f. Malice aforethought, express or implied (with specific intent or killing on purpose, with some bad will; planned in advance)
        4. Expansion of Blackstone's definition over time
            a. Malice aforethought—specific intent to kill, on purpose with spite, premeditated
            b. Addition of intentional killings that weren't premeditated (sudden killings in heat of passion)
            c. Addition of unintended killings if they occurred during commission of felony
            d. Addition of depraved heart murder (extremely reckless killings)
            e. Addition of intent-to-cause-serious-bodily-injury murders
        5. Express malice aforethought—Killings with the original Blackstone meaning: intentional and premeditated
        6. Implied malice aforethought—The four additional types of murder that developed.

Study Guide

B. **The Elements of Murder**—The elements of criminal homicide are act, intent, concurrence, causation, and harm.
   1. At common law, murder was the unlawful killing of another with malice aforethought.
      a. Express malice aforethought: fits original meaning of murder—intentional killings planned in advance
   2. Historically, the concept of "malice aforethought" was expanded to include implied malice. It consisted of five mental states—the specific intent to do one of the following:
      a. Kill another person (express malice aforethought)
      b. Seriously injure another person
      c. Commit specified dangerous felonies
      d. Forcibly resist a lawful arrest
      e. Create a higher than criminally reckless risk of death or serious bodily injury (depraved-heart murder)
   3. **Murder *actus reus***—Taking the life of or causing the death of another person (live human being). Defining the beginning and end of life is controversial and differs among jurisdictions (some include fetal murder and brain death).
      a. Includes all voluntary actions such as poisoning, striking, starving, and drowning
      b. Also includes voluntary omissions
      c. How the murderer kills doesn't matter in most cases (but could aggravate it)
   4. **Murder *mens rea***—Varies over time and from jurisdiction, but typically
      1. Purposely (intentionally)
      2. Knowingly
      3. Recklessly
      4. Negligently
   5. Causation—Acts that set in motion a chain of events that amount to cause in fact or legal cause of the death of another
   6. Criminal harm resulting in the death of another
C. **The Kinds and Degrees of Murder**—Murder is the most serious form of criminal homicide.
   1. Originally murder was never divided into degrees and all murders were capital offenses.
   2. Dividing murder into degrees was a product of not wishing to execute all persons convicted of criminal homicide, following the tradition of letting judges mitigate penalties by use of "benefit of clergy."
   3. Many statutes followed the same common-law scheme in dividing up premeditated and felony murder.
   4. The Model Penal code doesn't use the degrees, but does divide murder according to mental attitude.
   5. Today, most jurisdictions have two degrees of homicide (some have three).

D. **First-degree Murder**
   1. **Death Penalty**—Discretionary in all states authorizing the death penalty
      a. Highly complex
      b. Several constitutional limitations
         i. Mandatory death sentences are banned.
         ii. Unguided discretionary death penalty sentences are banned.
         iii. Mitigating factors are required.
         iv. Additional aggravating factors are allowed.
      c. Most states have adopted MPC's recommendation of bifurcation and a criterion for decision.
   2. **First-degree murder *mens rea*** (a capital offense in states with the death penalty)
      a. Premeditated, deliberate killings
      b. Atrocious, brutal, or cruel murders (in capital cases)
      c. Specific-intent-plus-real-premeditation-deliberation definition
      d. Equivalent-of-specific-intent definition
      e. *Cases: Commonwealth v. Drum*
      f. *Case: Byford v. State*
      g. *Case: State v. Snowden*
   3. **First-degree murder *actus reus***
      a. Generally the manner of killing doesn't matter.
      b. Manner could be critical if it could be a capital offense.
      c. Some states have statutes making heinous, atrocious, and cruel first-degree murder capital offenses.
      d. *Case: Duest v. State*
      e. *Case: Commonwealth v. Golston*

E. **Second-degree murder**
   1. Divide murder for purposes of determining capital and non-capital punishment.
   2. Divide between intentional and unintentional murder—second-degree murders are unintentional murders.
      a. **Depraved-heart murder**
         i. Unintentional killing without premeditation
         ii. Killings resulting from the intent to do serious bodily injury
         iii. Killings resulting from the resisting of lawful arrest
         iv. Killings that occur during the commission of felonies
         v. *Case: People v. Thomas*
      b. **Felony murder**—Unintentional death that occurs while committing dangerous felonies
         i. Intent to commit the underlying crime satisfies the ***mens rea* of felony murder**
         ii. Felony murder has three **rationales**
            (a) Deterrence

(b) Reduce violence
(c) Punish wrongdoers
iii. Four states have abolished it
iv. When someone besides the defendant caused the death
(a) Third-party exception prevents felony murder conviction
(b) Resisting victim exception allows felony murder conviction
v. *Case: People v. Hudson*
vi. *Case: People v. Phillips*

F. **Corporation murders**
1. Corporations can legally commit murder.
2. Usually, prosecutions of corporations for criminal homicide don't succeed.
3. Examples: Fort Pinto; Autumn Hills Convalescent Centers
4. *Case: People v. O'Neil*

IV. **Manslaughter** is divided into two types.
A. Two types: voluntary or involuntary
B. Elements of **voluntary manslaughter**
1. *Actus reus*—taking the life or causing the death of another person
2. *Mens rea*—intent to kill or cause serious bodily harm
3. **Adequate provocation**
a. Is a circumstance element
b. Occurs in the **sudden heat of passion before there was a reasonable time for the passion to cool off**
(1) Objective test of cooling off
(2) Case: *State v. Flory*
c. Caused both the passion and the killing
d. Is specified by law
(1) Fighting (mutual combat)
(2) Assault and battery
(3) Trespass
(4) Adultery (paramour rule)
e. Response must be reasonable to ordinary people.
f. Never consists of words
4. **Causation**—The acts that triggered the chain of events that led to the death
5. Result—The death of another
6. **Provocation by Words**
a. Last-straw rule
b. Words can never provoke rule (most states)
(1) *Dennis v. State*
7. **Provocation by Intimates**
a. Paramour rule
b. *Case: Commonwealth v. Schnopps*
c. *Case: People v. Washington*

C. **Involuntary manslaughter** is the killing of another person unintentionally.
  1. **Criminal Negligence/Vehicular/Firearms Manslaughter**
      a. Requires the *mens rea* of either criminal recklessness or criminal negligence
      b. Occurs during the commission of unlawful acts (like reckless or negligent driving)
      c. *Case: State v. Mays*
  2. **Unlawful act manslaughter**
      a. Most jurisdictions no longer recognize the misdemeanor-manslaughter or unlawful act manslaughter doctrines.
      b. *Case: People v. Datema*
      c. *Case: Todd v. State*

CHAPTER SUMMARY

Criminal homicides are different from all other crimes because of the finality of the result—the death of the victim. Because of the seriousness of the harm and the penalty, this is probably the most complex area of substantive criminal law. Although the definitions vary from state to state, there are many common principles. All criminal homicides involve the killing of another person. The *mens rea* can include knowingly, intentionally, purposely, recklessly, and negligently. The *mens rea* must trigger the act, and the act must cause the death. The causation element has two components: cause in fact and legal cause.

The law of homicide has its origins in the common law. Early on, there were only three types of homicide: justifiable, excusable, and criminal. A justifiable murder was not punishable if the defendant could establish a justification such as self-defense. An excusable murder was not criminal if the defendant could establish an excuse such as an accident.

Murder was defined as killing with malice aforethought. The crime of murder was expanded by creating implied malice situations, such as the depraved-heart and felony murder. The common law also created the crime of voluntary manslaughter, which involved an intentional killing during the heat of passion.

The *actus reus* of criminal homicide is killing another person. Today, in many jurisdictions, a fetus can be the victim of a criminal homicide. Advances in medical science have changed the definition of death. Brain death qualifies as death even though the person may be able to continue breathing. Assisted suicide has always presented a dilemma, and euthanasia can take many forms. Doctor-assisted suicide is controversial, and those opposing it argue that it is intrinsically immoral and flaunts the sanctity of human life. Additionally, they argue that there is a slippery slope and that allowing mercy killings leads to allowing non-mercy killings. Those in favor of doctor-assisted suicide aren't necessarily in favor of death, but rather oppose pain and advocate for personal autonomy. Without some justification, doctor-assisted suicide is first-degree murder. The Court in *Gonzales v. Oregon* upheld Oregon's Death with Dignity Act and thus provided the justification which prevents doctors from being prosecuted for rendering assistance to those who wish to terminate their lives—under very specific circumstances.

The *mens rea* of criminal homicide is typically intentionally, knowingly, recklessly, or negligently (criminal negligence). There are, however, other types of murders. For instance, the intent to commit a qualifying felony substitutes for the intent to kill in felony murder. Many states have limited the felony murder doctrine to violent or dangerous felonies

Most of the law of criminal homicide is about grading the offense according to the elements of *mens rea*, *actus reus*, or mitigating or aggravating circumstances. The common law did not recognize degrees of murder. Pennsylvania was the first state to divide murder into two degrees. Most states have four basic types of murder: first-degree murder, second-degree murder, voluntary manslaughter and involuntary manslaughter. Grading murder into first- and second-degree is important because in some states only first-degree (or capital) murders qualify for the death penalty (or prison for life without parole in states without the death penalty). Second-degree murder is typically an unpremeditated but intentional killing.

Most murder statutes apply to corporations. However, in most cases, liability doesn't extend beyond the rare prosecution for involuntary manslaughter in outrageous cases. A voluntary manslaughter is an intentional, sudden killing triggered by an adequate provocation.

Provocation isn't an excuse for criminal homicide; it only reduces the punishment to allow for human weaknesses. Most jurisdictions have both objective and subjective requirements for the elements of voluntary manslaughter. Only certain types of provocation are deemed legally adequate. Usually, these are mutual combat, assault and battery, trespass, and adultery. Words alone are, in many states, not deemed an adequate provocation. However, in other states following the "last-straw rule," words may be sufficient provocation. Catching a spouse in the act of adultery is generally recognized as an adequate provocation. Further, the killer must not have cooled off from the sudden passion. If the killer did cool off, it is an intentional murder and not a voluntary manslaughter. Specifically, the elements of voluntary manslaughter are as follows. The *actus reus* is killing of another person. The *mens rea* is intent to kill or inflict serious bodily injury. The circumstances are sudden heat of passion flowing from an adequate provocation (or honest but unreasonable belief that killing was necessary in self-defense). The acts must cause the death of another.

Involuntary manslaughter is the least blameworthy form of criminal homicide. It involves unintentional (reckless or negligent) killing. Recklessness involves conscious creation of a serous and unjustifiable risk. Negligence involves unknowing creation of a substantial and unjustifiable risk.

The common law and early statutes recognized a form of involuntary manslaughter that involved an intentional killing during the course of committing a misdemeanor or an unlawful act. Most jurisdictions have severely limited or abolished this form of involuntary manslaughter.

Practice Test Bank

MULTIPLE CHOICE

1. Most states have _____.
   a. abolished felony murder
   b. limited the types of felonies which qualify to violent or dangerous felonies
   c. made felony murder a form of involuntary manslaughter
   d. made felony murder a form of voluntary manslaughter

2. Implied malice includes intent to _____.
   a. commit any felony or misdemeanor
   b. commit a dangerous misdemeanor
   c. commit any illegal act
   d. inflict serious bodily harm

3. The degree of murder or type of homicide is determined by the *actus reus*, special circumstances, and the _____.
   a. concurrence
   b. act
   c. harm
   d. *mens rea*

4. The term "homicide" is usually defined as _____.
   a. killing another live human being
   b. a criminal offense where the victim dies
   c. a murder or a suicide
   d. a murder

5. A murder that was perpetrated by means of planned, intentional poisoning of two elderly parents to collect life insurance would be a/n _____.
   a. second-degree murder
   b. involuntary manslaughter
   c. first-degree murder
   d. voluntary manslaughter

6. An unintentional criminal homicide that resulted from a conscious risk of harm greater than recklessness is usually termed a _____.
   a. felony murder
   b. depraved-heart murder
   c. voluntary manslaughter
   d. excusable homicide

7. With regard to cooling off for voluntary manslaughter, assuming the defendant did, in fact, honestly not cool off, most courts would also then apply a/n _____ test of cooling-off time.
   a. objective
   b. overt
   c. lenient
   d. subjective

8. Although it is no longer the case, a few states went further than most with the paramour rule. In these states, wife killings during adultery were _____.
   a. justifiable homicides
   b. voluntary manslaughter
   c. involuntary manslaughter
   d. depraved-heart murders

9. Originally, the benefit of the paramour rule could be claimed by _____.
   a. wives only
   b. both husbands and wives
   c. the spouse's paramour only
   d. husbands only

10. Conscious creation of a substantial and unjustifiable risk is _____.
    a. negligence
    b. gross negligence
    c. recklessness
    d. criminal negligence

11. If the defendant accidentally killed the store clerk during an armed robbery this would be a/n _____.
    a. felony murder
    b. excusable homicide
    c. involuntary manslaughter
    d. depraved heart murder

12. Common-law judges expanded the original definition of murder by creating the concept of _____ malice aforethought.
    a. express
    b. constitutive
    c. implied
    d. latent

13. At early common law, there was only one type of criminal homicide, homicide _____.
    a. committed during a felony
    b. that was neither excused nor justified
    c. depraved-heart murder
    d. in the form of manslaughter

14. As the common law developed, murder was distinguished from manslaughter in that murder required _____.
    a. malice aforethought
    b. adequate provocation
    c. heat of passion
    d. no *actus reus*

15. In 1794, _____ was the first state to separate murder into two degrees.
    a. Virginia
    b. New York
    c. Pennsylvania
    d. Massachusetts

16. As compared to traditional murder law, the felony murder rule doesn't require _____.
    a. malice aforethought or an intent or purpose to kill
    b. intent to commit a felony
    c. an *actus reus*
    d. that the defendant's acts cause the victim's death

17. The common-law crime of manslaughter was eventually divided into two separate types, _____.
    a. voluntary and involuntary
    b. deliberate and premeditated
    c. first and second degree
    d. with implied or express malice

18. The main difference between voluntary and involuntary manslaughter is that in involuntary manslaughter, the killing is _____.
    a. unintentional
    b. totally unforeseeable
    c. with implied malice
    d. with express malice

19. If the defendant killed another in an honest but unreasonable belief that the killing was necessary for self-defense, this would be the crime of _____.
    a. involuntary manslaughter
    b. voluntary manslaughter
    c. excusable homicide
    d. justifiable homicide

20. Voluntary manslaughter involves intentionally killing another in the sudden heat of passion which _____.
    a. was caused by a legally recognized adequate provocation
    b. was caused by a mental disease or defect
    c. caused the actor to be reckless
    d. gave the actor time to cool off

21. In most states, which of the following is not deemed to be a legally adequate provocation for voluntary manslaughter?
    a. verbal provocation
    b. mutual combat
    c. adultery by spouse
    d. assault and battery

22. The *mens rea* of involuntary manslaughter is usually _____.
    a. recklessly or negligently
    b. intentionally
    c. deliberate and premeditated
    d. implied malice

23. Which of the following is typically an aggravating circumstance that will justify infliction of the death penalty?
    a. torture of victim
    b. victim attempted to defend themselves
    c. victim was related to offender
    d. victim was a stranger

24. Over time, the substantive law of criminal homicide has _____.
    a. become more complex
    b. come to exclude corporations from liability for criminal homicide
    c. come to include more capital offenses
    d. allowed numerous blameworthy individuals to avoid punishment

25. Unlawful act manslaughter is sometimes also referred to as _____.
    a. voluntary manslaughter
    b. misdemeanor manslaughter
    c. felony murder
    d. depraved-heart murder

26. The _____ element of all homicides is the killing of another person.
    a. *mens rea*
    b. *actus reus*
    c. circumstances
    d. concurrence

27. In the first statute creating two degrees of murder (1794), (and in some current statutes), second-degree murder was defined as _____.
    a. a deliberate and premeditated killing
    b. a killing with malice aforethought
    c. intentional killing during the course of rape, robbery, etc.
    d. any murder that is not a first-degree murder

28. Felony murder requires intent to _____.
    a. kill
    b. inflict serious bodily injury
    c. inflict any bodily injury
    d. commit a felony

29. Felony murders are usually _____.
    a. first- or second-degree murders
    b. second-degree murders or voluntary manslaughters
    c. voluntary or involuntary manslaughters
    d. involuntary manslaughters or negligent homicides

30. In most jurisdictions, second-degree murder is a murder _____.
    a. with malice aforethought
    b. done intentionally but without premeditation
    c. done with premeditation but not intentionally
    d. done with recklessness aforethought

TRUE/FALSE

1. Unintentional murders are second-degree murders.
    a. true
    b. false

2. No corporation has ever been charged with a criminal homicide.
    a. true
    b. false

3. A defendant who cools off after the provocation and then intentionally kills is guilty of voluntary manslaughter.
    a. true
    b. false

4. Reckless or negligent criminal homicides are usually termed involuntary manslaughter.
    a. true
    b. false

5. Recklessness has both objective and subjective components.
    a. true
    b. false

6. At common law, murder was divided into first, second, and third degrees.
    a. true
    b. false

7. In some jurisdictions, murders that include aggravating circumstances (torture, heinous, atrocious, or cruel) are capital offenses.
    a. true
    b. false

8. Murder *mens rea* can include every state of mind included in the concept of malice aforethought.
    a. true
    b. false

9. Manslaughter was not a common-law crime.
    a. true
    b. false

10. Insulting gestures or words and racial slurs are adequate legal provocation for manslaughter.
    a. true
    b. false

11. At common law, a criminal homicide committed with malice aforethought is a murder.
    a. true
    b. false

12. All felony murders are intentional homicides.
    a. true
    b. false

13. Not all homicides are criminal.
    a. true
    b. false

14. Corporations cannot be guilty of criminal homicide.
    a. true
    b. false

15. Voluntary manslaughter is a form of unintentional homicide.
    a. true
    b. false

16. The trend in the law is to expand the illegal act manslaughter rule.
    a. true
    b. false

17. The Supreme Court has banned doctor-assisted suicides notwithstanding a state's death with dignity act.
    a. true
    b. false

18. Most, if not all, jurisdictions recognize brain death as a legal death.
    a. true
    b. false

19. An accidental killing, involving no fault on the actor's part, would be an excusable homicide.
    a. true
    b. false

20. In some states, a person can be guilty of the crime of killing a fetus.
    a. true
    b. false

21. A homicide committed in valid self-defense would be a justifiable homicide.
    a. true
    b. false

22. The common-law term "aforethought" refers to planning in advance.
    a. true
    b. false

23. The *actus reus* of homicide is killing another person or human being.
    a. true
    b. false

24. Most, if not all, involuntary manslaughters have two *actus reus* elements.
    a. true
    b. false

25. At common law, life (or becoming a person) began at conception.
    a. true
    b. false

FILL-IN-THE-BLANK

1. For a felony to qualify for the felony murder rule, most states require that the felony be a violent or _____ felony.

2. One of the most highly publicized cases of alleged corporate criminal homicides involved the _____ automobile.

3. A valid self-defense killing is a form of _____ homicide.

4. At common law, murder was killing someone with _____.

5. Insulting gestures and words are generally not legally adequate provocation for purposes of _____ manslaughter.

6. An accidental killing can be a murder and not an excusable homicide under the _____ murder rule.

7. The *mens rea* for involuntary manslaughter is recklessness or _____.

8. The unintentional killing form of manslaughter is _____ manslaughter.

9. An intentional killing that occurred under circumstances of imperfect self-defense is a _____ manslaughter.

10. The _____ rule is an exception to the felony murder rule.

11. A killing is with _____ if it is intentional and without excuse or justification.

12. The most serious form of murder today is capital or _____ murder.

13. Conscious creation of a serious and substantial risk is called _____.

14. Creating serious and substantial risks but not being aware of it is called _____.

15. An unintentional death caused by driving while intoxicated would be a form of _____ manslaughter.

Study Guide

ESSAY

1. Compare and contrast first-degree murder and second-degree murder.

2. Describe the felony murder rule.

3. Compare and contrast voluntary and involuntary manslaughter.

4. Compare and contrast justifiable, excusable, and criminal homicide.

5. Discuss the concept of express and implied malice aforethought as it applies to common law murder.

Study Guide

CHAPTER 9 ANSWER KEY

Multiple Choice

1. b. See pg. 305, LO 2, 4
2. d. See pg. 286, LO 4
3. d. See pg. 275, LO 2
4. a. See pg. 274, LO 2
5. c. See pg. 291, LO 2
6. b. See pg. 301, LO 8
7. a. See pg. 314, LO 6
8. a. See pg. 316, LO 6
9. d. See pg. 316, LO 6
10. c. See pg. 285, LO 8
11. a. See pg. 303, LO 4
12. c. See pg. 286, LO 4
13. b. See pg. 284, LO 1
14. a. See pg. 285, LO 4
15. c. See pg. 288, LO 2
16. a. See pg. 303, LO 2
17. a. See pg. 312, LO 4
18. a. See pg. 312, LO 6,8
19. b. See pg. 314, LO 1
20. a. See pg. 313, LO 6
21. a. See pg. 314, LO 6
22. a. See pg. 320, LO 8
23. a. See pg. 298, LO 2
24. a. See pg. 284, LO 1
25. b. See pg. 319, LO 9
26. b. See pg. 286, LO 1
27. d. See pg. 288, LO 2
28. d. See pg. 304, LO 2
29. a. See pg. 301, LO 2
30. b. See pg. 291, LO 4

True/False

1. T. See pg. 301, LO 2
2. F. See pg. 308, LO 5
3. F. See pg. 314, LO 6
4. T. See pg. 319, LO 8
5. T. See pg. 285, LO 8
6. F. See pg. 282, LO 2
7. T. See pg. 288, LO 4
8. T. See pg. 288, LO 4
9. F. See pg. 282, LO 4
10. F. See pg. 314, LO 6
11. T. See pg. 282, LO 4
12. F. See pg. 304, LO 4
13. T. See pg. 289, LO 1
14. F. See pg. 308, LO 5
15. F. See pg. 312, LO 7
16. F. See pg. 323, LO 9
17. F. See pg. 280, LO 3
18. T. See pg. 277, LO 3
19. T. See pg. 284, LO 1
20. T. See pg. 276, LO 3

21. T. See pg. 284, LO 1
22. T. See pg. 285, LO 4
23. T. See pg. 287, LO 4
24. F. See pg. 319, LO 8
25. F. See pg. 285, LO 3

Fill-in-the-Blank

1. dangerous. See pg. 303, LO 4
2. Ford Pinto. See pg. 308, LO 5
3. justifiable. See pg. 284, LO 1
4. malice. See pg. 282, LO 4
5. voluntary. See pg. 314, LO 6
6. felony. See pg. 303, LO 4
7. negligence. See pg. 320, LO 8
8. involuntary. See pg. 312, LO 8
9. voluntary. See pg. 312, LO 7
10. third-party exception. See pg. 303, LO 4
11. malice. See pg. 285, LO 4
12. first-degree. See pg. 289, LO 4
13. recklessness. See pg. 285, LO 4
14. negligence. See pg. 319, LO 8
15. involuntary. See pg. 323, LO 9

Essays

1. Compare and contrast first-degree murder and second-degree murder.

   Grading murder into first- and second- degree is a relatively modern approach. Because the harm in murder is always the same (death of the victim), often the grade of murder is based on the mens rea of the actor and the manner in which the murder was committed. First-degree murder is premeditated, deliberate, and willful intent-to-kill murders (and some states include felony murders). Only first-degree murders are eligible for the death penalty. Much of the case law surrounding first-degree murder concerns whether the actions were deliberate, willful, premeditated. (See, for example, Byford v. States.) Sometimes the issue is whether the act was heinous, atrocious or particularly cruel. If so, the murder may be first degree or aggravated murder. Second-degree murder in some states is the catch all for intentional killings or unintentional killings which do not warrant the death penalty but involve "implied malice" such as felony murder, depraved heard murder, intent-to-inflict-serious bodily injury murder. Other states have specific depraved heard second-degree murder statutes. Felony murders fall into either first-degree or second-degree murder statutes depending on the state. LO 2

2. Describe the felony murder rule.

The felony murder rule makes accidental deaths that occur during the commission of a felony either a first degree or second degree murder (depending on the state). When an individual is killed during the course of "an inherently dangerous" felony, or a felony listed in the statute, it does not matter that the criminal did not intend to cause the death of the victim. It suffices that the person intended to commit the underlying felony. One issue surrounding the felony murder rules is when a co-defendant is killed during the course of the felony. In People v. Hudson, the court upheld the defendant's felony murder conviction when a police officer shot and killed the codefendant. The parties argued the issue of causation and foreseeability at the appellate level and the majority found that Hudson was the proximate cause of the death of his partner. The other issue that arises in felony murder is the meaning of "inherently dangerous felony." In California, the courts say that the underlying felony should be looked at "in the abstract" (meaning not paying attention to the facts of the given case), and found that a doctor could not be guilty of felony murder when the underlying felony was fraud. Other states adopt a case by case approach and look at whether the acts in the case were dangerous. (This is similar to the foreseeability examination in Hudson. If the felony was committed in a dangerous way, then the death is more foreseeable.) LO 2, 4

3. Compare and contrast voluntary and involuntary manslaughter.

Voluntary manslaughter is an intentional killing done during the "heat of passion" in response to adequate and legally recognized provocation, without time to cool off. Involuntary manslaughter is unintentional killing done in a reckless or negligent way or during the course of an unlawful act (misdemeanor manslaughter). The difference between voluntary and involuntary manslaughter rests with the mens rea element, and the intent to kill is the key. The reason voluntary manslaughter is not murder is because of the recognition that on occasion people cannot control themselves, and it would be unjust to subject them to the penalties of first degree murder in light of the provocation they are responding too. The reason that involuntary manslaughter is considered a crime and not just an accident has to do with the recklessness or negligence of the individual. It would be bad policy to let people who create substantial and unjustifiable risks of harm to not suffer any punishment when their behavior causes the death of another. LO 6, 7, 8 and 9

4. Compare and contrast justifiable, excusable, and criminal homicide.

Killing another person is homicide, and it becomes criminal homicide when there is no excuse or justification for the killing. Earlier in the text you examined justification defenses. Included among those were self defense, defense of others, choice of evils (necessity), and execution of public duties. One example that highlights the difference between criminal homicide and justifiable homicide is to examine the death penalty. When a person is put to death as a result of their crime, the state sets a time and place for the execution, prisoners are given a "last meal" etc. There is no way to argue that this is not the premeditated, deliberate, and willful killing of another, but it is not murder, and the prosecutor does not file charges against the executioner. Why? Because the action is justified. Likewise, excusable homicides are killing done with an excuse defense (insanity, age, involuntary intoxication, syndrome defenses). If, for example, a person was given a sedative in their soda pop and had an adverse reaction and ran over a crowd of young children on the playground, he or she would not be guilty of criminal homicide if they were able to show that their intoxication was involuntary and unknown to them. It would be wrong to hold them responsible for the deaths if they had no culpability other than drinking a soda pop. Criminal homicides are killings for which it is appropriate for society to express its condemnation. LO 1

5. Discuss the concept of express and implied malice aforethought as it applies to common law murder.

At common law, the earliest definitions of criminal homicide involved that the killing be done with malice aforethought. This meant that in order for the crime to be murder it had to be an intentional killing planned in advance. As common law developed, judges added additional types of killing to the definition of malice aforethought: intentional killings without premeditation or reasonable provocation; unintentional killings during the commission of felonies; depraved heart killings; intent to inflict grievous bodily harm. The term express malice aforethought was reserved for the intentional killing planned in advance, but implied malice aforethought was found when the killing occurred in the other ways. LO 4

Chapter 10
Crimes against Persons II:
Criminal Sexual Conduct, Bodily Injury, and Personal Restraint

LEARNING OBJECTIVES

1. Understand that crimes against persons boil down to four types: taking a life; unwanted sexual invasions, bodily injury; and personal restraint.

2. Understand that voluntary and knowing consensual sexual behavior between two adults is legal, healthy and desired.

3. Understand that the vast majority of rape victims are raped by men they know.

4. Understand that during the 1970s and 1980s, sexual assault reform changed the face of criminal sexual assault law.

5. Understand that force beyond that required to complete sexual penetration or contact is not always required to satisfy the force requirement in rape.

6. Understand that rape is a general-intent crime.

7. Understand that statutory rape is a strict liability crime in most states.

8. Understand that assault and battery are two separate crimes.

9. Understand that domestic violence crimes since the early 1970s have been transformed from a private concern to a criminal justice problem.

10. Understand that stalking, although an ancient practice, is a new crime.

11. Understand that kidnapping and false imprisonment violate the right of locomotion.

KEY TERMS AND CONCEPTS

- **common law rape**—intentional, forced, heterosexual vaginal penetration by a man with a woman not his wife; p. 328

- **common law sodomy**—anal intercourse between two males; p. 328

- **sexual assault statutes**—expanded the definition of sex offenses to embrace a wide range of nonconsensual penetrations and contacts; p. 330

Chapter 10: Crimes Against Persons II: Criminal Sexual Conduct, Bodily Injury, and Personal Restraint

- **sexual assault or criminal sexual conduct statutes**—expanded the definition of sex offenses to embrace a wide range of nonconsensual penetrations and contact; p. 328

- **aggravated rape**—rape committed with a weapon, by more than one person, or causing serious physical injury to the victim; p. 328

- **unarmed acquaintance rape**—nonconsensual sex between people who know each other; rape involving dates, lovers, neighbors, co-workers, employers, and so on; p. 328

- **corroboration rule**—element in rape that the prosecution had to prove rape by the testimony of witnesses other than the victim; p. 330

- **rape shield statutes**—statutes that prohibit introducing evidence of victims' past sexual conduct; p. 330

- **prompt-reporting rule**—rape victims have to report the rape soon after it occurs; p. 330

- **marital rape exception**—legally, husbands can't rape their wives; p. 330

- **rape**—intentional sexual penetration by force without consent; p. 331

- *actus reus (rape)*—the act of sexual penetration; p. 332

- **force and resistance rule**—victims had to prove to the courts they didn't consent to rape by demonstrating that they resisted the force of the rapist; p. 332

- **utmost resistance rule**—the requirement that rape victims must use all the physical strength they have to prevent penetration; p. 334

- **reasonable resistance rule (in rape)**—the amount of force required to repel rapists to show non-consent in rape prosecutions; p. 334

- **extrinsic force (in rape)**—requires some force, in addition to the amount needed to accomplish the penetration; p. 335

- **intrinsic force (in rape)**—requires only the amount of force necessary to accomplish the penetration; p. 335

- **threat-of-force requirement**—prosecution must prove a sexual assault victim feared imminent bodily harm and that the fear was reasonable; p. 342

- **fraud in the fact (in rape)**—when a rapist fraudulently convinces his victim that the act she consented to was something other than sexual intercourse; p. 343

- **fraud in the inducement (rape)**—the fraud is in the benefits promised, not in the act; p. 343

- **general intent crime**—crime in which defendants intend to commit the act defined in the crime (with rape, the act is forcible sexual penetration); p. 343

- **honest and reasonable mistake rule (regarding consent in rape)**—a negligence mental element in rape cases in which the defendant argues that he honestly, but mistakenly, believed the victim consented to sex; p. 334

- **recklessness requirement (regarding consent in rape)**—adopted by some states in rape cases; it requires that the defendant has to be aware that there's a risk the victim hasn't consented to sexual intercourse; p. 334

- **statutory rape**—to have carnal knowledge of a person under the age of consent whether or not accomplished by force; p. 346

- **reasonable mistake of age**—a defense to statutory rape in California and Alaska, if the defendant reasonably believed his victim was over the age of consent; p. 346

- **simple rape (second degree)**—rape without aggravated circumstances; p. 346

- **aggravated rape**—(see above); rape involving either: serious bodily injury to the victim, a stranger rapist, rape in connection with another crime, an armed rapist, more than one rapist, or a victim who is a minor and the rapist is several years older; p. 346

- **battery**—unwanted and unjustified offensive touching; p. 346

- **assault**—an attempt to commit a battery or intentionally putting another in fear; p. 346

- **stalking**—intentionally scaring another person by following, tormenting, or harassing; p. 346

- **attempted battery assault**—consists of having the specific intent to commit a battery and taking substantial steps toward carrying it out, without actually completing the attempt; p. 348

- **threatened battery assault**—sometimes called the crime of "intentional scaring," it requires only that actors intend to frighten their victims, thus expanding assault beyond attempted battery; p. 348

- **conditional threats (in assault)**—not enough to satisfy the *mens rea* of assault because they're not immediate; p. 348

- **subjective fear only test**—asks, was the victim actually afraid? p. 358

- **objective fear only test**—asks, would a reasonable person be afraid? p. 358

- **intent to instill fear test**—asks, did the actor intend to instill fear? p. 358

- **cyberstalking**—the use of the internet, e-mail, or other electronic communications devices to stalk another person through threatening behavior; p. 358

- **right of locomotion**—the right to come and go without restraint; p. 362

- **kidnapping**—taking and carrying away another person with intent to deprive the other person of personal liberty; p. 362

- **asportation (in kidnapping)**—the carrying away of another's property; p. 362

- **false imprisonment**—the heart of the crime is depriving others of their personal liberty; p. 367

CHAPTER OUTLINE

I. Other than homicide, there are three kinds of crimes against persons—sexual, bodily injury, and restraint.
    A. Sex offenses (*e.g.*, rape)
    B. Bodily injury crimes (*e.g.*, assault)
    C. Personal restraint crimes (*e.g.*, kidnapping and false imprisonment)

II. **Sex Offenses**—Forcible rape was an offense at common law but has been modified greatly since then. The criminal justice system has struggled in dealing with acquaintance rapes and sexual assaults against men.
    A. **The history of rape law**
        1. Originally, only narrowly defined rape and sodomy
            a. Rape—Forced heterosexual vaginal penetration of a woman not married to the rapist
            b. Sodomy—Anal intercourse between males
        2. The elements of common-law rape
            a. Intentional vaginal intercourse
            b. Between a man and a woman not his wife
            c. Achieved by force or threat of serious bodily harm
            d. Without the woman's consent

3. Victims could testify against rapists, but the woman's credibility depended on three conditions that were difficult (if not impossible) to prove:
    a. Her chastity
    b. Whether she reported the rape promptly
    c. Whether the rape was corroborated by other testimony

B. **Criminal Sexual Conduct Statutes**
  1. Rape and related sex offense law reforms (1970s–80s)
      a. Changes in prosecution procedures
      b. Abolished the corroboration rule
      c. Relaxed the prompt-reporting rule
      d. Banned introduction of evidence of the victim's past sexual conduct through rape shield laws
      e. Changes in the definition of rape and related sex offenses
          (1) Marital rape exception (husbands can't rape wives) abolished in some states
  2. Sexual offenses consolidated into one statute
      a. All nonconsensual sexual penetrations and contacts included
      b. Sex offenses made gender-neutral
      c. Seriousness of offense divided into several degrees, graded by
          (1) Penetration (more serious) and contact (less serious)
          (2) Use of force (more serious)
          (3) Physical injury aggravates crime
          (4) Gang rapes are more serious.

C. **The elements of modern rape law**
  1. **Rape *actus reus*** —Two parts
      a. Sexual penetration, however slight
      b. Force and resistance standard—focused on the woman's consent
          (1) Utmost resistance standard (1600s–1950s)—Victims had to prove by resistance to the utmost that they didn't consent
          (2) Reasonable resistance standard (1950s–70s)—Amount of required resistance depended on the circumstances of each case.
          (3) Many new statutes have dropped the resistance requirement.
              (a) Stranger rape, resistance isn't really an issue
              (b) Acquaintance rape, resistance is critical
          (4) *Case: Jones v. State*
      c. By force or threat of force—Force
          (1) "Intrinsic" in some jurisdictions—Only the amount of physical exertion needed to achieve penetration in nonconsensual sex
          (2) "Extrinsic" in some jurisdictions—Some force in addition to the amount of exertion needed to achieve nonconsensual penetration

(3) *Case: Commonwealth v. Berkowitz*
(4) *Case: State in the Interest of M.T.S.*
d. By force or threat of force—Threat of Force
(1) Subjective fear requirement
(2) Objective fear requirement
e. Resistance and danger to victim
(1) 1970s-80s research indicated resistance may endanger victims
(2) Later research reflects that earlier findings were flawed
(a) Overrepresented stranger rape—violent convicted rapists
(b) Acquaintance rape out-numbers stranger rapes, and resistance usually succeeds with acquaintances
(c) Initial rapist violence provokes victim resistance rather than the other way around
(3) No force or threat required if victim is insane or tricked
(a) Fraud in the fact—is rape
(b) Fraud in the inducement—isn't rape
2. **Rape *mens rea*—**Rape is a general-intent crime: defendant must intend to commit the act of forcible sexual penetration
a. Different states of mind surrounding non-consent
b. Mistakes can be either reckless, negligent, or no-fault (strict liability) mistakes
c. Strict liability with respect to intent to use force
(1) *Case: Commonwealth v. Fischer*
d. Negligent mistake—honest but reasonable mistake rule
(1) *Case: People v. Mayberry*
e. Reckless mistake—Defendant has to be aware that there is a risk the victim hasn't consented to the intercourse
(1) *Case: Regina v. Morgan* (England)
3. Circumstance—Non-consent by the victim
a. Formal law—State has to prove non-consent beyond a reasonable doubt
b. Informal practice—Defendants raise consent by the victim as a defense
c. Consent doesn't have to be in writing
D. **Statutory rape**
1. Victim's immaturity substitutes for the element of consent
2. Strict liability as to age in most states
3. A few states allow a defense of reasonable mistake of age.
E. **Grading Degrees of Rape**
1. Simple rape
2. Aggravated rape is rape with injury, a stranger, another crime, an armed rapist, multiple rapists, or a minor victim.

Study Guide

III. Bodily injury crimes involve offensive touching or bodily harm.
    A. **Battery** is unwanted and unjustified offensive touching; assault is either an attempted or threatened battery.
    B. The elements of battery
        1. *Actus reus*
            a. Unlawful touching
            b. Only unauthorized offensive touching (parents and law enforcement officers are authorized)
        2. *Mens rea* varies as to whether it requires purposely, knowingly, recklessly, or negligently offensive touching.
    C. Grading the seriousness depends on:
        1. The degree of injury—mere touching, minor injury, or serious injury
        2. The circumstances of the touching
    D. **Assault** elements
        1. Assault requires no touching
        2. Kinds:
            a. Attempted battery assault elements—having the specific intent to commit battery and taking steps to complete it.
            b. Threatened battery assault elements—intentionally scaring the victim.
        3. Victim awareness
            a. Not important in attempted battery because the offense focuses on the physical injury.
            b. Indispensable in threatened battery because the offense focuses on fear of the victim.
        4. Conditional threats aren't enough for threatened battery assault.
    E. The Model assault and battery statute
        1. Part of the Model Penal Code
        2. Integrates, rationalizes, and grades assault and battery
        3. Takes into account *actus reus*, *mens rea*, circumstance elements, and criminal harm
    F. **Domestic Violence Crimes**
        1. Sample DV statute: Ohio
        2. *Case: Hamilton v. Cameron*
    G. **Stalking**—Involves intentionally scaring another by conduct which falls short of assault and battery
        1. **Anti-stalking statutes**—tremendous variation among states
        2. **Stalking *actus reus***
            a. All states require that the act be a repeated one.
            b. All states require some version of visual or physical proximity.
            c. About half the states include verbal or written threats, threats implied by conduct, threat, terrorist threat, or credible threat
            d. Some states list very specific behavior
        3. **Stalking *mens rea***
            a. Specific intent to commit the forbidden *actus reus*.

b. Some mental attitude (it varies) causing the bad result is also required.
c. Just more than half the states require subjective fault.
d. One-third of the states require objective fault.
4. **Bad result**—placing the victim in fear
 a. Subjective and objective fear (most states and the model code)
 b. Subjective fear only test
 c. Objective fear only test
 d. Intent-to-instill-fear test
5. **Cyberstalking**—using the internet to stalk another
 a. *Case: State v. Hoying*

IV. **Personal restraint crimes**: kidnapping and false imprisonment
  A. Laws protect the fundamental right of locomotion—the right to move about and come and go as we please.
  B. **Kidnapping**
   1. Elements of common-law kidnapping:
    a. Seizing, carrying away (asportation of), and confining another person
    b. By force or threat of force, fraud, or deception
    c. Intent to deprive the other person of her or his liberty
   2. Elements of modern kidnapping law
    a. **Kidnapping** *Actus reus*—Asportation requirement recognizes even practically no movement of the victim.
     (1) *Case: People v. Chessman*
     (2) *Case: People v. Allen*
    b. **Kidnapping** *Mens rea*—The specific intent to confine, significantly restrain, or hold victims in secret without the victim's consent.
   3. **Grading the seriousness** of kidnapping
    a. Simple
    b. Aggravated—aggravating circumstances include kidnapping for the purpose of
     (1) Sexual invasion
     (2) Obtaining a hostage
     (3) Obtaining ransom
     (4) Robbing the victim
     (5) Murdering the victim
     (6) Blackmail
     (7) Terrorizing the victim
     (8) Achieving political aims
  C. **False imprisonment**
   1. *Actus reus*—Keeping another person from moving freely (no asportation requirement)
   2. *Mens rea*—Having the specific intent to confine or restrain another person without their consent

CHAPTER SUMMARY

Crimes against persons involve four types: taking a life (homicide), unwanted sexual invasions (rape and sex offenses), bodily injury (assault and battery), and personal restraint (kidnapping and false imprisonment). In one form or another, all of these were common-law crimes.

Sex offenses are serious even if there is no physical injury because they violate intimacy, privacy, and bodily integrity in a way typical physical injuries cannot. The criminal justice system handles rapes by strangers and men with weapons well, but it doesn't do as well with the overwhelming number of rapes by men who know their victims, including date rape.

The old rape law defined a crime of forcible sexual penetration that only men could commit against women who weren't their wives. The elements of rape at common law were: 1) intentional vaginal intercourse; 2) between a man and a woman who was not his wife; 3) achieved by force or a threat of severe bodily harm; 4) without the woman's consent.

Modern statutes have expanded the crime of rape and other sex crimes in criminal sexual conduct statutes. These new offenses include a list of gender-neutral sex offenses involving unwanted sexual penetrations and contacts. Rape in most jurisdictions today has four elements: 1) the *actus reus* of sexual penetration; 2) the *actus reus* of force, or threat of force, to accomplish sexual penetration (or some substitute such as unconsciousness, mental impairment, etc.); 3) the *mens rea* of intentional sexual penetration; and 4) the circumstance of the lack of victim consent.

One controversial issue is whether there should also be a specific intent element in rape. The leading case on the point is the controversial English case of *Regina v. Morgan* (1975). Morgan and three companions were drinking in a bar. When they failed to find female companionship, Morgan invited the others to come home with him to have sexual intercourse with his wife. Morgan told the others that she would want to have sex with them and would only pretend to resist. He told them not to worry if she struggled because she liked rough sex. The Sixth House of Lords (England's highest court) overturned the convictions because the defendants didn't specifically intend to have sexual intercourse without the victim's consent. Why? Because the defendants believed that Morgan's wife wanted sex and wanted the struggle.

When American courts face the intent question, they vary in their response. Many come down between the English specific-intent rule and strict liability on the issue of intent or knowledge to have sex without the victims consent. Some of these courts have adopted a reckless or negligent standard with regard to the consent problem.

Current rape law has shifted the emphasis from the resistance of victims to lack of consent. The traditional emphasis on physical violence (or threats thereof) to satisfy the element of force in the *actus reus* of rape is shifting in modern rape law to the sufficiency of non-consent to unwanted sexual activity.

According to the law, the prosecution has to prove non-consent by the victim beyond a reasonable doubt. However, as a matter of strategy, defendants claim victim consent as a defense.

Most current statutes divide rape into two degrees: simple (second-degree) rape and aggravated (first-degree) rape. Aggravated rape involves at least one of the following circumstances: victim suffers serious bodily injury, stranger rape, rape occurs in conjunction with another crime, rapist is armed, there are multiple offenders, or the victim is a minor while the rapist is significantly older. All other rapes are "simple" rapes with lesser penalties.

Much of the law of rape and rape prosecutions has changed over the years. The marital exception and prompt report rule have been abolished in many jurisdictions. Corroboration of the victim's testimony is no longer required. Rape shield laws limit the ability of the defense to bring out evidence of the victim's prior sex life. Utmost resistance by the victim is no longer required. Reasonable resistance is enough.

Bodily injury crimes include unlawful nonsexual contacts (battery) or threats of them (assault). The elements of battery are negligently, recklessly, knowingly, or purposely causing and unlawful, offensive touching of another. The grading of the seriousness of a battery depends on the amount of injury and the circumstances of the touching.

An assault requires no touching. There are two kinds of assault: attempted battery (having the specific intent to commit battery and taking steps to complete it) and threatened battery (intentionally scaring the victim). In both types, the victim must be aware of the defendant's conduct.

Domestic violence crimes have historically been prosecuted under assault and battery statutes. Because family violence has been shown to be far more than just a private concern to a criminal justice problem, some states have enacted specific domestic violence crimes. These generally apply the assault and battery crimes to situations involving domestic partners or other family members. Ohio's statute, by way of example, shows that repeat domestic violence results in increased punishment and elevation of assault and battery from misdemeanor level to felony level.

Although stalking has occurred for centuries, in 1990 California enacted the first criminal stalking statute. Most states have since followed suit, but there is tremendous variation in these statutes. Stalking involves repeated, unwanted, and threatening conduct which either places the victim in fear or would cause a reasonable person to fear. Stalking is widespread and has major negative effects on its victims. Cyberstalking is a type of stalking in which the stalker uses the internet, e-mail, or electronic communication devices to threaten the victim.

Kidnapping and false imprisonment are crimes against the right to come and go as we please. At common law, kidnapping consisted of six elements: 1) seizing, 2) carrying away (asportation of) and 3) confining 4) another person 5) by force, threat of force, fraud, or deception 6) with the intent to deprive the other of their liberty.

The critical difference between false imprisonment and kidnapping is that the *actus reus* of asportation (carrying away) of victims is required in kidnapping. Modern interpretations have rendered the asportation requirement of kidnapping almost meaningless.

Kidnapping is usually divided into two degrees: simple and aggravated. The most common aggravating circumstances include kidnapping for the purpose of sexual invasion, taking a hostage, getting ransom, terrorizing the victim, and achieving political goals. The penalty for aggravated kidnapping is typically life imprisonment and, until recently, even death.

The elements of false imprisonment are restraining another person's liberty, with specific intent to restrain. The Model Penal Code requires the restraint to "interfere substantially with the victim's liberty," but in most states, any interference with another person's liberty suffices. In many states, false imprisonment means forcibly, by threat, or secretly confining, abducting, imprisoning, or restraining another person against their will and without legal authority.

Chapter 10: Crimes Against Persons II: Criminal Sexual Conduct, Bodily Injury, and Personal Restraint

Practice Test Bank

MULTIPLE CHOICE

1. Asportation is an element of kidnapping. Asportation refers to _____.
    a. confining
    b. alleviating
    c. carrying away
    d. restraining

2. The crime of kidnapping has _____ *mens rea* element(s).
    a. no
    b. one
    c. two
    d. three

3. False imprisonment and kidnapping are _____ crimes.
    a. specific-intent
    b. strict liability
    c. *mala prohibita*
    d. inchoate

4. The *actus reus* of false imprisonment is _____.
    a. carrying away
    b. threats
    c. abducting
    d. restraint

5. One difference between false imprisonment and kidnapping is that false imprisonment _____.
    a. is a felony
    b. is a strict liability crime
    c. has no asportation element
    d. has only one *actus reus*

6. Prior to recent reforms, proof of lack of consent in rape prosecutions _____.
    a. was irrelevant to the crime of rape
    b. could be established by verbal resistance alone
    c. required proof of physical resistance
    d. required that the defendant show physical signs of being forcibly resisted

7. A battery is an unlawful _____.
    a. attempted assault
    b. felony
    c. aggravated assault
    d. offensive touching of another

8. Modern assault and/or battery statutes often _____.
   a. have made them capital offenses
   b. have negligence and recklessness as a *mens rea*
   c. have made them strict liability crimes
   d. have eliminated purposeful as a *mens rea*

9. The extrinsic force standard of rape requires that the rapist have used _____.
   a. only the force necessary to accomplish the penetration itself
   b. force beyond that necessary to penetrate the victim
   c. only a reasonable amount of force to accomplish the penetration itself
   d. only reasonable force to overcome the victim's resistance

10. In *Regina v. Morgan*, Britain's highest court held that the defendants were not guilty of rape because _____.
    a. they reasonably believed the victim was old enough to give valid consent
    b. did not use force on the victim
    c. they reasonably believe the victim consented
    d. the statute had no specific intent requirement

11. In statutory rape cases, the rule in most states is that _____.
    a. there is a defense that the victim was promiscuous
    b. a reasonable mistake as to consent is a defense
    c. there is no *mens rea* in the crime
    d. there is no mistake of age defense

12. Under the common law, _____.
    a. there were only two sex crimes—rape and sodomy
    b. there were no sex crimes
    c. rape was the only sex crime
    d. sodomy was the only sex crime

13. In the 1950s, courts began to relax the traditional _____ victim resistance standard and replaced it with a reasonable resistance standard for rape victims.
    a. maximum
    b. utmost
    c. contingent
    d. foreseeable

14. Rape shield statutes _____.
    a. limit evidence of the victim's reputation or past sexual conduct
    b. shield the victim from the media
    c. prohibit cross examination of the rape victim
    d. protect the defendant from prejudicial pretrial publicity

15. In many jurisdictions today, rape statutes have modified the common law by _____.
    a. excluding any defense of victim consent
    b. making rape a capital felony
    c. making the offense gender neutral
    d. eliminating the marital exception

16. Many states now have an offense called felonious or _____ assault which is an assault plus other elements such as causing serious bodily injury, using a deadly weapon, or assaulting a peace officer.
    a. grand
    b. aggravated
    c. mitigated
    d. serious

17. The Model Penal Code is different from both the common law and many state statutes in that the Model Penal Code definition of simple assault _____.
    a. has no offensive touching *actus reus*
    b. provides that assault can be committed vicariously
    c. makes assault a strict liability crime
    d. has no *actus reus* element

18. The offense of _____ rape involves an adult having sex with a child, even if the child consents.
    a. child indecency
    b. criminal contact
    c. statutory
    d. minority

19. Traditionally, all assaults were _____.
    a. felonies
    b. *mala prohibita*
    c. misdemeanors
    d. strict liability crimes

20. In common-law rape trials, the victims must have _____ in order to get a conviction.
    a. reported the rape promptly
    b. been unmarried
    c. been over the age of fourteen
    d. been under the age of twelve

21. The crime of rape generally _____.
    a. requires that actual extrinsic force be used against the victim
    b. includes threats of imminent force
    c. has no circumstance element
    d. has no *actus reus* element

22. In many modern rape, sexual assault, and criminal sexual conduct statutes, such as that in Minnesota, _____.
    a. a female could be guilty of a penetration crime
    b. the marital exception is retained
    c. the corroboration requirement is retained
    d. have only one degree of offense

23. In most statutes today, _____.
    a. the formerly separate offenses of assault and battery are combined
    b. all assaults are felonies
    c. all batteries are misdemeanors
    d. the common-law offenses of battery and aggravated assault are combined

24. Offensive physical contact of another is _____.
    a. always criminal
    b. the *actus reus* of battery
    c. the *actus reus* of assault
    d. the *mens rea* of mayhem

25. Intentionally spitting in someone's face to insult them _____.
    a. cannot be a crime
    b. could be an assault
    c. can be a battery
    d. can be an aggravated assault

26. If a person's dog attacks and injures a victim, the person _____.
    a. cannot be guilty of any crime unless the person intended that the victim be injured
    b. can only be sued civilly by the victim. There is no crime.
    c. is guilty of battery only if the victim provoked the animal
    d. can be guilty of an assault or battery

27. Intentionally and repeatedly following a person to scare or harass them is usually referred to as the crime of _____.
    a. intimidation
    b. stalking
    c. terroristic threats
    d. habitual harassment

28. The societal value offended by kidnapping and false imprisonment is personal _____.
    a. privacy
    b. solitude
    c. liberty
    d. integrity

29. Kidnapping can be committed by force, threat of force, and _____.
    a. confounding or compounding
    b. mendacity or veracity
    c. fraud or deception
    d. culpability and mendacity

30. States have enacted domestic violence statutes which are often variations on _____.
    a. assault and battery crimes
    b. false imprisonment crimes
    c. rape crimes
    d. coercion

TRUE/FALSE

1. In the Model Penal Code, and most states, simple assault is a felony.
    a. true
    b. false

2. Cyberstalking constitutes approximately 50 percent of all stalking.
    a. true
    b. false

3. The crimes of kidnapping and false imprisonment are specific-intent crimes.
    a. true
    b. false

4. Certain types of motives can turn a simple kidnapping into an aggravated kidnapping.
    a. true
    b. false

5. False imprisonment always requires actual use of force.
    a. true
    b. false

6. Modern interpretations of the asportation element of kidnapping require only slight movement of the victim or render it virtually meaningless.
    a. true
    b. false

7. At common law, the offense of kidnapping had only three elements.
    a. true
    b. false

8. At common law, a man could not be guilty of raping his wife.
   a. true
   b. false

9. Rape law reform began seriously in the 1920s.
   a. true
   b. false

10. In some jurisdictions, an aggravated rape is one where the rapist is armed or the victim suffers serious bodily injury.
    a. true
    b. false

11. The *actus reus* of assault is offensive touching.
    a. true
    b. false

12. Domestic violence has always been viewed as a serious societal concern
    a. true
    b. false

13. Intercourse obtained by fraud in the inducement is not rape
    a. true
    b. false

14. One difference between false imprisonment and kidnapping is that only kidnapping requires asportation of the victim.
    a. true
    b. false

15. At common law, the crime of rape was punishable by death.
    a. true
    b. false

16. At common law, rape was a specific-intent crime.
    a. true
    b. false

17. If the rape victim is mentally deficient, incapacitated by alcohol or drugs, or otherwise not capable of giving a valid consent, it can still be rape even though no force was used or threatened.
    a. true
    b. false

18. Beginning in the 1990s, most states began repealing their rape shield laws.
    a. true
    b. false

19. Over time, the reasonable resistance standard came to be replaced by an utmost resistance standard.
    a. true
    b. false

20. Stalking is a relatively recent phenomenon.
    a. true
    b. false

21. In most modern rape laws, lack of consent of the victim is not a circumstance element.
    a. true
    b. false

22. The extrinsic force standard requires more force than the intrinsic force standard.
    a. true
    b. false

23. Only a few states allow the defense of reasonable mistake of age in statutory rape cases.
    a. true
    b. false

24. Victim consent is a defense to statutory rape.
    a. true
    b. false

25. In a statutory rape case, the prosecution must prove some force or threat of force by the defendant to convict.
    a. true
    b. false

FILL-IN-THE-BLANK

1. The term _____ means carrying away.

2. _____ rape involves sex with a young person, even without force.

3. The only two common-law sex offenses were rape and _____.

4. The circumstance element of most modern rape laws is _____ of the victim.

5. The *actus reus* of rape is sexual _____ of the victim.

6. In some states, a reasonable mistake of fact with regard to the victim's _____ is a defense to statutory rape.

7. Intentionally restraining someone's liberty is the offense of _____ imprisonment.

8. The *actus reus* of traditional assault is a/n _____ or threatened battery.

9. Rape _____ laws limit evidence about a rape victim's past and reputation.

10. The _____ standard requires more force than just the force needed to penetrate the victim.

11. Most sex crime statutes today are _____ neutral.

12. If mistake as to the victim's age is a defense to rape, the mistake or belief must be _____.

13. In general, assaults or batteries that cause _____ bodily injury are felonies.

14. _____ threats cannot be an assault, because the threat of harm is not immediate.

15. The _____ force standard requires only the force necessary to cause penetration of the victim.

ESSAY

1. Discuss the four types of crimes against persons.

2. Over time, how has the law of rape changed with regard to force and consent?

3. Compare and contrast the crimes (and elements) of kidnapping and false imprisonment.

4. Compare and contrast the crimes of assault and battery.

5. Discuss the prevalence of acquaintance rape and attempts to combat acquaintance rape.

Chapter 10: Crimes Against Persons II: Criminal Sexual Conduct, Bodily Injury, and Personal Restraint

CHAPTER 10 ANSWER KEY

Multiple Choice

1. c. See pg. 362, LO 11
2. b. See pg. 366, LO 11
3. a. See pg. 367, LO 11
4. d. See pg. 367, LO 11
5. c. See pg. 367, LO 11
6. c. See pg. 332, LO 6
7. d. See pg. 346, LO 8
8. b. See pg. 347, LO 8
9. b. See pg. 335, LO 5
10. c. See pg. 345, LO 6
11. d. See pg. 346, LO 7
12. a. See pg. 328, LO 4
13. b. See pg. 334, LO 5
14. a. See pg. 330, LO 4
15. d. See pg. 330, LO 4
16. b. See pg. 349, LO 8
17. a. See pg. 349, LO 8
18. c. See pg. 346, LO 7
19. c. See pg. 349, LO 8
20. a. See pg. 330, LO 4
21. b. See pg. 332, LO 5
22. a. See pg. 331, LO 4
23. a. See pg. 346, LO 8
24. b. See pg. 347, LO 8
25. c. See pg. 347, LO 8
26. d. See pg. 348, LO 8
27. b. See pg. 356, LO 10
28. c. See pg. 362, LO 11
29. c. See pg. 362, LO 11
30. a. See pg. 350, LO 9

True/False

1. F. See pg. 349, LO 8
2. F. See pg. 358, LO 10
3. T. See pg. 367, LO 11
4. T. See pg. 366, LO 11
5. F. See pg. 367, LO 11
6. T. See pg. 364, LO 11
7. F. See pg. 362, LO 11
8. T. See pg. 330, LO 4
9. F. See pg. 330, LO 4
10. T. See pg. 346, LO 4
11. F. See pg. 349, LO 8
12. F. See pg. 350, LO 9
13. T. See pg. 343, LO 5
14. T. See pg. 367, LO 11
15. T. See pg. 328, LO 2
16. F. See pg. 331, LO 6
17. T. See pg. 342, LO 5
18. F. See pg. 330, LO 4
19. F. See pg. 334, LO 5
20. F. See pg. 356, LO 10
21. F. See pg. 332, LO 5
22. T. See pg. 335, LO 5

Study Guide

23. T. See pg. 346, LO 7
24. F. See pg. 346, LO 7
25. F. See pg. 346, LO 7

Fill-in-the-Blank

1. asportation. See pg. 362, LO 11
2. Statutory. See pg. 346, LO 7
3. sodomy. See pg. 328, LO 4
4. nonconsent. See pg. 332, LO 5
5. penetration. See pg. 333, LO 7
6. age. See pg. 346, LO 7
7. false. See pg. 367, LO 11
8. attempted. See pg. 348, LO 8
9. shield. See pg. 330, LO 4
10. extrinsic force. See pg. 335, LO 5
11. gender. See pg. 331, LO 4
12. reasonable. See pg. 346, LO 7
13. serious. See pg. 347, LO 8
14. Conditional. See pg. 348, LO 8
15. intrinsic. See pg. 335, LO 5

Essays

1. Discuss the four types of crimes against persons.

   Crimes against persons involve taking a life (criminal homicide), unwanted sexual invasions (rape, sodomy, sexual contact, sexual assault and other sexually invasive offenses), bodily injury and threats of bodily injury (battery, assault, menacing) and personal restraint (kidnapping and false imprisonment). There is variance among the states as to the grades of the crimes, often based upon the level of mens rea and the degree of harm experienced by the victim. Modern statutes concerning stalking and domestic violence are new approaches to older crimes against persons that attempt to resolve some of the difficulty in prosecuting these offenses. LO 1

2. Over time, how has the law of rape changed with regard to force and consent?

   Rape law has changed over time with regard to the force and consent requirements which seem to be intertwined. Although lack of consent has always been the pivotal issue in determining whether the contact is rape, many recent sexual assault statutes have shifted the emphasis away from whether there was consent by the victim because they work to the disadvantage of women who acquiesced to threatened violence. Similarly, the Model Penal Code eliminated the consent as an element in the rape law. The law's development is seen by its transition from the utmost resistance standard to the reasonable resistance standard as a show of lack of consent. Currently, many states have dropped the resistance requirement completely in stranger rapes. The element of force or threat of force is part of the actus reus requirement of rape both historically and under modern statutes (except for statutory rape). States vary on whether the intrinsic force used to accomplish the rape, or some additional extrinsic force, is necessary to satisfy the force requirement. The resistance issue playas part in the force discussion in the same manner it did as to the issue of consent. LO 4, 5

3. Compare and contrast the crimes (and elements) of kidnapping and false imprisonment.

   Kidnapping and false imprisonment are both crimes of personal restraint. They differ in that kidnapping requires the element of asportation whereas false imprisonment does not. Asportation means that the victim is moved a substantial distance from one area to another, but how far that distance is varies by state and in the end is a jury question. Both kidnapping and false imprisonment require that the offender intends to deprive the victim of personal liberty (to come and go as we please-the right of locomotion). The carrying away requirement of kidnapping is not present in false imprisonment. False imprisonment is compelling another person to remain where he doesn't want to remain. These can be forcible detentions, but many statutes find false imprisonment with any interference with the person's liberty. L0 11

4. Compare and contrast the crimes of assault and battery.

   Battery involves causing physical harm or injury to another. It requires unwanted and unjustified offensive touching that involves some injury. Assault is either threatened battery or attempted battery, and does not involve injury. The mens rea for battery varies from statute to statute, and batteries may be graded based upon the mens rea of the offender. Similarly, the degree of injury may determine the grade of the battery. The mens rea for attempted battery assault is the intent to commit a battery (purposeful and intentional behavior) and for threatened battery assault is the intent to frighten the victim. Attempted battery assault involves incomplete physical injury whereas threatened battery assault is directed at psychological or emotional harm. LO 8

5. Discuss the prevalence of acquaintance rape and attempts to combat acquaintance rape.

In the 1970s and 1980s the crime of rape underwent many modifications due, in part, to the recognition that many, if not most, were non-violent (though non-consensual). Nonconsensual sex between acquaintances make up the majority of rapes, but the criminal justice system has had difficulty in addressing "unarmed acquaintance rape." Victims are less likely to report, prosecutors less likely to prosecute, and jurors less likely to convict when the sexual encounter is between acquaintances. Unfortunately, the prevalence of "date rape" is high, and reporting is very, very low. Foreman's survey shows that one in five college women reported being physically forced to have sexual intercourse by her date. Of non-reported rapes, Williams found that 80 percent of the women who did not report indicated they had been raped by men they knew. LO 3

Chapter 11
Crimes Against Property

LEARNING OBJECTIVES

1. Know that crimes against other people's property are of three types: taking property, damaging or destroying property, and invading property.

2. Understand that the crime of theft grew out of the general social concern with violent crimes against persons.

3. Know that the federal mail fraud statute defines false pretenses much more broadly than common law fraud.

4. Know that it's illegal to receive stolen property only if you intend to keep it permanently.

5. Appreciate that the heart of robbery is the use of actual or threatened force to obtain someone else's property right now.

6. Understand that extortion differs from robbery in that the threat is to use force some time in the future.

7. Know that arson is a felony; criminal mischief is a misdemeanor.

8. Understand that the heart of both burglary and criminal trespass is invading other people's property, not taking, destroying, or damaging it.

9. Understand that criminal trespass used to be limited to unauthorized invasions of physical property, but now it includes unauthorized access to electronic information systems.

10. Know that identity theft is the most prevalent crime in the United States.

11. Appreciate that intellectual property theft results in billions of dollars in losses each year.

KEY TERMS AND CONCEPTS

- **theft**—the consolidated crimes of larceny, embezzlement, and false pretenses; p. 372

- **robbery**—taking and carrying away another's property by force or threat of force with the intent to permanently deprive the owner of possession; p. 372

- **fraud**—abuse of trust generally involving an intentional misrepresentation that causes another to turn over property or money; p. 372

- **receiving stolen property**—benefiting from someone else's property without having participated in the wrongful acquisition in the first place; p. 372

- **arson**—intentionally burning a house or other structure; p. 372

- **conversion**—illegal use of another's property; p. 373

- **criminal mischief**—misdemeanor of damaging or destroying other people's property; p. 372

- **burglary**—breaking and entering a building with intent to commit a crime inside the building; p. 401

- **criminal trespass**—the crime of invading another person's property; p. 406

- **cybercrime**—crimes committed through the internet or some other computer network; p. 372

- **larceny**—taking and carrying away another person's property without the use of force with the intent to permanently deprive its owner of possession; p. 373

- **tangible property**—personal property (not real estate); p. 373

- **intangible property**—property that lacks a physical existence (examples include stock options, trademarks, licenses, and patents); p. 373

- **embezzlement**—the crime of lawfully gaining possession of someone else's property and later converting it to one's own use; p. 374

- **abuse-of-trust crimes (in property crime)**—crimes committed by caretakers; p. 374

- **white-collar crimes**—crimes growing out of opportunities to get someone else's property provided by the perpetrator's occupation; p. 374

- **obtaining property by false pretenses**—in modern law, it's often called "theft by deceit," and it means having the specific intent to obtain property by deceit and lies; p. 374

- **consolidated theft statutes**—eliminate the artificial need to separate theft into distinct offenses according to their *actus reus*; p. 375

- **common law fraud**—the precursor for the crime of false pretenses. It involved the actor knowing making false representations with the intent to obtain property by deceit; p. 378

- **federal mail fraud statute**—statute which broadened the definition of fraud and includes using the mail to perpetuate schemes to defraud for the purpose of obtaining money or property; p. 378

- **Ponzi schemes**—A Ponzi scheme is a fraudulent investment operation that pays returns to investors from their own money or money paid by subsequent investors rather than any profit earned; p. 381

- **extortion (blackmail)**—misappropriation of another's property by means of threats to inflict bodily harm in the future; p. 390

- **burning (in arson)**—setting a building on fire, and the fire actually reaches the structure; p. 396

- **general-intent definition (of arson)**—the mens rea of arson which requires the actor intend only to start the fire and not necessarily to intend the resulting harm; p. 397

- **first-degree arson**—burning homes or other occupied structures where there is danger to human life; p. 397

- **second-degree arson**—burning unoccupied structures, vehicles and boats; p 397

- **breaking (in burglary)**—at common law the breaking element of burglary required a violent entry (knocking down doors and smashing windows). Now many statutes do not require the breaking element; p. 402

- **entering (in burglary)**—another element of burglary that has changed overtime. Even as early as the 1700s this element had broad definition and many modern statutes do not require entering--these statutes substitute unlawful remaining for the unlawful entering; p. 402

- **surreptitious remaining element**—entering a structure lawfully with the intent to commit a crime inside; p. 403

Study Guide

- **intellectual property**—information and services stored in and transmitted to and from electronic data banks; a rapidly developing area of property crimes; p. 408

- **identity theft**—stealing another person's identity for the purpose of getting something of value; p. 408

CHAPTER OUTLINE

I. Taking other people's property
  A. **History of property crimes**
     1. General concern about violent crimes led to crime of common-law robbery.
        a. Taking someone else's property by force
     2. Larceny
        a. Taking and carrying away
        b. Intent to permanently deprive someone else of their property
        c. Tangible personal property (property valuable itself, like a ring)
        d. Intangible personal property (paper that represents something of value like stocks, bonds, checks)
     3. Embezzlement (first white-collar crime)
        a. Keeping (converting) property lawfully obtained
        b. "Converting" substitutes for "taking" in larceny
        c. Caretakers (bailees) taking someone else's property that was handed over to them voluntarily (like bank clerks)
           (1) Abuse-of-trust crimes
           (2) White-collar crimes
     4. False pretenses (theft by deceit)
        a. Tricking (deceiving) someone into giving up their property
        b. Deceiving substitutes for taking in larceny and converting in embezzlements.
  B. **Larceny and Theft**
     1. Modern consolidated theft statutes—turn away from history to logic in consolidating embezzlement larceny, and false pretenses into one crime of theft: getting other people's money by taking, converting, or deceiving
     2. Elements
        a. Purposefully (intentionally), or knowingly
        b. Taking and carrying away, converting, or swindling
        c. Someone else's property
        d. *Case: People v. Olivo, Gasparik, and Spatzier*
  C. **Theft by False Pretenses**
     1. Purposefully taking by deceit or lies
     2. Common law fraud
     3. Elements summarized
        a. Knowingly misrepresenting a fact

    b. Intending that the victim be unaware that it is a misrepresentation
    c. Intending that the victim rely and act upon the misrepresentation
    d. Offender obtains victim's property due to victim's reliance on the misrepresentation
  D. Federal Mail Fraud Statute
    1. Devising a scheme which uses mail to execute a scheme to defraud in order to obtain money or property
    2. Used to prosecute Madoff for ponzi scheme
    3. Ponzi scheme: Deceiving individuals into believing they are investing in something of value when they are not and then using the money of later investors to repay initial investors
    4. Civil and criminal liability for violation of federal mail fraud statutes
      a. *Case: U.S. v. Madoff*
      b. *Case: U.S. v. Coughlin*
  E. Robbery—Crimes against persons and property
    1. **Robbery *actus reus***—taking and carrying away someone else's property by force or threat of immediate force
      a. *Case: State v. Curley*
      b. *Case: Commonwealth v. Zangari*
    2. **Robbery *mens rea***—intent to take property from another person by force or threat of immediate force
    3. **Degrees of Robbery**—measured by
      a. Force (kind and degree) used
      b. Injury (kind and degree) inflicted
  F. Extortion (blackmail)
    1. Circumstance of time distinguishes extortion from robbery
    2. Extortion elements
      a. *Actus reus*—taking someone else's property by threat of a variety of future harms
      b. *Mens rea*—intent to take someone else's property by threat of future harm
  G. Receiving Stolen Property
    1. It is a crime not only to take someone else's property but also to "receive" (accept) property already stolen.
    2. *Actus reus*—receiving means controlling (not necessarily physically) property.
    3. *Mens rea* varies from knowingly to recklessly to negligently, depending on the state.
    4. *Mens rea* also includes the intent to keep the property permanently.
      a. *Case: Sonnier v. State*

II. Damaging and destroying other people's property
  A. Arson
    1. **Arson *actus reus*: burning**
      a. *Case: Williams v. State*

2. **Arson *mens rea*** — Intent to commit the act of burning or setting fire to a building (not necessary to intend to damage or destroy the building)
3. **The degrees of arson**
   a. First degree — Burning occupied buildings
   b. Second degree — Burning unoccupied structures

B. **Criminal Mischief**
1. **Criminal mischief *actus reus*** — Burning, exploding, flooding, or committing some other dangerous act; could include tampering (creating danger to property)
2. **Criminal mischief *mens rea*** — Varies tremendously amongst states
   a. *Case: Commonwealth v. Mitchell*

III. **Invading other people's property**

A. **Burglary**
1. **Common law burglary elements**
   a. Breaking and entering; of dwelling place of another; at night; with intent to commit a felony therein.
2. **Burglary *actus reus*** — entering or remaining in (and in a few states "breaking into") someone else's "structure"
   a. Breaking — Common law requirement with broad definition, most states no longer "breaking."
   b. Entering — Common law requirement broadly defined, some states no longer require unlawful entering, other states don't require entering at all
   c. Surreptitious remaining — Entering lawfully and then waiting inside to commit a crime
   d. Circumstances — Is the structure occupied? Is it another's place? Is it nighttime?
   e. *Case: Jewell v. State*
3. **Burglary *mens rea*** — Specific-intent crime
   a. Intent to commit the breaking, entering, or remaining
   b. Intent to commit a crime once inside the structure
4. **Degrees of burglary**
   a. According to seriousness
   b. According to the type of structure

B. **Criminal Trespass** — Heart of crime is unwanted presence
1. **The elements of criminal trespass**
   a. Unauthorized entering or remaining on the premises of another
2. **The degrees of criminal trespass**
   a. MPC has three: misdemeanor, petty misdemeanor, and violation

C. **Cybercrimes**
1. **Identity theft**
   a. Currently one of the most prevalent crimes — taking someone else's property by first stealing their identity.
   b. Huge consequences, but difficult to catch

        c. Family members, friends, and neighbors get information from credit cards, utility services, bank accounts, etc.
        d. *Case: Remsburg v. Docusearch, Inc.*
    2. **Intellectual Property Theft**
        a. Taking people's ideas
        b. Protected by copyright laws, laws on trademarks, trade secrets, patents, theft, damage, and destruction of intellectual property
        c. Hackers and cybercriminals
        d. *Case: U. S. v. Ancheta*

CHAPTER SUMMARY

Crimes against property fall into one of three categories: taking it, damaging or destroying it, or invading it. In recent centuries, technology has afforded many new ways to steal. The new crimes created to deal with the new types of property crime are really only new ways of committing the three original types of crimes. Computer and internet crimes consist of taking, damaging or destroying, or invading other people's computers or the information stored on them.

Historically, all crimes of taking property descend from larceny, which means sneaking away with, or stealing, someone else's property. However, as times changed, other crimes developed to address the fact that sometimes people wrongfully take property entrusted to them, called embezzlement, or trick people into obtaining title of the property, termed false pretenses. Modern consolidated theft statutes now deal with the various ways people acquire other's property (sneaking away, converting, through fraud). Theft (or larceny) is a specific-intent crime; it requires the intent to permanently deprive the other person of their property.

Robbery is a crime against persons and their property. It involves taking someone else's property from their person by force or the threat of immediate force. Robbery consists of three elements. The *actus reus* components are: 1) the taking and carrying away, 2) by immediate force or the threat of immediate force, 3) another person's property from their body or presence. The *mens rea* is the intent to permanently deprive the victim of their property by immediate force or the threat of immediate force. The circumstance element is that the property is taken from the victim's person or presence.

Extortion, also called blackmail, is a crime against persons and their property. Theft by extortion is taking someone else's property by threats of future harm. Time separates extortion from robbery. Robbery is a threat to hurt someone right now if they don't give up their property, while extortion is a threat to hurt someone later. The elements of extortion consist of *mens rea,* the specific intent to take someone else's property by means of threats, and *actus reus,* a specific threat by which the taking of property is accomplished.

Obtaining property already stolen by someone else is still regarded as a crime. Traditionally, it was called receiving stolen property.

Arson, which means damaging or destroying other people's buildings by fire or explosives, is a felony. Criminal mischief, which means destroying or tampering with other people's property or causing money loss by "expensive practical jokes" or false threats, is a misdemeanor. Criminal mischief includes three types of harm to tangible property: 1) destruction or damage by fire, explosives, or other "dangerous acts" (the original malicious mischief); 2) tampering with tangible property so as to endanger it; and 3) deception or threat that causes monetary loss.

The elements of common-law burglary from which our modern burglary emerged included: 1) breaking and entering (*actus reus*), 2) the dwelling of another (circumstance element), 3) in the nighttime (circumstance element), 4) with the intent to commit a felony inside (*mens rea*).

Modern burglary has outgrown its common-law origin of just protecting homes. Now, you can "burglarize" all kinds of structures, even vehicles, at any time of the day. The breaking and entering elements have been eliminated or modified, and the predicate crimes do not always have to be a felony.

A less serious crime related to burglary is criminal trespass. The *actus reus* of criminal trespass is the unauthorized entering of or remaining on the premises of another. The *mens rea* varies, including 1) knowingly entering or remaining without authority invitation, license privilege, or legality; 2) specific intent to enter or remain without authority for some unlawful purpose (a few states); or 3) strict liability.

Although relatively new, cybercrime is the most common crime in America. It consists of identity theft and intellectual property theft. Identity theft involves taking another's property by stealing their name and personal information (their identity). Intellectual property theft is taking someone's ideas or creative endeavors. Cybercrime involves the use of computers to gain access to identity, ideas, or creative endeavors. Cybercriminals are smart, skilled, and motivated; and catching intellectual property and identity thieves is very difficult.

PRACTICE TEST BANK

MULTIPLE CHOICE

1. A person who receives stolen property and then resells it is called a _____.
   a. unlawful receiver
   b. unlawful wholesaler
   c. larceny receptor
   d. fence

2. At common law, the offense of burglary _____.
   a. could only be committed at night
   b. included all types of buildings
   c. required entering but not breaking
   d. was a strict liability crime

3. Under modern approaches to burglary and assuming all the elements, if the burglar entered the building unlawfully, in an unusual fashion, such as coming down the chimney, this _____.
   a. could not be a burglary because there was no breaking
   b. could be a burglary but only if the building was occupied
   c. could still be a burglary
   d. is not a burglary because there was no unlawful entry

4. In many states, and the Model Penal Code, the *actus reus* of arson requires _____.
   a. only that the defendant start a fire
   b. that some part of the building be charred
   c. that some damage to the building occur
   d. that some part of the building be burned

5. At common law, the intent to commit a crime in the dwelling required that the intended crime be _____.
   a. a crime of violence
   b. a felony
   c. any form of theft
   d. any property crime

6. In contrast to earlier burglary law, by 1900 in most statutes _____.
   a. the breaking element became a mere technicality
   b. the breaking element evolved into a strict liability offense
   c. the requirement of intent to commit a crime in the building was eliminated
   d. the requirement that the building be occupied at the time of the burglary was eliminated

7. In addition to the unlawful entry version of burglary, the Model Penal Code and some jurisdictions also have a/n _____ version of burglary.
    a. surreptitious remaining
    b. constructive concealment
    c. constructive burglary
    d. entry by deceit

8. In the case of *U.S. v. Madoff*, the defendant unlawfully got rich by _____.
    a. stealing someone's identity
    b. embezzling bank funds
    c. receiving stolen property from the largest heist in America
    d. engaging in a Ponzi scheme and violating the federal mail fraud statute.

9. In *Remsburg v. Docusearch*, the information given to Youens enabled him to _____.
    a. use the victim's identity to purchase airline tickets
    b. plant a worm in a computer
    c. obtain a social security number and get gainful employment
    d. find and kill someone

10. Most states have attempted to better organize theft law by enacting _____ statutes.
    a. omnibus larceny
    b. comprehensive larceny
    c. complete theft
    d. consolidated theft

11. The specific-intent element of receiving stolen property is _____.
    a. knowing the property is stolen
    b. receiving property
    c. deceiving the true owner
    d. finding property that is stolen

12. A trademark is a type of _____.
    a. tangible property
    b. intellectual property
    c. identity property
    d. personal property

13. Criminal trespass can be accomplished through entry _____.
    a. onto land only
    b. onto land and into buildings
    c. onto land, into buildings, and through computers
    d. into buildings only

14. The court in *Jewell v. State* found that Jewell could be liable for burglary because _____.
    a. the house had never been Barry Jewell's because Bridget had bought it in her name
    b. the court found that the statute's requirement "of another" was satisfied by unauthorized entry
    c. the court found that Jewell and the victim were divorced
    d. Jewell obviously had the intent to commit assault when he entered through the kitchen window

15. Which of the following is NOT a reason for the nighttime requirement of common-law burglary?
    a. It was easier to commit crimes at night.
    b. It is harder to identify suspects you've seen at night.
    c. Nighttime intrusions frighten victims more than daytime intrusions.
    d. At common law, there were no police officers at night.

16. Federal mail fraud is _____.
    a. a civil offense
    b. a civil and criminal offense
    c. a criminal offense
    d. only a proposed law and thus neither a civil nor criminal offense.

17. The offense of burglary has _____ *mens rea* elements.
    a. two
    b. three
    c. four
    d. five

18. Which of the following elements of common-law burglary is retained in most modern statutes?
    a. The burglary occurred at night.
    b. The entry must be unlawful.
    c. The building must be a dwelling.
    d. There must be an actual, physical breaking.

19. Under modern statutes, the crime the burglar intended to commit inside the building _____.
    a. must be a crime that is *mala prohibita*
    b. has been expanded beyond the common-law rule of felonies only
    c. is limited to crimes of theft
    d. must be a felony as also required at common law

20. If a person is apprehended while unlawfully on someone else's property, but there is no evidence of another crime, or intent to commit another crime, the proper charge would be _____.
    a. burglary
    b. criminal trespass
    c. attempted invasion of privacy
    d. discrepancy

21. The offense of burglary is a crime that has _____.
    a. no *mens rea* elements
    b. a general-intent component but not a specific-intent element
    c. a specific-intent, but not a general-intent
    d. both specific- and general-intent elements

22. The specific-intent of robbery is intent to _____.
    a. harm the victim
    b. permanently deprive the victim of the property
    c. commit a crime
    d. obtain title to the property

23. One of the circumstance elements of burglary is _____.
    a. type of structure
    b. constructive breaking
    c. intent to enter unlawfully
    d. surreptitious remaining

24. Which of the following are *mens rea* elements of burglary?
    a. intent to damage or destroy the building
    b. intent to break and enter or surreptitiously remain
    c. intent to deprive the owner of possession and ownership of the structure
    d. intent to surprise and harm the persons in the structure

25. As compared to burglary, criminal trespass has _____.
    a. fewer elements
    b. greater penalties
    c. more elements
    d. a longer history

26. The *mens rea* in most types of arson is intent to _____.
    a. destroy a building by fire
    b. enter a building to start a fire
    c. set a fire to a building
    d. break into a building and start a fire

27. The defendant walks into the bank while it is open to the public and hides in the public restroom. After the bank closes he attempts break into the vault. This is the _____ type of burglary.
    a. privileged entry
    b. surreptitious remaining
    c. false pretenses
    d. constructive entry

28. Many incidents that were burglaries at common law would today _____.
    a. be criminal trespasses
    b. not be crimes
    c. be *mala in se* crimes
    d. also be burglaries

29. The law of criminal trespass has been expanded beyond its traditional coverage to now include _____ trespass.
    a. real estate
    b. personal property
    c. computer
    d. curtilage

30. The practice of employees and insiders altering or manipulating data, credit limits, or other financial information is called _____.
    a. piggybacking
    b. sniffing
    c. data diddling
    d. a salami attack

TRUE/FALSE

1. At common law, walking through a wide open door into a home to commit a felony therein was a burglary.
    a. true
    b. false

2. To be guilty of burglary, the burglar does not have to complete the crime he intended to commit.
    a. true
    b. false

3. The modern definition of burglary is narrower than the common-law definition.
    a. true
    b. false

Study Guide

4. The two offenses that involve both thefts and force or threat of force are robbery and burglary.
   a. true
   b. false

5. Picking a pocket without any additional action or force by the defendant is not a robbery.
   a. true
   b. false

6. In some states, a purse snatching, where the victim is not threatened and does not resist, and the purse is not otherwise attached to the person, is not a robbery.
   a. true
   b. false

7. Intellectual property theft requires the use of computers.
   a. true
   b. false

8. Robbery requires that the robber threaten to use force immediately.
   a. true
   b. false

9. The *mens rea* of extortion is the specific intent to obtain property by deceit.
   a. true
   b. false

10. The definition of arson has contracted as compared to its definition at common law.
    a. true
    b. false

11. Most arson statutes create specific-intent crimes.
    a. true
    b. false

12. The *actus reus* of arson is to set fire to a structure.
    a. true
    b. false

13. Extortion is a strict liability crime.
    a. true
    b. false

14. Many states divide arson into one or more degrees or types.
    a. true
    b. false

15. Surreptitious remaining is a type of extortion.
    a. true
    b. false

16. Abuse-of-trust crimes, such as embezzlement, eventually became white-collar crimes.
    a. true
    b. false

17. For common-law burglary, a *mens rea* element was that the crime occurred at night.
    a. true
    b. false

18. Until the 1900s, the *actus reus* of burglary consisted of only constructive breaking.
    a. true
    b. false

19. At common law, the breaking element of burglary was by a surreptitious remaining element.
    a. true
    b. false

20. Robbery is a crime against both persons and property.
    a. true
    b. false

21. Robbery has a specific-intent element.
    a. true
    b. false

22. Robbery has a circumstance element.
    a. true
    b. false

23. While picking a pocket, the thief is grabbed by the victim. The thief pushes the victim away and takes the wallet. This is a robbery.
    a. true
    b. false

24. Most robbery victims are physically harmed.
    a. true
    b. false

25. Identity theft involves the violation of copyright and trademark laws.
    a. true
    b. false

FILL-IN-THE-BLANK

1. The common law *mens rea* of arson was that it be done willfully and _____.

2. Some states have removed the unlawful _____ element to create a new form of burglary by surreptitious remaining.

3. The Model Penal Code limits the crime of burglary to _____ structures or vehicles.

4. _____ is the crime committed most often in the United States of America.

5. The illegal use or keeping of someone else's property is called _____.

6. The form of theft involving lies or deception is called _____.

7. The MPC divides arson into two degrees, based on the defendants' _____.

8. A _____ is a series of minor computer crimes (such as hacking into a computer and taking one penny from each account) which is difficult to detect.

9. The *actus reus* of common-law burglary is breaking and _____.

10. Many states have combined a number of types of theft into one statute that is termed a _____ theft statute.

11. Personal property, which can be physically held, is called _____.

12. _____ is the unlawful entry or remaining on property or in a building of another.

13. If a pickpocket must push or shove the victim to get the wallet, the crime becomes one of _____.

14. _____ is permanently keeping someone's property when you only have a temporary right to possess it.

15. Trade secrets, information, programs, and data are known as _____ property.

ESSAY

1. Compare and contrast intellectual property crimes and identity theft crimes. How has the rise of computer use enhanced these crimes?

2. Compare larceny, embezzlement, and false pretenses.

Study Guide

3. Compare the crimes of burglary and criminal trespass.

4. Compare and contrast robbery and extortion.

5. Compare and contrast arson, and criminal trespass.

CHAPTER 11 ANSWER KEY

Multiple Choice

1. d. See pg. 392, LO 4
2. a. See pg. 402, LO 8
3. c. See pgs. 402-403, LO 8
4. a. See pg. 396, LO 7
5. b. See pg. 402, LO 8
6. a. See pg. 402, LO 8
7. a. See pg. 403, LO 8
8. d. See pgs. 378-379, LO 3
9. d. See pg. 409, LO 9
10. d. See pg. 375, LO 2
11. a. See pg. 392, LO 4
12. b. See pg. 408, LO 2
13. c. See pg. 406, LO 9
14. b. See pg. 405, LO 8
15. d. See pg. 405, LO 8
16. b. See pg. 378, LO 3
17. a. See pg. 403, LO 8
18. b. See pg. 402, LO 8
19. b. See pg. 405, LO 8
20. b. See pg. 406, LO 8
21. d. See pg. 405, LO 8
22. b. See pg. 389, LO 5
23. a. See pg. 403, LO 8
24. b. See pg. 405, LO 8
25. a. See pg. 407, LO 9
26. c. See pg. 397, LO 7
27. b. See pg. 403, LO 8
28. d. See pg. 402, LO 8
29. c. See pg. 406, LO 9
30. c. See pg. 413, LO 10

True/False

1. F. See pg. 402, LO 8
2. T. See pg. 405, LO 8
3. F. See pg. 402, LO 8
4. F. See pg. 385, LO 5
5. T. See pg. 387, LO 5
6. T. See pg. 387, LO 5
7. F. See pg. 408, LO 11
8. T. See pg. 387, LO 5
9. F. See pg. 390, LO 6
10. F. See pgs. 396-397, LO 7
11. F. See pg. 397, LO 7
12. T. See pg. 396, LO 7
13. F. See pg. 390, LO 6
14. T. See pg. 398, LO 7
15. F. See pg. 403, LO 5, 8
16. T. See pg. 374, LO 2
17. F. See pg. 403, LO 8
18. F. See pg. 402, LO 8
19. F. See pg. 402, LO 8
20. T. See pg. 385, LO 5
21. T. See pg. 389, LO 5
22. T. See pg. 386, LO 5

23. T. See pg. 387, LO 5
24. F. See pg. 390, LO 5
25. F. See pg. 408, LO 10

Fill-in-the-Blank

1. maliciously. See pg. 397, LO 7
2. entry. See pg. 403, LO 8
3. occupied. See pg. 403, LO 8
4. Identity theft. See pg. 408, LO 10
5. conversion. See pg. 373, LO 2
6. false pretenses. See pg. 374, LO 2
7. blameworthiness. See pg. 397, LO 7
8. salami attack. See pg. 413, LO 10
9. entering. See pg. 402, LO 8
10. consolidated. See pg. 375, LO 2
11. tangible property. See pg. 373, LO 1
12. Criminal trespass. See pg. 406, LO 9
13. robbery. See pg. 387, LO 5
14. Embezzlement. See pg. 374, LO 2
15. intellectual. See pg. 408, LO 11

Essays

1. Compare and contrast intellectual property crimes and identity theft crimes. How has the rise of computer use enhanced these crimes?

   Identity theft involves stealing another's personal information for illegal gain or to harm the victim whereas intellectual property theft involves stealing another's ideas for illegal gain. Both of these crimes have been expanded in an unprecedented way by the internet. The storage of information on national and international databases makes victims particularly vulnerable. LO 10 11

2. Compare larceny, embezzlement, and false pretenses.

Larceny was the original common law crime of theft. It involved sneaking away the tangible property of another. Over time, there was a need to respond to the new ways that people were taking the property of another. The crime of embezzlement arose to cover situations in which an individual was initially lawfully in possession of the property, but then unlawfully converted for his own use and permanently depriving the lawful owner of the property. The crime of false pretenses arose to deal with the situation when an individual misrepresented something in order to unlawfully get ownership of the property of another. For example, if you sold a painting you know is not a Van Gogh as a Van Gogh for millions of dollars you make a material misrepresentation in order to deprive the other person of their property. In modern times, most states no longer distinguish between larceny, embezzlement, and false pretenses, choosing to enact consolidated theft statutes covering the various ways thieves come into possession of the property of another. LO 2

3. Compare the crimes of burglary and criminal trespass.

Criminal trespass and burglary are both crimes of invading another's property. The crime of burglary adds the element of the intent to commit a crime while on the property. At common law, there were very specific requirements for burglary including the elements of breaking, entering, at night, dwelling, of another, with the intent to commit a felony. Many of those elements have been relaxed under modern statutes. Now, it is often sufficient that a person enter lawfully but remain unlawfully. States vary on the nature of the predicate crime. Some require that it be theft, others that it must be a felony, still others allow intent to commit any crime (misdemeanor or felony—other than trespass). LO 8

4. Compare and contrast robbery and extortion.

Robbery is taking property of another by force or threat of force. Extortion is taking the property of another by some future threat. For example, robbery would involve a person taking another's wallet after demanding, "Your money or your life." Extortion would involve a person saying, "If you don't give me $10,000 I will send Guido to break your kneecaps next week." Both robbery and extortion involve taking someone else's property by threat of force, but extortion threatens future harm. Additionally, extortion can involve threats of not only physical harm but also would include threats to embarrass the other. LO 1, 6

5. Compare and contrast arson and criminal trespass.

Arson and criminal mischief are both crimes that damage or destroy another's property. Arson involves setting fire to another's property. Common law arson required the property be another's dwelling, and that the fire had to reach the structure. Modern arson statutes tend to grade arson based upon the type of structure and the amount of damage. Arson also includes explosions. At common law, arson was considered a "general intent" crime meaning that the person needed to intend to light something on fire and need not intend to destroy the property. Now, modern statutes tend to grade arson based to some extent on the intent of the offender. Criminal mischief involves damaging the tangible property of another. One extension of criminal mischief that doesn't necessarily involve the destruction of property includes using deception or threat to cause someone to suffer a monetary loss. State statutes on arson and criminal mischief vary greatly as to the mens rea requirement and occasionally as to the actus reus requirement. LO 1, LO 7

Chapter 12
Crimes Against Public Order and Morals

LEARNING OBJECTIVES

1. To understand how disorderly conduct crimes ("quality of life") are aimed at bad manners in public.

2. To know how efforts to control bad manners in public underscore the tension between order and liberty in constitutional democracies.

3. To understand that the "broken windows" theory claims "quality of life" crimes are linked to serious crime.

4. Appreciate that the widespread consensus among all classes, races, and communities that "street people" and "street gangs" bad behavior should be controlled has shaped the content of the criminal law.

5. To understand how most people are more worried about bad public manners than they are about serious crimes.

6. To know how "victimless" crimes against public decency (the ancient "crimes against public morals") are a hot-button issue between those who believe the criminal law should enforce morality and those who believe the nonviolent behavior of competent adults is none of the law's business.

KEY TERMS AND CONCEPTS

- **disorderly conduct crimes**—crimes including individual disorderly conduct and group disorderly conduct; p. 420

- **quality of life crimes**—breaches of minimum standards of decent behavior in public; p. 420

- **order**—behavior in public that comports with minimum community standards of civility; p. 420

- **liberty**—the right of individuals to go about in public, free of undue interference; p. 420

- **crimes against public order**—crimes that harm the public peace generally (for example, disorderly conduct) also known as "bad manner crimes" or "quality of life" crimes; p. 420

- **victimless crimes**—crimes without complaining victims (for example, recreational illegal drug users); p. 420

- **actual disorderly conduct**—completed disorderly conduct (fighting); p. 421

- **constructive disorderly conduct**—acts that tend toward causing others to breach the peace; p. 421

- **unlawful assembly**—ancient crime of three or more persons gathering together to commit an unlawful act; p. 422

- **rout**—three or more people moving toward the commission of a riot; p. 422

- **riot**—disorderly conduct committed by more than three persons; p. 422

- **broken-windows theory**—theory that minor offenses or disorderly conduct can lead to a rise in serious crime; p. 424

- **vagrancy**—ancient crime of poor people wandering around with no visible means of support; p. 425

- **loitering**—remaining in one place with no apparent purpose; p. 425

- **preliminary injunction**—a temporary order issued by a court after giving notice and holding a hearing; p. 431

- **panhandling**—stopping people on the street to ask them for food or money; p. 431

- **time, place, and manner test**—three-part test to determine whether a statute places legitimate limits on the First Amendment right of free speech; p. 431

- **public nuisance injunctions**—an action in which city attorneys ask the courts to declare gang activities and gang members public nuisances and to issue injunctions to abate their activities; p. 440

- **civil gang injunctions**—non criminal lawsuits brought by cities to bar gang members from gang activities; p. 442

CHAPTER OUTLINE

I. Disorderly conduct crimes can involve group or individual activity.
    A. Historically, these were largely ignored misdemeanors, punishment was minor, convictions rarely appealed.
    B. Now considered important in the criminal justice system because they affect a large number of defendants, involve much public activity, and influence people's view of public justice.
    C. **Individual disorderly conduct** in Model Penal Code
        1. *Actus reus*—Three kinds
            a. Fighting
            b. Making unreasonable noise, using offensive language
            c. Creating hazardous or offensive conditions
        2. *Mens rea*—Acting purposely, knowingly, or recklessly
        3. Special individual disorderly conduct sections in Model Penal Code
            a. Knowingly spreading false alarms
            b. Appearing drunk in public (no *mens rea* requirement)
            c. Loitering or prowling (no *mens rea* requirement)
            d. Purposely or recklessly obstructing highways or other public passages
            e. Purposely disrupting lawful meetings, processions, or gatherings
    D. **Group disorderly conduct** ("riot")
        1. Background
            a. Three ancient misdemeanor crimes (unlawful assembly, rout, riot)
            b. Riot Act of 1714—Made riot a felony
            c. "Reading the riot act" comes from this act
        2. Elements
            a. *Actus reus*—Participate in disorderly conduct
            b. *Mens rea*
                (1) Have specific intent or purpose to commit or facilitate the commission of a felony
                (2) Have the purpose to prevent or coerce an official action
                (3) Have knowledge that any participant used or plans to use a deadly weapon

II. Quality-of-life crimes involved both constitutional and criminological concerns.
    A. Broken-windows theory
        1. Theory—There's a link between "minor" quality-of-life offenses (public drunkenness, panhandling, graffiti, vandalism, prostitution, loitering) and serious crimes (rape, robbery, burglary).
        2. Reality
            a. National debate concentrates on serious crime; local officials and public more worried about quality-of-life offenses.
            b. Empirical findings mixed as to link between serious crime and disorder.

(1) Some find a causal relationship (Kelling, Skogan)
(2) Others find common origins but not a causal link (Sampson and Radenbush)
B. Disconnect between national focus (on serious crime) and local concern (on quality of life crimes).
C. Since the 1980s, state statutes and city ordinances have been used to fight the crimes against public order and preserve quality of life in communities.
D. Courts balance social and community interest in individual liberty and privacy.
E. **Vagrancy and Loitering**
1. Two early offenses aimed at roaming around (vagrancy) with no visible means of support and standing around (loitering)
2. Vagrancy and loitering have been tailored to meet modern problems of "bad public manners" of street people and gangs.
3. **Vagrancy**—Due process (void-for-vagueness) restricts power to criminalize vagrancy
   a. *Case: Papachristou v. City of Jacksonville (1972)*
4. **Loitering**
   a. *Case: Kolender v. Lawson (1983)*
5. Vagrancy and loitering can overcome the vagueness objection if they're defined to include more than just roaming around or standing around.
6. San Francisco's efforts to legislate against these quality-of-life crimes
   a. *Case: Joyce v. City and County of San Francisco*
H. **Panhandling**
1. Panhandling statutes call the ancient crime of public begging into service to control "aggressive" begging by "street people."
2. Bans on panhandling don't apply to "organized charities" like the Salvation Army.
3. Panhandling is "speech" protected by the First Amendment.
   a. Right to panhandle is "commercial speech" and so it's less protected than other types of speech.
   b. States can control time, place (subways), and manner ("aggressive") of panhandling.
   c. States have limited ability control the content of panhandling.
4. *Case: Gresham v. Peterson*
I. **Gang Activity**
1. "Bands of loitering youth" scare ordinary people.
2. *Case: City of Chicago v. Morales*
3. Anti-gang ordinances raise due process questions (liberty and void-for-vagueness).
4. Anti-gang ordinances meet due process and liberty requirements if they define loitering more specifically than "hanging out with no apparent purpose" (permissible to ban loitering "for the purpose of committing a crime").
5. **Civil remedies**, such as having injunctions to abate public nuisances, have been used to control gangs.
6. *Case: People v. Acuna*

Chapter 12: Crimes Against Public Order and Morals

       7. Civil Gang Injunctions Research:
          a. youth crime rates are low, but media coverage and fear of gang activity is very high.
          b. Justice Policy Institute
          c. Maxson, Hennigan, and Sloand: positive evidence of short term effects (from injunctions) but no significant changes mid or long term.
          d. Grogger: violent crime decreases in the first year after an injunction
          e. *Case: City of Saint Paul v. East Side Boys and Selby Siders*

III. Victimless crimes are a controversial topic.
    A. Applies only to adults—Refers to crimes committed by adults who don't see themselves as victims
    B. **Victimless crime controversy**
        1. Referring to these crimes as "victimless" is controversial and involves the debate over the proper relationship between law and morality.
        2. The Wolfendon Report in 1950s England recommended decriminalizing private sexual conduct between consenting adults (homosexuality and prostitution).
    C. **Prostitution and Solicitation**—Today, both patrons and prostitutes (male or female) commit prostitution, and it is a crime almost everywhere in the U.S.

CHAPTER SUMMARY

Issues of public order include both individual disorderly conduct crimes, such as fighting or making unreasonable noise, and group disorderly conduct crimes, such as unlawful assembly, rout, and riot. Public order crimes also include "bad manner" crimes known as quality-of-life crimes. These ancient crimes, such as vagrancy and loitering, have been applied to new situations like street gangs. Public order crimes highlight the tension between order and liberty and include the controversial category of "victimless" crimes, such as prostitution and solicitation.

The Model Penal Code was very influential in shaping the current law. The code limits conduct that qualifies as disorderly conduct *actus reus* to three kinds: 1) fighting in public; 2) making unreasonable noise or using abusive language; and 3) creating a "hazardous or physically offensive condition" like strewing garbage, setting off "stink bombs," or turning off lights in crowded public places. The code was also unusual in that it had a *mens rea* element.

Group disorderly conduct consisted of three misdemeanors at the common law: unlawful assembly, rout, and riot. All three were aimed at preventing the ultimate evil of open disorder and breach of the public peace. Unlawful assembly was committed when a group of at least three persons joined together for the purpose of committing an unlawful act. If the group of three or more started toward achieving their purpose, they committed the crime of rout. If the group actually committed an unlawful violent act, or performed a lawful act in a "violent or tumultuous manner," they committed the crime of riot (if there were twelve of them). Committing riot didn't require the group to plan their unlawful violent act in advance. It was enough that once together they came up with the plan of violence.

Some disorderly conduct crimes are now called quality-of-life crimes, but they're still aimed at the same conduct—"bad manners" in public places. Efforts to control bad manners in public underscore the tension between order and liberty in constitutional democracies. Order is acting in accordance with ordinary standards of good manners and decency. Liberty is freedom to come and go and do as we like without government interference. The U.S. Supreme Court has used the term "ordered liberty" to describe this need for both.

Quality-of-life crimes are minor offenses, but the broken-windows theory claims (based on mixed empirical results) that they're linked to serious crime. In the 1980s, two scholars noted a deep public need for what they called a lost sense of public "good manners," especially in our largest cities. Professors James Q. Wilson and George L. Kelling (1982) suggested that what were labeled "petty crimes" weren't just "bothering" law-abiding people; they were connected to serious crime. They called this connection between disorderly conduct and serious crime the broken-windows theory. According to Kelling, research conducted since the article was written in 1982 has demonstrated a direct link between public disorder and crime. Others argue that both disorder and serious crime are caused by the same factors and that disorder does not always lead to serious crime.

There is widespread public support among all classes, races, and communities for controlling the offensive behaviors of "street people" and "street gangs." Most people are more worried about bad public manners (loitering, panhandling, public drunkenness, and prostitution) than they are about serious crimes (rape, robbery, burglary, and assault).

A number of state and city governments have passed criminal laws to regulate gang behavior. In some places, it's a crime to participate in a gang. Some statutes and ordinances have stiffened the penalties for crimes committed by gang members. Others make it a crime to encourage minors to participate in gangs. Some have applied organized crime statutes to gangs. A few have punished parents for their children's gang activities. Cities have also passed ordinances banning gang members from certain public places, particularly city parks.

Laws against loitering, vagrancy, panhandling, and non-criminal gang activity raise serious issues of due process (void-for-vagueness) and violation of First Amendment rights. Many loitering, vagrancy, panhandling, and anti-gang laws have been found to be unconstitutional. However, carefully written laws that are specific and content-neutral about time, place, and manner restrictions can be constitutional if other outlets for expression are available.

Government ability to regulate speech, including panhandling, varies with the type of public property involved. In traditional public forums, government power is weakest. Traditional public forums include public parks and streets. Government power is at an intermediate level in designated public forums, which are public places that the government has set aside or designated for speech activities. Auditoriums or public bulletin boards would be examples. Government power is strongest in nonpublic forums such as government office buildings and military bases.

In addition to criminal penalties, cities have also turned to civil remedies to control gang activity. For example, the government has requested and received public nuisance injunctions that declare gang activities and gang members to be public nuisances and order the "abatement" (stopping) of the public nuisance. Civil gang injunctions have been found to reduce gang activity in the short term but not in the long run. They have also been found to reduce violent crime in the first year after their implementation.

"Victimless" crimes (the ancient "crimes against public morals") are a controversial issue. It pits those who believe the criminal law should enforce morality against those who believe the private, nonviolent, consensual behavior of competent adults is none of the law's business. The Wolfendon Report, a British report from the 1950s, recommended that private consensual adult homosexuality and prostitution be decriminalized.

Victimless crimes include crimes between consenting adults, and/or crimes in which the victim does not perceive themselves as being a victim. A number of types of offenses have been termed victimless. Among these are substance abuse, internet censorship, loitering, prostitution, sodomy, seatbelt law violations, helmet law violations, bans on bungee jumping, and laws against assisted suicide. Crimes involving a willing buyer and seller, such as prostitution, drug, and firearms crimes can also be victimless crimes.

Prostitution is an ancient business, prospering in all cultures at all times, in spite of being illegal. It's also a crime nearly everywhere in the United States. Prostitution used to be reserved for the act of selling sexual intercourse for money and only selling, not buying, sex was included. Now, it means all contacts and penetrations as long as they're done with the intent to gratify sexual appetite. Both patrons (buyers) and prostitutes (sellers) can commit prostitution. In the past, the law recognized only women as prostitutes. Now both men and women who sell sex are prostitutes.

It's a crime not only to buy and sell sex, but also to solicit prostitution (sometimes called promoting prostitution, "pimping," or "pandering"). Soliciting prostitution means getting customers for prostitutes and/or providing a place for prostitutes and customers to engage in sex for money. Prostitution and promoting prostitution are misdemeanors in most states, but it's a serious felony when circumstances such as minors and violence are involved.

Practice Test Bank

MULTIPLE CHOICE

1. The _____ theory suggests that public order crime should be policed aggressively because it eventually triggers increases in more serious crimes, and therefore, stopping public order crimes is important in protecting the quality of life in a community.
    a. shattered dreams
    b. un-mended fences
    c. broken-windows
    d. cracked sidewalks

2. Crimes against morals and public order are termed _____ crimes.
    a. public disturbance
    b. breach of the peace
    c. public life
    d. quality-of-life

3. Broken-windows theory was formulated by _____.
    a. Boyce and Hart
    b. Wilson and Kelling
    c. LaFave and Scott
    d. Fulbright and Jaworski

4. Starting in the 1960s, courts began striking down vagrancy laws because they violated the _____ doctrine.
    a. cruel and unusual punishment
    b. void-for-vagueness
    c. *ex post facto* law
    d. *res ipsa loquitur*

5. One of the First Amendment requirements for a valid time, place, and manner regulation is that the regulation _____.
    a. be content-neutral
    b. serve any type of government interest
    c. be limited to places that are nonpublic forums
    d. apply only to symbolic speech

6. The term "panhandling" means _____.
    a. threatening others
    b. aggressive marketing
    c. begging
    d. stealing housewares

7. Because begging is clearly speech, attempts to regulate it must meet the requirements of the _____ Amendment.
   a. First
   b. Fourth
   c. Fifth
   d. Eighth

8. In attempting to deal with gang problems, many cities have utilized the civil remedy a _____.
   a. public order crimes injunction
   b. public nuisances injunction
   c. quality-of-life crimes injunction
   d. breaches of the peace abatement

9. In contrast to the broken-windows theory, Skogan suggests that disorder _____.
   a. and more serious crime are not related in any way
   b. and more serious crime may both be caused by some other factor
   c. is caused by serious crime
   d. causes more serious crime

10. One of the reasons the 7th Circuit Court of Appeals upheld the anti-panhandling ordinance in *Gresham v. Peterson* was because the ordinance _____.
    a. met the standards of the rational basis test
    b. banned panhandling totally at all times and places
    c. banned panhandling only where the other person was touched by the panhandler
    d. did not ban panhandling at all times and places

11. In *Chicago v. Morales*, the U.S. Supreme Court held that the city's anti-gang ordinance was unconstitutional because it _____.
    a. violated equal protection in that it discriminated against gang members
    b. discriminated against young people in violation of equal protection
    c. was unconstitutionally vague
    d. was an unreasonable interference with First Amendment rights

12. The expression 'reading the riot act' comes from the British Riot Act of _____.
    a. 1615
    b. 1714
    c. 1813
    d. 1912

13. The crime of vagrancy refers to _____.
    a. persons standing around with no obvious purpose
    b. being poor and being seen in public
    c. being homeless
    d. poor people roaming around with no visible means of support

14. The crime of loitering refers to _____.
    a. being without any visible means of support or employment
    b. being homeless
    c. remaining in one place with no apparent purpose
    d. panhandling

15. Traditional vagrancy and loitering statutes were struck down by the U.S. Supreme Court because such statutes violated the _____.
    a. void-for-vagueness doctrine
    b. First Amendment
    c. right of interstate travel
    d. Eighth Amendment

16. Under the First Amendment, panhandling is deemed to be _____ speech, which gets only a low level of protection.
    a. symbolic
    b. political
    c. expressive
    d. commercial

17. Which of the following is not generally included in a civil gang injunction?
    a. an order prohibiting gang members from wearing gang colors.
    b. an order prohibiting gang members from interacting with one another.
    c. an order prohibiting gang members from entering certain areas of the city.
    d. an order prohibiting gang members from engaging in violent crime.

18. The term "victimless crime" typically only applies to behavior by _____.
    a. the poor
    b. minors
    c. adults
    d. gang members

19. In Britain, in the 1950s, the _____ Report recommended decriminalizing prostitution and consensual homosexual behavior.
    a. Whittendon
    b. Whittington
    c. Wolverton
    d. Wolfendon

20. Most modern prostitution laws _____.
    a. cover both the buyer and seller
    b. are limited to selling sexual penetrations
    c. are felonies for the first offense
    d. apply only when a minor is involved

21. Today's disorderly conduct statutes grew out of the common-law crime of _____.
    a. disturbing the public peace
    b. breach of the peace
    c. public indecency
    d. public disorder

22. The Model Penal Code approach to disorderly conduct differs from prior approaches in that the code includes _____.
    a. an *actus reus* element
    b. felony punishment
    c. a *mens rea* element
    d. starting a riot

23. At common law, the offense of unlawful assembly involved ____ or more persons joined together for the purpose of committing an unlawful act.
    a. two
    b. three
    c. four
    d. five

24. At common law, if the people committing an unlawful assembly starting moving toward achieving an illegal purpose the offense became a _____.
    a. riot
    b. rout
    c. unlawful gathering
    d. unlawful congregation

25. Under the British Riot Act of 1714, the felony offense of riot required participation of _____ or more persons.
    a. three
    b. six
    c. nine
    d. twelve

26. Government power to regulate speech and soliciting is weakest in public streets and parks which are known as _____.
    a. nonpublic forums
    b. forums by designation
    c. traditional public forums
    d. free speech zones

27. Research on gangs and gang activity has revealed _____.
    a. gang activity decreased permanently after the imposition of a civil gang injunction
    b. youth crime is relatively low, but fear of gang crime and media attention to gang problems have increased
    c. law enforcement and community partners contribute equally and have the same degree of influence in implementation of gang control programs
    d. gang control programs are narrowly tailored and correspond closely with the type of behavior they are addressing

28. In any society, there is a tension between _____.
    a. liberty and freedom
    b. order and stability
    c. license and promiscuity
    d. liberty and order

29. A pimp would be guilty of the crime of _____.
    a. pimpery
    b. promoting prostitution
    c. public indecency
    d. public obscenity

30. Conduct that conveys a message is called nonverbal expression or _____.
    a. expressive conduct
    b. expressive symbolism
    c. communicative behavior
    d. symbolic behavior

TRUE/FALSE

1. Public order and decency crimes are relatively new offenses.
    a. true
    b. false

2. Order and liberty are values that can be in conflict.
    a. true
    b. false

3. The broken-windows theory was originally formulated by Stephen and Mill.
    a. true
    b. false

4. Many vagrancy and loitering laws were struck down under the due process theory of void-for-vagueness.
    a. true
    b. false

5. Loitering means to remain in one place with no apparent purpose.
   a. true
   b. false

6. At one time, all states had laws against vagrancy and loitering.
   a. true
   b. false

7. One of the reasons why enforcing laws against quality-of-life crimes is controversial is because it seems to target the poorest and weakest members of the community.
   a. true
   b. false

8. The Model Penal Code does not contain any disorderly conduct or breach of the peace crimes.
   a. true
   b. false

9. Quality-of-life crimes were enacted primarily in cities rather than in the country.
   a. true
   b. false

10. The Wolfendon Report recommended that prostitution not be decriminalized.
    a. true
    b. false

11. Crimes against public order and morals are sometimes referred to as quality-of-life crimes.
    a. true
    b. false

12. The term "panhandling" means begging.
    a. true
    b. false

13. Among the various types of forums, First Amendment rights are strongest in nonpublic forums.
    a. true
    b. false

14. Expressive conduct is not protected by the First Amendment.
    a. true
    b. false

15. Commercial speech is not protected by the First Amendment.
    a. true
    b. false

16. To be constitutional, time, place, and manner regulations must apply everywhere in the city or state.
    a. true
    b. false

17. To be constitutional, time, place, and manner regulations must not be based on the content of the speech.
    a. true
    b. false

18. A preliminary injunction is a temporary court order designed to freeze the status quo pending a full trial.
    a. true
    b. false

19. *City of Saint Paul v. East Side Boys and Shelby Siders* involved restricting gang members from associating with one another during a community festival.
    a. true
    b. false

20. Under old English law, an unlawful assembly consisted of at least three people.
    a. true
    b. false

21. Under old English law, those who participated in an unlawful assembly could later be guilty of the offense of rout if they started toward achieving their unlawful goal.
    a. true
    b. false

22. Under the English Riot Act of 1714, it took at least ten people to form a riot.
    a. true
    b. false

23. The U.S. Supreme Court has never struck down a vagrancy or loitering law.
    a. true
    b. false

24. San Francisco was a city that enforced quality-of-life crimes against street people.
    a. true
    b. false

25. Victimless crimes always involve minors.
   a. true
   b. false

FILL-IN-THE-BLANK

1. First Amendment rights are strongest in _____ forums.

2. As compared to other forums, First Amendment rights are weakest in _____ forums.

3. Of the three types of forums, First Amendment rights have intermediate strength in _____ forums.

4. Panhandling is _____ speech.

5. To be valid under the First Amendment, time, place, and manner restrictions must serve _____ government interests.

6. The _____ theory suggests that tolerance of minor offenses can lead to more serious crimes.

7. The government can place _____, _____, and _____ restrictions on speech in public places.

8. A/n _____ is a court order to do or stop doing something.

9. _____ is remaining in one place with no apparent purpose.

10. Streets, sidewalks, and public parks are termed _____ forums.

11. The U.S. Supreme Court's term, ordered _____, reflects the need to balance the values of freedom and order.

12. Public _____ law provides a civil remedy for many quality of life problems.

13. In *Chicago v. Morales*, the U.S. Supreme Court invalidated a loitering ordinance aimed at _____.

14. Loitering and vagrancy laws were frequently found unconstitutional under the _____ doctrine.

15. Nonverbal expression is also called _____ conduct.

ESSAY

1. Discuss the research regarding the link between social disorder and serious crimes. Explain the broken-windows theory and provide examples.

2. Compare and contrast individual disorderly conduct and group disorderly conduct. Give examples.

Chapter 12: Crimes Against Public Order and Morals

3. What is the void-for-vagueness doctrine and what impact did it have on traditional loitering and vagrancy laws?

4. Discuss the types of restrictions that the government can place on panhandling. Compare and contrast the three types of First Amendment forums.

5. Discuss the main points of the controversy regarding "victimless" crimes.

Study Guide

CHAPTER 12 ANSWER KEY

Multiple Choice

1. c. See pg. 424, LO 3
2. d. See pg. 420, LO 1
3. b. See pg. 424, LO 3
4. b. See pg. 426, LO 2
5. a. See pg. 433, LO 2
6. c. See pg. 431, LO 4
7. a. See pg. 431, LO 2
8. b. See pg. 440, LO 4
9. b. See pg. 424, LO 3
10. d. See pgs. 433-434, LO 2
11. c. See pg. 436, LO 4
12. b. See pg. 423, LO 1
13. d. See pg. 425, LO 1
14. c. See pg. 425, LO 1
15. a. See pg. 426, LO 2
16. d. See pg. 432, LO 2
17. b. See pg. 442, LO 4
18. c. See pg. 444, LO 6
19. d. See pg. 445, LO 6
20. a. See pg. 446, LO 6
21. b. See pg. 421, LO 1
22. c. See pgs. 421-422, LO 1
23. b. See pg. 422, LO 1
24. b. See pg. 422, LO 1
25. d. See pg. 423, LO 1
26. c. See pg. 431, LO 2
27. b. See pg. 441, LO 6
28. d. See pg. 420, LO 2
29. b. See pg. 446, LO 6
30. a. See pg. 434, LO 2

True/False

1. T. See pg. 425, LO 1
2. T. See pg. 420, LO 2
3. F. See pg. 424, LO 3
4. T. See pg. 426, LO 1
5. T. See pg. 425, LO 5
6. T. See pg. 425, LO 5
7. T. See pg. 427, LO 1
8. F. See pg. 420, LO 1
9. T. See pg. 424, LO 1
10. F. See pg. 445, LO 5
11. T. See pg. 420, LO 6
12. T. See pg. 431, LO 6
13. F. See pg. 431, LO 2
14. F. See pg. 432, LO 2
15. F. See pg. 432, LO 2
16. F. See pg. 431, LO 2
17. T. See pg. 431, LO.4
18. T. See pg. 428, LO 4
19. T. See pg. 443, LO 1
20. T. See pg. 432, LO 1
21. T. See pgs. 422, LO 1
22. F. See pg. 423, LO 1

Chapter 12: Crimes Against Public Order and Morals

23. F. See pg. 426, LO 2
24. T. See pg. 427, LO 5
25. F. See pg. 444, LO 6

Fill-in-the-Blank

1. traditional public. See pg. 431, LO 4
2. nonpublic. See pg. 431, LO 4
3. designated public. See pg. 431, LO 4
4. commercial. See pg. 432, LO 4
5. significant. See pg. 431, LO 4
6. broken-windows. See pg. 424, LO 3
7. time, manner, place. See pg. 431, LO 4
8. injunction. See pg. 428, LO 5
9. Loitering. See pg. 425, LO 1
10. traditional public. See pg. 431, LO 4
11. liberty. See pg. 420, LO 2
12. injunction . See pg. 440, LO 5
13. street gangs. See pg. 436, LO 4
14. void-for-vagueness. See pg. 426, LO 4
15. expressive. See pg. 432, LO 4

Essays

1. Explain the broken-windows theory and provide examples.

   Wilson and Kelling's broken windows theory suggests a connection between disorderly conduct/quality of life crimes band serious crime. They found a link between order and crime. Skogan cautions that the connection is not necessarily a causal one, but agrees that disorder needs to be taken seriously because it plays a role in neighborhood decline. Harcourt found a weak-to-no-causal link between disorder and serious crime. Sampson and Raudenbush found that disorder and serious crime have common causes but not any direct causal relation with each other. LO 3

2. Compare and contrast individual disorderly conduct and group disorderly conduct. Give examples.

Individual disorderly conduct is common law breach of peace and includes fighting in public, making unreasonable noise, or engaging in conduct that provokes others to engage in disorderly conduct. The most common use of disorderly conduct is the ban on fighting in public. Group disorderly conduct consists of three common law crimes: unlawful assembly (three or more people joining for the purpose of committing an unlawful act), rout (taking steps toward achieving their purpose of committing an unlawful act), and riot (the group actually committing the lawful violent act or performing a lawful act in a violent manner). Because riots involve especially alarming and dangerous behavior, all states still have the crime of riot, and it is generally a felony offense whereas most disorderly conduct crimes are misdemeanor offenses. LO 1,2

3. What is the void-for-vagueness doctrine and what impact did it have on traditional loitering and vagrancy laws?

The void for vagueness doctrine (also discussed in Chapter 2) flows from the requirement of due process. Individuals need to be put on notice what type of behavior will violate the law. If the law is too vague then they cannot conform their behavior and may fall into law breaking. Another concern when laws are vaguely written is that they encourage arbitrary law enforcement. Vagrancy and loitering laws which were popular prior to the 1950s were challenged on void for vagueness grounds, primarily because of their uneven administration (arbitrary law enforcement). Vagrancy and loitering laws tended to be used to punish and control displaced poor, and the Court has since struck down many of these statutes based on void-for-vagueness grounds. LO 2, 4

4. Discuss the types of restrictions that the government can place on panhandling. Compare and contrast the three types of First Amendment forums.

Panhandling, asking others for food or money, is speech. Although it is protected by the First Amendment to the U.S. Constitution, it is nevertheless subject to time, place, and manner restrictions. These restrictions must not be based on the content of the speech, they must serve a governmental interest, and they must allow for other channels of expression. Additionally, speech in public forums (streets, sidewalks, parks) is "more protected" than speech in nonpublic forms (airports, bus stations, subways, shopping malls)—this means that the government has more power to put restrictions on speech in nonpublic forums. Finally, because panhandling is considered commercial speech, it is subject to more restriction than other types of speech. (LO 5)

5. Discuss the main points of the controversy regarding "victimless" crimes.

The controversy surrounding "victimless" crimes exists because of the tension between personal autonomy and the governments' interest in protecting the public good, which is often read as public morals. The controversy exists because there is a polarization among individuals who believe that the criminal law should enforce morals to purify society and individuals who believe that non-violent behavior by consenting adults is none of the criminal law's business. LO 6

Chapter 13
Crimes Against the State

LEARNING OBJECTIVES

1. Understand how defining and applying crimes against the state reflects the enduring idea of balancing security and freedom during wartime emergencies.

2. Know that treason is a fundamental weapon against present allegiance and support to foreign enemies.

3. Appreciate that crimes against potential terrorist attacks are subject to the limits placed on traditional criminal law.

4. Know that the most commonly prosecuted crime against the state since September 11, 2001, is "providing material support or resources" to terrorists or terrorist organizations.

5. Appreciate that "providing material support or resources" is open to constitutional challenges.

KEY TERMS AND CONTENT

- **USA Patriot Act**—act passed by Congress following September 11, 2001, creating some new (and enhancing the penalties for existing) crimes of domestic and international terrorism; p. 451

- **treason**—crime of levying war against the United States or of giving aid and comfort to its enemies; p. 452

- **adherence to the enemy (in treason)**—breaking allegiance to your own country; p. 453

- **treason *actus reus***—levying war against the United States, or giving aid and comfort to enemies of the United States; p. 454

- **treason *mens rea***—intentionally giving aid and comfort for the purpose of betraying the United States; p. 454

- **sedition**—the crime of "stirring up" treason by words; p. 456

- **seditious speech**—"stirring up" treason by means of the spoken word; p. 456

- **seditious libel**—writings aimed at "stirring up" treason; p. 456

- **seditious conspiracy**—agreement to "stir up" treason; p. 456

- **Smith Act of 1940**—U.S. statute aimed at Communists who advocated the violent overthrow of the government; p. 456

- **sabotage**—damaging or destroying property for the purpose of hindering preparations for war and national defense during national emergencies; p. 457

- **espionage**—the crime of spying for the enemy; p. 457

- **terrorism**—in the nonlegal sense, it means the use of violence and intimidation in the pursuit of political aims; p. 458

- **Anti-Terrorism and Effective Death Penalty Act (AEDPA)**—law defining new crimes of domestic terrorism and increasing the penalties for domestic terrorism crimes; p. 459

- **international terrorism**—terrorist acts dangerous to U.S. citizens committed outside the United States; p. 459

- **domestic terrorism**—terrorist crimes committed inside the United States; p. 460

- **weapons of mass destruction**—any destructive device used to commit acts of terror; p. 460

- **conduct transcending national boundaries**—element in new antiterrorism crime statute that cites acts of terrorism that take place partly outside and partly inside the United States; p. 460

- ***actus reus* of harboring or concealing (terrorists)**—harboring or concealing persons who have committed or are about to commit a list of terrorist-related crimes. 461

- ***mens rea* of harboring or concealing (terrorists)**—knowing that the *actus reus* of harboring or concealing was about to be committed; p. 461

- **material support**—element in terrorist crimes that consists of helping terrorists or terrorist organizations; p. 462

- **proximity crimes**—ban conduct because of its closeness to other crimes; p. 463

- **training**—training terrorists to commit terrorist acts; p. 467

- **expert advice or assistance**—providing help to terrorists by a variety of means; p. 467

- **personnel**—personnel staff, employees, workforce, workers, labor force, human resources, manpower, wage labor; p. 467

CHAPTER OUTLINE

I. **Treason**
    A. Distrust of treason laws and the **American Revolution**
        1. The only crime defined in the Constitution
    B. **After the Revolution**, the new government was fragile because it was new and needed time for loyalty and allegiance to take hold.
        1. England, Spain, France, and Native American nations threatened from all sides.
        2. Traitors, spies, and other disloyal individuals and groups threatened from within.
    C. Authors of the Constitution had mixed feelings about treason.
        1. They were tough on traitors who broke allegiance and were disloyal.
        2. Their own ancestors had fled from religious persecution and prosecution for treason.
        3. Treason was broadly defined in England to include thoughts and feelings that led to prosecution of innocent people.
        4 Two concerns:
            a. Repression of peaceful opposition to government
            b. Conviction of the innocent because of perjury, passion, and/or insufficient evidence
    D. Treason is defined in the body of the Constitution, where it's very difficult to change.
    E. Elements of treason
        1. *Actus reus*
            a. Levying war against the U.S.
            b. Giving aid and comfort to enemies of the U.S.
        2. *Mens rea*
            a. Intent to give aid and comfort
            b. The purpose of betraying the U.S. by means of aid and comfort
        3. Proof
            a. Two witnesses to *actus reus*
            b. Confession in open court
            c. *Case: Cramer v. U.S.*

II. **Sedition, Sabotage, and Espionage**
    A. **Sedition**
        1. Ancient crime of "stirring up" treason (advocate violent overthrow of government) by
            a. Speeches
            b. Writing (libel)
            c. Conspiracy
        2. In the U.S. Code, sedition includes only advocating the violent overthrow of the government and seditious conspiracy involves only conspiracies that advocate violence.
        3. Smith Act of 1940

B. **Sabotage**
   1. Damaging and/or destroying property related to war and defense material, buildings, and utilities (which includes transportation and harbors)
   2. Producing defective property related to war and defense
   3. Elements
      a. *Actus reus*
         (1) Destroy
         (2) Damage
         (3) Obstruct
         (4) Interfere
         (5) Contaminate
         (6) Produce defective war or national defense materials
      b. *Mens rea*
         (1) Purposely obstruct (or any other acts in *actus reus*)
         (2) Knowingly obstruct (or any other acts in *actus reus*)
         (3) Negligently obstruct (or any other acts in *actus reus*)
      c. Circumstance
         (1) At war
         (2) During national emergency

C. **Espionage (spying)**
   1. Definition of espionage—Secret intelligence gathering by spies about foreign people, activities, and enterprises for political and military uses.
   2. U.S. Code espionage elements (at any time)
      a. *Actus reus*
         (1) Communicate
         (2) Deliver
         (3) Transmit
         (4) Attempt to communicate, deliver, or transmit intelligence (information harmful to the U.S.)
      b. *Mens rea*
         (1) Purposely injure
         (2) Reason to believe use of intelligence will injure
      c. Circumstances
         (1) Intelligence provided to foreign government
         (2) Foreign faction or party
         (3) Foreign military or naval force
         (4) Foreign representative, officer, agent, employee, subject, or citizen
   3. U.S. Code espionage elements (during war)
      a. *Actus reus*
         (1) Collect any intelligence useful to the enemy
         (2) Publish it
         (3) Communicate it
         (4) Attempt to do so
      b. *Mens rea*—Intent to communicate information to enemy
      c. Circumstance—Time of war

III. Antiterrorism Crimes
  A. A number of relatively new statutes involve fighting terrorism.
    1. General crimes applicable to terrorist acts
       a. Treason, sedition, sabotage, and espionage
       b. Murder, attempted murder, and conspiracy to murder also apply
    2. International Terrorism
    3. Domestic Terrorism
  B. **The use of weapons of mass destruction**
    1. Elements
       a. *Actus reus*
          (1) Use
          (2) Threaten to use
          (3) Attempt or conspire to use
       b. *Mens rea*—Without lawful authority (voluntarily)
       c. Circumstance(s)
          (1) Against a U.S. "national" outside the U.S.
          (2) Against any "person" inside the U.S.
          (3) Against any property inside or outside the U.S.
    2. Definition of "weapon of mass destruction"
       a. "Any destructive device"—Explosive, incendiary, poison gas, bomb, grenade, rocket, missile, mine, or similar device
       b. Any weapon intended to cause death or serious bodily injury by poisonous chemicals or precursors
       c. Any weapon involving a disease mechanism
       d. Any weapon designed to release radiation or radioactivity at levels harmful to human life
  C. **Acts of terrorism transcending national boundaries**
    1. Definition—Conduct occurring partly inside and partly outside the U.S.
    2. Types of conduct (*actus reus*)
       a. Commit violent crimes against any person inside the U.S.
       b. Create a substantial risk of serious bodily injury by destroying or damaging property within the U.S.
       c. Threatening, or attempting, or conspiring to commit (a) or (b)
    3. Circumstances
       a. Victims—U.S. government, members of uniformed services, officials, employees, and agents of the U.S.
       b. Property owned or leased by the U.S.
    4. Penalties
       a. Death for killing or death resulting from the act
       b. Up to life for kidnapping
       c. Up to 35 years for maiming
       d. Up to 30 years for assault
       e. Up to 25 years for damaging or destroying property
  D. **Harboring or concealing terrorists**
    1. *Actus reus*—Harboring or concealing persons who have committed or are about to commit a list of terrorist-related crimes

2. *Mens rea*—Knowing (or a reasonable person should have known) the crimes were going to be committed
3. Penalty—Fine and up to 10 years imprisonment

E. **Providing material support to terrorists and/or terrorist organizations**
1. Prosecutions for violating Section 2339B are most frequent in practice.
2. Material support crimes created after the Oklahoma City bombing in the Anti-Terrorism and Effective Death Penalty Act (AEDPA) of 1996
3. Amendment increased the AEDPA penalty in the USA Patriot Act (Uniting and Strengthening America by Providing Appropriate Tools to Intercept and Obstruct Terrorism) of 2001.
4. The 300+-page Patriot Act is devoted mainly to criminal procedure—Surveillance and intelligence, law enforcement information sharing, search and seizure, detention, and interrogation.
5. Providing support to individuals or groups are proximity crimes because of their closeness to other crimes (44 other federal crimes) that terrorists might commit.
6. Material support to individual terrorists
   a. *Actus reus*
      (1) Provide material support to individual terrorist
      (2) Conceal or disguise nature, location, source, or ownership of material support or resources
   b. *Mens rea*—Intending or knowing support or resources to be used in preparing or committing list of crimes helpful to terrorists
7. Material support to terrorist organizations
   a. *Actus reus*—Provides material support or resources to terrorist organizations
   b. *Mens rea*—Knowingly provides material support
   c. Case: *U.S. V. Lindh*
8. Most-argued issues in material support cases
   a. Due process—term "material support" is void-for-vagueness
      (1) Case: *Humanitarian Law Project v. Reno,*
   b. First Amendment—Providing material support violates right to free speech and association.
9. Intelligence Reform and Prevention of Terrorism Act of 2004—Congressional response to court's decisions finding terminology void for vagueness
   a. Case: *Humanitarian Law Project v Mukasey*

CHAPTER SUMMARY

To maintain themselves, governments everywhere have always had to rely on laws to protect them against foreign enemies and ensure the allegiance and loyalty of their citizens. During times of national emergency we must try to strike the proper balance between security and freedom.

Treason is an ancient crime and it is the only crime defined in the U.S. Constitution. Article III provides: "Treason against the United States, shall consist only in levying War against them, or, in adhering to their Enemies, giving them Aid and Comfort. No Person shall be convicted of Treason unless on the Testimony of two Witnesses to the same overt Act, or on Confession in open Court." The treason sections in the U.S. Code flesh out these terms.

It is a crime against the state not only to commit treason but also to encourage others to overthrow the government by violence. Advocating the violent overthrow of the government is called sedition.

Sabotage is the crime of destroying or damaging property with the intent of interfering with and hindering preparations for war and defense during national emergencies. Espionage is another term for spying for the enemy. It includes gathering information harmful to national security and defense and communicating that information to hostile groups or nations.

Some of the recent legislation on these topics is part of the USA Patriot Act, which is the best known of the recent acts. It is an acronym for "Uniting and Strengthening America by Providing Appropriate Tools Required to Intercept and Obstruct Terrorism." Aimed at terrorists, it was passed and signed into law on October 16, 2001, after the devastating September 11th attacks on the World Trade Center and the Pentagon. The new laws divide terrorism into two kinds—international and domestic. Domestic terrorism involves acts within the U.S., while acts outside the U.S. are deemed international terrorism.

A number of sections of the U.S. Code are available for prosecuting crimes related to terrorists and terrorist organizations. Among the crimes specifically aimed at terrorism are U.S. Code Title 18, Chapter 113B, "Terrorism", the Anti-Terrorism and Effective Death Penalty Act (AEDPA) (1996), and the USA Patriot Act (2001). The U.S. Code divides terrorism into international terrorism and domestic terrorism.

Among the offenses in these new laws are: 1) the use of certain weapons of mass destruction; 2) harboring or concealing terrorists; 3) providing material support to terrorists; and 4) providing material support or resources to designated foreign terrorist organizations. The fourth-listed law has probably been the one most utilized by the government.

A number of legal challenges have been launched against these laws. The two most utilized challenges are due process (void-for vagueness) and First Amendment freedom of speech and association. In *U.S. v. Lindh,* Lindh failed to get his indictment thrown out on vagueness and overbreadth challenges, and he subsequently entered a plea. In *Humanitarian Law Project v. Reno,* the court held that the term "personnel" in the act was vague. In response, Congress amended the material support provisions in the Intelligence Reform and Prevention of Terrorism Act of 2004 (IRTPA). However, in *Humanitarian Law Project v. Mukasey* (2009), the court similarly held while "personnel" was no longer vague, other parts of IRTPA were constitutionally impermissible.

Chapter 13: Crimes Against the State

Practice Test Bank

MULTIPLE CHOICE

1. In response to the terrorist attacks of September 11, 2001, Congress passed the _____.
    a. AEDPA
    b. RICO Act
    c. Act to Prevent Terrorist Attacks
    d. USA Patriot Act

2. The crime of espionage involves _____.
    a. sabotage
    b. obstructing the war effort
    c. spying
    d. aiding or giving comfort to enemies of the government

3. Many anti-terrorism laws are included in the 1996 _____.
    a. International Terrorists Act
    b. USA Patriot Act
    c. Anti-terrorism and Effective Death Penalty Act
    d. Act for the Prevention of Terrorist Acts against the U.S.

4. The crime of _____ involves encouraging others to overthrow the government by violence.
    a. conduction
    b. sedition
    c. espionage
    d. treason

5. According to the U.S. Supreme Court in the Cramer case, _____ saboteurs is not treason.
    a. mere association with
    b. corresponding with
    c. aiding and abetting
    d. discussing politics

6. The crime of _____ involves damaging or destroying property to hinder preparation for war or national defense.
    a. treason
    b. espionage
    c. sedition
    d. sabotage

275

Study Guide

7. U.S. Code sections 2339A and 2339B of Title 18 make it a crime to provide _____ to terrorist organizations or terrorists.
    a. aid and assistance
    b. cover and concealment
    c. material support
    d. aid and comfort

8. The AEDPA was passed partly in response to the 1996 bombing of the _____ in Oklahoma City, Oklahoma.
    a. federal building
    b. U.S. arsenal
    c. Post Office
    d. airport

9. The offense of _____ is defined as levying war, adhering to enemies, or giving aid or comfort to the enemies of a nation.
    a. terrorism
    b. sedition
    d. espionage
    d. treason

10. One of the most famous American treason cases involved Julius and Ethel _____ who were executed for treason.
    a. Cramer
    b. Hess
    c. Alexander
    d. Rosenberg

11. The offense of _____ is the only one defined in the U.S. Constitution.
    a. espionage
    b. treason
    c. sabotage
    d. sedition

12. Terrorist acts committed in the U.S. are referred to as _____ terrorism.
    a. homeland
    b. internal
    c. domestic
    d. secondary

13. The most infamous domestic terrorist of recent years was _____.
    a. Karl Cramer
    b. Bernhard Goetz
    c. Timothy McVeigh
    d. George Siemens

14. The U.S. Constitution provides that a conviction of treason must be based on _____.
    a. a written confession or admission by a foreign government
    b. corroboration by physical evidence or testimony of three witnesses
    c. confession in open court or the testimony of two witnesses to an overt act
    d. proof beyond a reasonable doubt of remuneration from an enemy nation

15. Seditious speeches are termed seditious _____.
    a. conspiracy
    b. slander
    c. speech
    d. libel

16. The purpose element of the crime of treason is _____.
    a. to betray the U.S.
    b. remuneration
    c. revenge
    d. obtaining perquisites from foreign nations

17. The Intelligence Reform and Prevention of Terrorism Act was a response to
    a. the events of September 11, 2001
    b. the Supreme Court's ruling the Patriot Act unconstitutional
    c. the holding of several federal courts that the material support provisions of the AEDPA/Patriot Act violates the constitution
    d. the Circuit Court's holding in *Humanitarian Law Project v. Mukasey*

18. The two constitutional issues involved in the crime of providing material support to terrorists are _____.
    a. void-for-vagueness and First Amendment freedom of association
    b. *ex post facto* and bill of attainder
    c. Fifth and Eighth Amendment
    d. procedural and substantive due process

19. The crime of treason has _____ *mens rea* elements.
    a. two
    b. three
    c. four
    d. five

20. Weapons capable of killing numerous individuals by use of disease, poisons, and radioactivity are called weapons of _____.
    a. multiple homicide
    b. mass murder
    c. mass destruction
    d. multiple murder

21. Destruction and damaging are among the possible _____ elements of sabotage.
    a. *mens rea*
    b. circumstance
    c. *actus reus*
    d. concurrence

22. Treason is a _____ crime.
    a. strict liability
    b. vicarious liability
    c. specific-intent
    d. mandatory death penalty

23. The circumstance element of sabotage is _____.
    a. during war or national emergency
    b. while enemies are spying on the nation
    c. while the defendant is a citizen of the U.S.
    d. the information will aid the enemy in attacking the U.S.

24. Most of the USA Patriot Act deals with _____.
    a. sentences for terrorists, including expedited death penalty appeals
    b. creating new crimes
    c. punishing sedition
    d. procedural matters such as surveillance, search and seizure, etc.

25. The *mens rea* of providing material support to terrorist organizations is doing so _____.
    a. intentionally
    b. knowingly
    c. recklessly
    d. negligently

26. The U.S. Code separates spying into two separate crimes—_____.
    a. time of peace and time of war
    b. committed by U.S. citizen or non-citizen
    c. domestic or transnational
    d. overt and covert

27. The U.S. Constitution _____.
    a. leaves Congress free to create new definitions of treason
    b. leaves the courts free to create new crimes of treason
    c. prohibits the death penalty for treason
    d. limits the definition of treason

28. The current U.S. Code definition of sedition is limited to _____.
    a. seditious libel
    b. conspiracies that advocate violence against the government
    c. acts during actual time of war
    d. acts that are intended to aid enemies of the U.S.

29. The first sedition act in the U.S. was controversial because it included speech that _____.
    a. might be protected by the First Amendment
    b. encouraged young men to avoid fighting the French
    c. criticized the War of 1812
    d. advocated immediate, violent overthrow of the government

30. The Smith Act involved laws against _____.
    a. espionage
    b. spying
    c. treason
    d. sedition

TRUE/FALSE

1. The primary aim of the USA Patriot Act is to fight international terrorism.
   a. true
   b. false

2. Sedition is the only crime defined in the U.S. Constitution.
   a. true
   b. false

3. Espionage consists of inciting others to violently overthrow the government.
   a. true
   b. false

4. Treason is an ancient crime.
   a. true
   b. false

5. Espionage means destroying government property.
   a. true
   b. false

6. Advocating the violent overthrow of the government is called treason.
   a. true
   b. false

7. Under U.S. law, espionage is only a crime during wartime.
   a. true
   b. false

8. In the U.S., treason can be punishable by death.
   a. true
   b. false

9. Under the U.S. Code, seditious conspiracy can be punishable by death.
   a. true
   b. false

10. The USA Patriot Act provides that it is a crime to conspire or attempt to provide material support to terrorist organizations or terrorists.
    a. true
    b. false

11. Sedition is a strict liability crime.
    a. true
    b. false

12. The U.S. Constitution specifies the type of proof required to convict of treason.
    a. true
    b. false

13. The right of peaceful association is protected by the Fourth Amendment.
    a. true
    b. false

14. The most commonly prosecuted crime against the U.S. since September 11, 2001, is harboring or concealing terrorists.
    a. true
    b. false

15. Timothy McVeigh was a domestic terrorist.
    a. true
    b. false

16. Julius and Ethel Rosenberg were executed for allegedly passing American atomic secrets to the Russians.
    a. true
    b. false

17. According to the U.S. Constitution, one of the ways treason may be proved is by confession in open court.
    a. true
    b. false

18. According to the U.S. Constitution, one of the ways treason may be proven is by the testimony of at least three witnesses to the same overt act.
    a. true
    b. false

19. The first U.S. sedition law was passed in 1917.
    a. true
    b. false

20. The first U.S. sedition law was limited to active advocacy of violent overthrow of the government.
    a. true
    b. false

21. In the 1700s, Britain had no laws against treason.
    a. true
    b. false

22. Murdering the president of the United States would be an act of sabotage.
    a. true
    b. false

23. The crime of espionage involves information.
    a. true
    b. false

24. Sabotage is a strict liability crime.
    a. true
    b. false

25. Espionage during time of war is a vicarious liability crime.
    a. true
    b. false

Study Guide

FILL-IN-THE-BLANK

1. _____ is the more common term for espionage.

2. _____ is advocating the violent overthrow of the government.

3. The U.S. Code prohibits providing _____ support to terrorists or terrorist organizations.

4. Destroying or damaging government property to interfere with national defense is called _____.

5. Making war or aiding those who make war on one's own country is called _____.

6. The USA _____ Act was passed quickly after the terrorist attacks of September 11, 2001.

7. _____ to the enemy means breaking allegiance to your own country and supporting an enemy country.

8. In *U.S. v. Lindh,* John Lindh tried to get the indictment against him dismissed on the ground that the material support provisions are _____.

9. Under recent legislation, implements of biological, chemical, or nuclear warfare are termed weapons of _____.

10. Under section 2339 of the U.S. Code, it is a crime to _____ or conceal terrorists.

11. The *mens rea* of providing material support to terrorist organizations is _____.

12. Damaging or destroying is the *actus reus* of the crime of _____.

13. Seditious writings are called seditious _____.

14. Laws prohibiting providing support for terrorist organizations may run afoul of the _____ Amendment's freedom of association.

15. The _____ doctrine may invalidate some anti-terrorism laws.

282

ESSAY

1. Compare and contrast sabotage and espionage. Provide examples.

2. Compare and contrast treason and sedition. Provide examples.

3. What does the U.S. Constitution say about the crime of treason?

4. Discuss the Congressional Acts that deal with both domestic and international terrorism? Discuss some the things that are crimes under each.

5. What Constitutional challenges have been raised to the felony of providing material support to terrorists or terrorist organizations? How successful have those challenges been?

CHAPTER 13 ANSWER KEY

Multiple Choice

1. d. See pg. 451, LO 4
2. c. See pg. 457, LO 1
3. c. See pg. 459, LO 4
4. b. See pg. 456, LO 1
5. a. See pg. 455, LO 2
6. d. See pg. 457, LO 1
7. c. See pg. 459, LO 4
8. a. See pg. 462, LO 3
9. d. See pg. 452, LO 2
10. d. See pg. 455, LO 2
11. b. See pg. 452, LO 2
12. c. See pg. 460, LO 3
13. c. See pg. 462, LO 3
14. c. See pg. 452, LO 2
15. c. See pg. 456, LO 1
16. a. See pg. 454, LO 2
17. c. See pg. 465, LO 5
18. a. See pg. 463, LO 4
19. a. See pg. 454, LO 2
20. c. See pg. 460, LO 4
21. c. See pg. 457, LO 1
22. c. See pg. 454, LO 2
23. a. See pg. 457, LO 1
24. d. See pg. 462, LO 3
25. b. See pg. 463, LO 4
26. a. See pg. 458, LO 1
27. d. See pg. 452, LO 2
28. b. See pg. 456, LO 1
29. a. See pg. 456, LO 1
30. d. See pg. 456, LO

True/False

1. T. See pg. 451, LO 3
2. F. See pg. 452, LO 1
3. F. See pg. 457, LO 1
4. T. See pg. 452, LO 2
5. F. See pg. 457, LO 1
6. F. See pg. 456, LO 2
7. F. See pg. 458, LO 1
8. T. See pg. 452, LO 2
9. F. See pg. 456, LO 1
10. T. See pg. 459, LO 4
11. F. See pg. 456, LO 1
12. T. See pg. 452, LO 2
13. F. See pg. 456, LO 1
14. F. See pg. 462, LO 4
15. T. See pg. 462, LO 4
16. T. See pg. 455, LO 2
17. T. See pg. 452, LO 1
18. F. See pg. 452, LO 1
19. F. See pg. 456, LO 1
20. F. See pg. 456, LO 1
21. F. See pg. 453, LO 2
22. F. See pg. 457, LO 1
23. T. See pg. 459, LO 1
24. F. See pg. 457, LO 1
25. F. See pg. 458, LO 1

Study Guide

Fill-in-the-Blank

1. Spying. See pg. 457, LO 1, 2
2. Sedition. See pg. 456, LO 1, 2
3. material. See pg. 459, LO 4
4. sabotage. See pg. 457, LO 2
5. treason. See pg. 452, LO 2
6. Patriot. See pg. 459, LO 3
7. Adhering. See pg. 452, LO 2
8. void-for-vagueness. See pg. 463, LO 1
9. mass destruction. See pg. 460, LO 3
10. harbor. See pg. 461, LO 3
11. knowing. See pg. 463, LO 3
12. sabotage. See pg. 457, LO 1
13. libel. See pg. 456, LO 4
14. First. See pg. 465, LO 5
15. void-for-vagueness. See pg. 465, LO 4

Essays

1. Compare and contrast sabotage. Provide examples.

    Sabotage is purposefully (or willfully) damaging or destroying property for the purpose of interfering with and hindering preparations for war and defense during national emergencies. Sabotage would be the appropriate crime to charge when an individual set off an explosion that took down a transmission tower if we were at war or there was a national emergency. As a crime, sabotage seems to be the most restrictive because it focuses on being at war or having an actual national emergency. The idea is that one is purposefully trying to impede the country in its efforts to defend itself. Espionage is spying either during times of peace or during war. If one spies during peace time, then it entails gathering information and turning it over with the intent to hurt the United States or help a foreign country. Espionage during war involves gathering and turning over information about the military actions that may be useful to the enemy. Sabotage and espionage are both aimed at hurting the United States in its ability to protect itself, but they are accomplished in very different manners—sabotage being a direct attack on a physical place, and espionage using information that can then be used by the enemy. LO 1

Chapter 13: Crimes Against the State

2. Compare and contrast treason and sedition. Provide examples.

The constitutional crime of treason involves levying war against the United States or giving enemies of the United States aid and comfort. To commit treason, one must intentionally give aid with the purpose of betraying the United States. Sedition means to stir up others to overthrow the government by violence. The crimes are not mutually exclusive, but sedition is not punishable by death whereas treason is. It is possible to commit sedition without committing treason (stirring up others to levy war or not giving aid to the enemy), and it is possible to commit treason without committing sedition (individually committing acts which give the enemies of the U.S. aid and comfort without stirring up anyone to violently overthrow the government). LO 1, 2

3. What does the U.S. Constitution say about the crime of treason?

Treason is the only crime mentioned in the Constitution. The framers walked a tight rope in writing treason into the Constitution: they had to take a strong position against those who were against the new government, but they also had to account for the fact that they too would have been guilty of treason in England. So, they limited the behavior which constituted treason, made it a very serious crime, and worked in some protections, such as limiting legislatures and courts from creating new means of treasons, requiring two witnesses to an overt act or open confession, and included it in the Constitution where it could not easily be modified. LO 2

4. Discuss the Congressional Acts that deal with both domestic and international terrorism. Discuss the things that are crimes under each.

In addition to the crimes found in the U.S. Code (murder, conspiracy, assault/battery, etc) Congress has passed three Acts which are somewhat intertwined dealing with domestic and international terrorism. The Anti-Terrorism and Effective Death Penalty Act (1996) (AEDPA) was enacted in response to the domestic terrorist attack on the Oklahoma City Federal Building. The U.S. Patriot Act was enacted in response to the attacks of September 11, 2001 that were also domestic attacks (target inside U.S., although individuals committing attacks were not U.S. citizens). Finally, Congress enacted the Intelligence Reform and Terrorism Prevention Act which amended the AEDPA after some of its provisions were found by lower federal appellate courts to violate the Constitution. Many of AEDPA's provisions on terrorism were incorporated into the Patriot Act, and much of the IRTPA were just modifications of these earlier acts. The crimes that are specified in these acts are: use of weapons of mass destruction; acts of terrorism transcending national boundaries, harboring or concealing terrorists, providing material support to terrorists, providing material support or resources to designated foreign terrorist organizations. LO 4

5. What Constitutional challenges have been raised to the felony of providing material support to terrorists or terrorist organizations? How successful have those challenges been?

The legality of the AEDPA, the US Patriot Act, and the IRTPA have been challenged based on due process grounds of void-for-vagueness, void for overbreadth, but so far, no case has reached the Supreme Court. In particular, the language found in the crime of providing material support to terrorists has given plaintiffs such as John Lindh and the Humanitarian Law Project fodder for their suits. The terms "training," "personnel," "expert advice or assistance," and "service" have been challenged for being overly vague. In 2000, in Humanitarian Law Project v. Reno, the court did find that the terms were vague which resulted in a Congressional amendment (IRPTA). In 2009, the 9th Circuit Court of Appeals in Humanitarian Law Project v. Mukasey, found that the 2004 amendment, IRTPA, still contained language that violated the U.S. Constitution though the amendment did fix some of the troubling language from the material support crime found in AEDPA. LO 3